Masculinities and Markets

Masculinities and Markets

RACED AND GENDERED URBAN
POLITICS IN MILWAUKEE

BRENDA PARKER

THE UNIVERSITY OF GEORGIA PRESS
Athens

Parts of chapter 2 appear in "Feminist Forays in the City: Imbalance and Intervention in Urban Research Methods," *Antipode* 48, no. 5 (Nov. 2016): 1337–58.

Chapter 6 was published in slightly different form as "Reproduction . . . Amplified: Life's Work for African American Women in Milwaukee" in *Precarious Worlds: Contested Geographies of Social Reproduction*, edited by Katie Meehan and Kendra Strauss (Athens: University of Georgia Press, 2015), 118–36.

© 2017 by the University of Georgia Press
Athens, Georgia 30602
www.ugapress.org
All rights reserved
Set in 10/12.5 Minion Pro by Graphic Composition, Inc., Bogart, Georgia

Most University of Georgia Press titles are
available from popular e-book vendors.

Printed digitally

Library of Congress Cataloging-in-Publication Data

Names: Parker, Brenda K., author.
Title: Masculinities and markets : raced and gendered urban politics in Milwaukee / Brenda Parker.
Description: Athens : University of Georgia Press, 2017. | Series: Geographies of justice and social transformation ; 32 | Includes bibliographical references and index.
Identifiers: LCCN 2016034611 | ISBN 9780820335117 (hardback : alk. paper) | ISBN 9780820350325 (pbk. : alk. paper) | ISBN 9780820350318 (ebook)
Subjects: LCSH: Urban policy—Wisconsin—Milwaukee. | Public welfare—Wisconsin—Milwaukee. | Local government—Wisconsin—Milwaukee. | Women—Political activity—Wisconsin—Milwaukee. | Community development—Wisconsin—Milwaukee.
Classification: LCC HN80.M58 P37 2017 | DDC 307.7609775/95—dc23 LC record available at https://lccn.loc.gov/2016034611

CONTENTS

Acknowledgments   *vii*

CHAPTER 1   Masculinities and Markets: An Introduction   *1*

CHAPTER 2   Reconsidering History: Gender, Race, and Neoliberal Narratives in U.S. Cities   *21*

CHAPTER 3   From Sewer Socialism to "Sewers for Sale": Milwaukee's Journey toward Neoliberalism   *44*

CHAPTER 4   Rationalities of Rule: New Urbanism, Neoliberalism, and Gendered Governance   *79*

CHAPTER 5   Could the Violent Femmes Save Milwaukee? Richard Florida, the Young Professionals of Milwaukee, and Embodied Creativity   *97*

CHAPTER 6   Getting By in Milwaukee: Amplified Lives and Labors for Low-Income African American Women   *117*

CHAPTER 7   "This Land Is Our Land": Race, Gender, Neoliberalism, and Contested Urban Politics   *134*

CONCLUSION   Feminist Urban Narratives, Politics, and Imaginaries   *166*

Notes   *179*

Bibliography   *191*

Index   *223*

ACKNOWLEDGMENTS

In a small way, this book is like a city—it has been created from multiple blue-prints, designers, and thinkers. Yet it comes alive only through the people who inhabit it with their words, practices, and actions, and the networks of scholar-ship and support that surround its author.

This means I owe the most thanks to the people of Milwaukee, who shared their voices, their vulnerabilities, and their aspirations, sometimes directly and sometimes as members of the public that I observed. My hope is that by writing this book, I can somehow contribute to the spirit and the practice of a better Milwaukee, even from afar. My critiques come with the understanding that true city building, the kind that accounts for and cares for not just buildings, but also the collective—people of every stripe and size—is difficult labor. I applaud the many people in Milwaukee who have dedicated their lives to this work, with humor, grit, and love.

So many fabulous academic colleagues and friends have also helped this book along, by engaging with important ideas, reading chapters or drafts, edit-ing, providing inspiration from their own scholarship, and helping me tame and craft my prose. In Milwaukee, I am indebted to Marc Levine and John Gurda, who shared their thoughts with me in interviews and whose publications and perspectives informed this work. Blyth Meier, a Milwaukee artist and wonderful friend, generously provided the photo that graces the cover of this book. Jane Collins, Teresa Cordova, Kim Coulter, Mona Domosh, Marc Doussard, Judith Kenny, Leslie Kern, Wendy Larner, Heather McLean, Oona Morrow, Kris Olds, Jamie Peck, and Nik Theodore provided important feedback and friendship. My feminist political economy comrades in geography, Ann Bonds, Kate Derick-son, Reecia Orcezk, Kendra Strauss, and Marion Werner, have animated several ideas in this book, and helped me to clarify my perspectives. So too have my "between hope and despair" feminist urban scholar group: Sendi Alcidonis, Asma Ali, Fran Klodawsky, Tiffany Myrdahl, and Ebru Ustundag. Rachel Weber, Karen Su, Michelle Boyd, and Anna Guaverra are fellow writing muses, admirable scholars, and trusted colleagues. Megan Heim LaFrombois provided critical assistance with research and editing. More generally, I am grateful to the many feminists across generations and geographies who have shaped and inspired this book with visions of justice, collectivity, and care.

The Department of Urban Planning and Policy and the College of Urban Planning and Public Administration at the University of Illinois at Chicago has provided a supportive, collegial, and enjoyable environment for my work as well as important resources. I am grateful to my bright, caring, and generous colleagues there. The Institute for Research on Race and Public Policy and the Great Cities Institute at UIC also provided essential funding and intellectual support to help me write this book.

The University of Georgia Press and anonymous reviewers shared extensive and incisive feedback on previous drafts. A special thanks to my sharp and witty editor, Mick Gusinde-Duffy, and the Editorial Board who had faith in this project and provided important guidance. I also owe my appreciation to Bethany Snead, David Edward Desjardines, and John D. Joerschke at UGA Press, and to Joseph Dahm for his precise and patient editorial assistance.

And then there were the people who held me up so I could write it all down. Many are mentioned above as both colleagues and loyal friends, but I would add Sarah Keith, Holly Van Havermaat, Joy Wright, Haley Gross, Maureen McLachlan, Hazel Brown, Janet Smith, Moira Zellner, and Valerie Werner. I also want to thank the Parkers, from whom I learned to fight for what I believe in, and my second family of wonderful and caring in-laws.

To my three children, Lily, Liam, and Emmett, whose vivacious, joyful, and intense presence slowed the publication of this book, but made its feminist mission all the more urgent: in writing this book, hopefully I have taught you to work persistently for your accomplishments and for a better world, but to love, laugh, and play along the way. To Matt Clifford—fellow academic, utopian dreamer, wise critic, and love of my life—thank you for fiercely believing in me.

Masculinities and Markets

CHAPTER ONE

Masculinities and Markets

An Introduction

> Just this one time, you leave your child in the car while you go to work. You swear
> you will never do it again. But you can't afford to lose your job or get your benefits
> sanctioned, so you do it.
>
> **LOW-INCOME MOTHER, MILWAUKEE**

> We're not San Francisco. We're not Los Angeles. We can't ask for things like
> affordable housing and union wages *and* downtown development. That will shut
> down the market.
>
> **ELECTED OFFICIAL, MILWAUKEE**

In the broadest sense, this book is about the practices, politics, and places that surround the decisions and dilemmas articulated in the epigraphs to this chapter. I trace the ways in which urban politics and discourses in Milwaukee, Wisconsin, and other cities have changed or stayed the same and how they affect the lives of ordinary people. I quote a woman explaining her decision about child care because this book is an unabashedly feminist endeavor. It illuminates and challenges urban inequalities in gender, race, neoliberal capitalism, and other power relations.

This mother's dilemma—whether to leave her child in a precarious position or to risk losing her job or her public assistance—and the notion that cities must choose between development and benefits for citizens are related to a broader shift toward urban neoliberalism in the United States. This shift was perhaps most salient in the 1980s, but it has diverse geographical and historical roots and variations.

Neoliberalism involves changes in how governments, markets, and citizens act and are perceived. Among other things, it entails extending market logics into many arenas of political and social life. Competition, efficiency, free trade, and other market values come to supersede the practice and perceived value of collective politics, public service, and social welfare provision (e.g., Brown 2015;

Larner 2000; Moody 1997; Peck and Theodore 2002). Rhetoric so embedded in the American psyche that it seems redundant to state it here has justified and accompanied neoliberal policies. It includes claims about independence and freedom through the market, the necessity of "self-sufficiency," the value of efficiency, and the need for liberation from bureaucracy. In concert with other processes, neoliberalism has restructured subjectivities, citizenships, and attendant rights and benefits.[1]

Cities—key sites of neoliberal experimentation and social tensions—now prioritize growth, elite development, privatization, lean government, and the creation of a capital-friendly urban climate (Brenner and Theodore 2002). In the past twenty to thirty years, U.S. cities have transferred public goods to private companies and expanded public-private partnerships. Private contractors provided nearly 20 percent of all urban services throughout the United States in 2007, with cities like Indianapolis and Philadelphia contracting up to 50 percent of all services (Warner and Hefitz 2007). It is now commonplace for privately led bodies (e.g., business associations and developers catering to a largely wealthy, white, and male membership) to determine the allocation of public tax dollars. For Milwaukee, Wisconsin, this represents a turn from the "Sewer Socialism" of the early 1900s. Under Sewer Socialism, Milwaukee's government built planned homes; paid and required living wages; and invested in education, care, and "social reproduction" and recreation while providing infrastructure such as sewers and water. Even during the Great Depression, Milwaukee's government refused to cut services to the bone. Yet, by the 1980s, the city had privatized its sewers along with many other programs. The Milwaukee official quoted in the chapter epigraph conveys the now common sentiment that the city needs to encourage downtown development *rather* than be concerned with poor citizens. While the official implies that bigger cities like Chicago don't have to make such difficult choices, urban leaders have abandoned the poor in U.S. cities of all sizes as they have embraced neoliberal policies.[2]

In some ways, the public barely takes notice of these shifting practices and philosophies in U.S. cities. Meanwhile, scholars, critics, and activists have struggled to document and make sense of urban governance in its current manifestations, such as privatization and intensified competition among cities, welfare reform, and the effects of bond ratings on governance. Among other topics, scholars of urban neoliberalism have considered its differentiated geographies (Is neoliberalism the same in Latin American and the United States? Is it the same in Chicago and Milwaukee?) and its boundaries (When did it start? How is it different from other urban practices? Have we reached a postneoliberal moment?). In some cases at odds with each other, academics have examined both generalized features of neoliberalism as well as local contingencies, variations, contestations, and hybridities.[3] Some scholars have argued that we have made too much of neoliberalism—rattled it around like a child's toy now emptied of its value. Other geographers contend that it is an "illusion," or that our theorizations of neoliberalism give it more power and centrality than it actually possesses.[4]

This book argues that neoliberalism remains a useful concept for understanding discourses, practices, and policies in U.S. cities, which have not shifted toward a postneoliberal moment. However, neoliberal processes need cautious examination and reappraisal through varied epistemological and theoretical angles. Neoliberalism doesn't explain everything and is open to contestation. Neoliberalization processes are best understood as historically contiguous and in relation to other assemblages, practices, and power relations, and there remains a need to explore the "specific routines, practices, networks, and structures through which the neoliberal project has been constructed and sustained" (Peck 2006a, 731; also see Larner 2011).

Furthermore, contemporary theorizations of urban politics perhaps say too little about other forms of power and projects in cities. Gender relations, in particular, have remained rather quiet chimes in the cacophonous literature on U.S. urban neoliberalism and urban politics.[5] With some recent exceptions, race, ethnicity, and sexuality are also less pervasive themes, while cities continue to be comprehended as battlefields of class and capital.

In this book, I contribute to the scholarly discussions on urban neoliberalism in the United States. Most critically, I fill lacunae in the literature by conducting an intersectional analysis of urban politics that simultaneously pays attention to gender, race, the state, neoliberal capitalism, and other power relations. I specifically highlight gender relations, as they have recently been somewhat obfuscated in research on U.S. urban politics. Through a nuanced empirical case study of Milwaukee, I ask these questions: How do gender, race, neoliberalism, and other power relations shape the city and urban politics? Are white privileged masculinities being invigorated as much as markets?

By invoking masculinities, I do not suggest this book is only about men and/or women. I *do* reflect on the domination of men in cities (patriarchy), and I do highlight the experiences of many women. However, I also draw on research by urban theorist Ananya Roy, who suggests that "masculinist power implies much more than the power exercised by men; instead it indicates the construction of the idealized subject-citizen, a regulatory fiction whose presence delimits the field and agenda of politics" (Roy 2003, 108). In this way, even the city might be rendered masculine.

Thus, the book addresses gender and power quite broadly, and in relation to multiple inequalities, especially race. It explores what we imagine and value in cities, and with what effects. I examine how gendered, raced, and capitalist discourses (regulatory fictions) and material practices shape urban governance and development, housing, everyday life and labors, and resistance in Milwaukee. I consider who governs and how, and with what latitude and constraints.

This book contemplates the persistently meager presence of women as urban policy makers and leaders in the United States (Center for American Women and Politics 2014), and how cities embrace competition over connection and collaboration. It probes the raced and gendered subjectivities that are imagined, reified, and erased in urban development discourses about "creative cities" and "new urbanism." It conveys the precarity with which low-income African American women and households are getting by in cities, exploring the stark and intertwined dimensions of racism, sexism, and poverty. Albeit briefly, this book also explores how feminists and progressives—and the issues they fight for, like economic justice and affordable housing—are addressing these inequalities and transforming cities.

Sympathetically, this book challenges scholarship that blames or subsumes all forms of inequality in cities on and into "neoliberal" practices and policies. I suggest that these power relations and projects exist outside of and before neoliberalism, even as they collude with and are often embedded in neoliberal discourses and policies. There are also contradictions and new formations and assemblages of power to consider (see Larner 2011; Larner et al. 2013).

By invoking intersectionality (the study of race, class, gender, sexuality, and other interlocking power relations), this book does not argue that it is a new or unproblematic concept. But maybe there is no need to be vogue. As Barbara Tomlinson (2013) reminds us, the search for the *new* and the *perfect* in academia often distracts researchers from central organizing themes and needed work. Scholarship has made clear that U.S. cities have historically been constructed and expanded via colonial domination, racist exploitation, tumultuous capitalism, and patriarchal practices. The ongoing production of urban built environments is contingent on the production and assembling of these complex inequalities, in sometimes novel ways.[6] This book acknowledges that power relations entail continuity, change, and contestation. I aim to capture the historical legacies and contemporary reworkings and amplifications of gendered and raced neoliberalism and other power relations with some detail and rigor.

I examine these intersectional power relationships by telling an in-depth tale about Milwaukee at specific moments in time. To some, this midsized, midwestern, declining industrial city may seem an unusual or innocuous case. However, Milwaukee's blend of "ordinary" and "extraordinary" characteristics makes it a rich site for analysis. By "ordinary," I mean that Milwaukee's experience parallels other Rust Belt cities in that its economy has moved from industrial to service-oriented, and that it is a midsized city with a diverse ethnic and racial population. Like many cities, it has a deep history of activism with regard to gender, race, and workers' rights.

By "extraordinary," I mean that Milwaukee has historically experimented with its urban politics. It has a bold Socialist past, and implemented neoliberal policies like welfare reform and privatization earlier than many other cities and in somewhat radical forms. Milwaukee is among the most racially segregated cities in the United States, has the country's fourth highest child poverty rate, and has a blend of progressive and regressive politics. Milwaukee offers us a city that we might relate to—a place where it is possible to explore the core and the outer edges of raced, gendered neoliberal urban politics and to reflect deeply about urban governance and inequality in the United States. In other words, Milwaukee resonates beyond its space and time.

This book contributes to dialogues about gender, race, and urban politics. It also engages with questions about how to conduct feminist research in the city, recognizing of course that "feminism" and "city" are not unitary or stable concepts. However, I argue that *urban feminist materialism*, which draws on the strengths of antiracist feminism, political economy, and Foucauldian approaches to power, can reveal complex and subterranean power relations and practice (see Hennessy and Ingraham 1997; Naples 2003). It can help reveal the way that gender, race, and other inequalities operate in cities, in ways that are embedded in, connected to, but also extend beyond neoliberalism and beyond one place. I call my epistemological strategy a *feminist partial political economy of place*. Drawing from historical and current literatures, it has at least four dimensions: (1) emphasis on gendered and intersectional power relations in cities; (2) deep qualitative research and reflexive, *partial* approaches to knowledge production and related practices of power; (3) reliance on feminist concepts of relationality to look beyond particularities and examine commonalities, structures, and opportunities for activist intervention; and (4) the use of theoretical toolkits (Wright 2006) in order to observe, interpret, and challenge material-discursive power relations in complex and revealing ways.

Finally, this book imagines within and beyond a temporal moment. It features two decades of neoliberalism in Milwaukee, but also examines raced and gendered power in the city's Socialist era and envisions a postneoliberal future, asking, for example, whether it might be free of sexism and racism. In this way, the book is aspirational, imagining better futures for all people in cities. My hopes, among many, are that local governments can encourage good jobs and affordable housing as surely as they support downtown development, and for mothers not to have to choose between their jobs and their children's safety.

At the Margins of Urban Political Theory: Feminism, Gender, and Intersectionality

How we theorize cities deeply informs how we make and change them, including what spaces are designed and undone, what problems are made pressing, and what voices and bodies are deemed important. Theories of neoliberalism are connected to research on urban politics in fields like geography, urban planning, and urban sociology. These theories, such as urban regime theory and urban growth machine theory, have provided the schematics by which Western scholars often conceptualize and analyze cities and urban governance. Corresponding activities in cities involve the construction and dissemination of urban policies and development schemes, ideologies, and discourses about the city, the allocation of material resources, and the decisions and discourses of developers, to name a few.

Many of these and other urban processes are gendered and raced in constitution and effect. However, with some exceptions, North American scholarship on planning and urban politics, much of it of political-economy persuasion, typically does not interrogate gender relations, sexism, or patriarchy.[7] Feminist urbanists have critiqued these silences, and a body of feminist urban political scholarship exists. However, this work often occupies a parallel urban landscape, and is not taken up in the dominant canon of urban scholarship. While race has been a more prominent topic in the literature, it is less commonly examined in conjunction with gender and other power relations.

These empirical silences are matched by epistemological omissions and narrow orientations in much U.S. urban scholarship. These include confined constructs and methods, and prevailing political economic approaches that insist that cities grind on the axis of capital and class. The result is a knowledge base that fails both activists and academics as we seek to build better cities.

As such, this book grapples with questions about how to provide feminist renderings of urban politics that are sensitive to intersectional power relations. How should we understand the interactions among gender, race, state power, neoliberalism capitalism, and other relations? Over the years, I have struggled with how a nuanced, geographically sensitive account of urban politics in Milwaukee might speak "back" to mainstream urban theories. Drawing on a range of feminist contributions, this section outlines the theoretical and methodological sensibilities that framed my explorations and suggests some ways forward for urban research.

First, I acknowledge there is no single feminist approach or method to studying cities, although feminists usually challenge gender and other power relations in research and practice. Years ago, Gillian Rose argued that consensus is not necessary to feminism: "Different strategies are needed for different circumstances. We do not have to take sides when we have had so little say in the rules of the game" (1993, 83). The diversity of feminist approaches has made women's lives and the intimate and everyday visible and valuable research topics. Urban feminists have debated and challenged spatial and structural dimensions of gender inequality in cities; used governmentality approaches to probe urban subjectivities and techniques of governance; examined agency and resistance in complex ways; destabilized discursive constructs of gender, women, "capitalism," and the "global"; and detailed the unequal, material consequences of sexual and urban neoliberal violences. Feminists have deeply engaged with power and politics in knowledge production. Some feminist urban research focuses explicitly on women and gender; other research brings feminist epistemological and methodological strategies to broader urban topics. *All of these techniques are valuable.* As Hesse-Biber (2012, 4) points out, "multiple feminist lenses wake us up to layers of sexist, racist, homophobic, and colonialist points of view."

However, mainstream urban political scholarship has often ignored the role of intersecting power relations in cities and the rich and diverse contributions of feminists.[8] The result is often narrowed epistemologies, empirics, and erasures, even as there is a growing emphasis on diversity, contingency, relationality, and assemblage in literatures on urban politics (McGuirk 2012). Too often, urban political economy approaches have privileged class inequalities over other forms of oppression.

Since the 1970s, feminists have critiqued this silence, showing how cities are spun not only on the axis of capital, but also by heterosexist, gendered, and raced relations. In the 1970s, for example, feminists began to detail gendered accumulation processes and divisions of labor in cities. Some argued that the built environment featured designs that differentially served men and women, often leaving women vulnerable to violence. Such designs were the vision of predominately male planners and politicians who viewed the city in masculine, rational, and economic terms.[9] While critical geography research at the time, along with the popular urban growth machine theory that followed, argued that class- and land-based interests motivated urban actors, feminists have detailed how complexly situated identities, communities, and subjectivities have also shaped urban decision making (Clarke, Staeheli, and Brunell 1995; Gilbert 1999). In one example of how, as activists and scholars, feminists have illuminated and challenged intersectional power relations in cities, Dolores Hayden helped found the Woman's Building in Los Angeles around the time that David Harvey published *The Urban Experience.* The Woman's Building's intent was to provide "a social and physical place in the public world in which women can re-evaluate and re-create their gender identity, crossing boundaries of age, race, class, or ethnic origin" (Levrant de Bretteville 1981, 47).

Unfortunately, mainstream urban theorists have rarely considered the intersectional dimensions of urban elites, networks, and governance processes—topics of much urban theory. For example, urban regime theory argues that urban policies are shaped by the composition of a city's governing coalition, the nature of the relationships among its members, and the resources they mobilize (Stone 1989, 2). Gender is not seen as relevant, even though urban governing coalitions are generally saturated with men (usually white, heterosexual, and elite). Yet studies of gender and organizations reveal that "men and masculinized social practices, linked also to class-based and racialized practices, dominate organizational structures and practices and construct women and 'others' as out of place or inferior workers."[10] Additional studies have shown that the absence of women in governance is meaningful in representative, discursive, and material ways, especially as women have long been marginalized in politics.[11] While not all women are feminist, research shows that they are more likely to be so than men, and greater representation of women is often a necessary, if not completely sufficient, condition to transform urban governance. Studies of female-identifying elected officials (especially self-labeled feminists and progressives) show that they place priority on gender rights and family issues, are more likely to bring citizens into the governing process, are more responsive to outside groups, sometimes define power in cooperative rather than coercive terms, and will mitigate the most punitive aspects of welfare reform and incarceration. The latter is especially true among officials who are African American women.

The sidelining of gender, difference, intersectionality, and feminist insights and research is not just an issue of inclusion or equity but also an empirical and epistemological problem. Urban political theories have sometimes reproduced theories that are not reflexive, built on empirical cases, sensitive to messy nuances and everyday life, or attentive to complex power relations in cities and research practice.[12] Scholars of various stripes have made such critiques. Feminist geographer Linda Peake (2015) recently asked, "Where are the subjects" in global urbanisms? In a critique that still resonates, sociologist John Walton (1993, 318) argued decades ago that "a cocksure analytical style begins to enter the writing in which developed theory is used implicitly to 'read off' interpretations for empirical events" in political economy. Noel Castree has opined, "one [should] not *start* with a textbook definition of neoliberalism and *then* look for examples of it 'on the ground'" (2005, 543, emphasis original).

Feminists and antiracist scholars have pushed back against foregone conclusions of political economy and other types of academic "metavision." They have challenged the notion of an urban flaneur as a privileged, objective, detached male gazer and interpreter (Wilson 1991; Wright 2013), even as this subject seems to continually reappear in, for example, the hypermasculinized urban explorer culture (Mott and Roberts 2014).

In addition, dominant urban political scholarship can be a form of "everyday racism" (Gilroy 2000, 2013; Holland 2012) and "cultural misrecognition," where injustices are (re)produced in representation, interpretation, and communication (see Fraser 2013). Cultural misrecognition can include being disparaged in stereotypic public cultural representations and/or in everyday life, but also being silenced in authoritative and scholarly accounts (see Derickson 2015; Fraser 2013). Antiracist feminists and scholars point out that urban scholarship and politics often rely on liberal notions of a white, male, free subject and are inattentive to everyday and systemic racism (e.g., Holland 2012; Lorde 1984; McKittrick 2011). As Katherine McKittrick (2011) argues, research that does address racism, violence, and urbicide may naturalize, presume, and perhaps even profit from describing black death, instantiating an us/them framework and trajectory that it perhaps seeks to critique. Much critical urban theory, dominated by privileged white, male bodies and influenced by Marxist political economy "has done an inadequate job of reckoning in a meaningful way with how its own theories and knowledge production practices are themselves implicated in cultural marginalization and misrecognition" (Derickson 2015).

Feminists have argued for situated and partial knowledges that engage in deep empirical work, clarify the standpoint from which they are produced, blur binaries, engage and make visible the historically marginalized, and avoid all-inclusive claims about knowledge, causality, structure, or the world.[13] McKittrick (2011), among others, has argued for narratives that attend to "human life," include diverse racial and sexual perspectives, and politicize "place-life" and "place-death" differently (see also Gilmore 2007; Woods 2002). In spite of these contributions, dominant urban research retains a strongly masculinist bias.

Much feminist urban research suffers from its own imbalances and silences, remaining a work in progress. In practice, feminist urban researchers have often but not always chosen geographic scales like households, bodies, and neighborhoods, and used qualitative, reflexive methods that facilitate sustained contact with research subjects. These strategies may be more amenable to feminist *praxis*—politically engaged, nonexploitative empirical research that reveals and challenges unjust relations, often starting with the "everyday" (e.g., Rankin 2009; Swarr and Nagar 2010). However, in some cases, feminist urban researchers have overemphasized the "situated" and been reluctant to explore broader causal patterns and generalizations (Fincher 2006). At times, feminist urbanists have avoided engagement with structural arguments, and critics have posed that Anglo-American feminist geography has insufficiently engaged with the material (Bondi and Rose 2003; di Leonardo 1993; Parker 2011). In addition, feminists privileged by race, geography, and other power relations sometimes fail to include or credit other voices and perspectives; make claims that don't match others' experiences; are blinded by their own privilege; or engage in voyeuristic or violent descriptions.[14]

An Intervention: Urban Feminist Partial Political Economies of Place

To address some of these silences and imbalances, in this book I use an urban feminist partial political economy of place (FPEP) approach informed by intersectional feminist and urban literatures. This approach is reflexive, critical, and multivalent, drawing from varied literatures. It is imperfect, but aspirational. FPEP has at least four related dimensions: (1) attention to gendered, raced, and intersectional power relations and structures, including affinities and alliances;

(2) reliance on partial, place-based, materialist approaches to research that attend to power in knowledge production; (3) emphasis on feminist concepts of *relationality* to examine connections among sites, scales, and subjects and to emphasize "life" and possibility; and (4) the use of theoretical toolkits to observe, interpret, and challenge material-discursive power relations in complex ways.

DIFFERENT BODIES . . . DIFFERENT BURDENS: STUDYING INTERSECTIONALITY IN CITIES

As other scholars have posited and I argue in this book, gender remains a lived reality in cities (Jarvis 2009; Jupp 2014) and an important but rather obscured dimension of urban politics. Or, as feminist scholars have variously asserted, it is time for a gender revolution (Campbell 2014) and to notice sexism and patriarchy and "get angry again" (e.g., Gill 2011; Valentine, Jackson, and Mayblin 2014). This argument emerges amid a general climate in the United States that remains somewhat hostile to feminism, a lukewarm interest among urban academics and students in feminist approaches (see Parker 2016), and complex critiques from radical, queer, postcolonial, and antiracist feminists. This latter group has argued that feminist activism and scholarship can be elitist or ignore inequalities like race, ethnicity, or citizenship. Feminist scholars worry that a focus on gender cements binary categories like women and men, and that we should focus on broader agendas of difference in cities. I take these critiques seriously, but argue that, combined with or co-opted by more hostile or conservative impulses, they may help contribute to the erasure of sexist and patriarchal practices.[15]

I recognize the need for diverse studies of various urban inequalities and the limits of some feminist research. One approach I take to this is to study "individual" and "intersectional" strands of power. As Gill Valentine (2007, 19), argues, "In our contemporary concern to theorize the intersection of categories we must not lose sight of the fact that the specific social structures of patriarchy, heteronormativity, oralism and so on that so preoccupied feminists of the 1970s still matter. As such, this article ends with a call for feminism and specifically feminist geography, to re-engage with questions of structural inequalities and power, while at the same time retaining a concern for theorizing the relationship between multiple categories and structures." An FPEP approach recognizes that power falls on and is articulated, embraced, and resisted differently by different bodies and institutions. As black and Chicana feminists first articulated years ago, urban experiences of gentrification, work, migration, state violence, and incarceration are all mediated by race, gender, geography, sexuality, class, ethnicity, citizenship, and life stage, for example.[16] As I explore in the pages to follow, in U.S. cities, race—often in conjunction with neighborhood—affects every facet of life and associated outcomes, including income, health, education, and exposure to the prison-industrial complex.

However, interlocking power relations and their cumulative interactions can be difficult to observe and impossible to tangle apart, especially as lived experiences or identities. Inequality takes different forms in different cities, even where economic conditions seem to be similar (McCall 2005; McDowell 2008). Categories like race and gender are not stable but socially produced, unmoored, and maintained through practices that operate at and across different temporal and spatial scales (McKittrick 2006, 2011; Puar 2012). Even in cities with similar economic conditions, practices like racism and their outcomes might be somewhat different (McCall 2005; McDowell 2008). Also, constructions of difference are produced in and operate across different scales. Gender, for example, is reproduced in homes through gendered divisions of labor, but also in advertising that encourages women and men to buy different products or act feminine or masculine, and by governments that regulate reproductive rights. Thus, conducting "intersectional" research that examines multiple power relations and forms of difference is fraught with difficulty in practice and characterized by controversy (e.g., Cho, Crenshaw, and McCall 2013; Crenshaw 1989; Holland 2012; McKittrick 2006, 2011; Puar 2012). For example, should we focus on difference between or among categories? Does our research flatten or fragment social experience as we either collapse social categories or try to list or add them (Russell 2007)? Does an intersectionality approach "fix" power relations, assume permanence, or deny the performativity of identity? Should we conduct sustained long-term analysis of individual lives to fully capture the multiple power relations, avoid categories, or focus on specific categories and quantifiable differences like earnings or education?[17]

There is no simple solution to these questions, and myriad approaches to intersectionality are needed. In this book, I explore practices and inequalities surrounding race, gender, and class/poverty in Milwaukee. In some ways, I capture additional forms of difference and power, such as heteronormativity and geography. By conducting lengthy qualitative interviews and participant observation, I was able to listen to and reflect some of the ways that people in Milwaukee experience, articulate, and engage with multiple and cumulative power relations in their daily lives. For example, I show how my African American interviewees reject and sometimes laugh at neoliberal discourses about work and responsibility and how they enact power in daily life. Rather than focusing on individual identities, however, I explore diffuse power relations in different scales and spaces, occasionally using quantitative data to articulate uneven outcomes related to violence, incarceration, and poverty that result from these workings. As Chun, Lipsitz, and Shin (2013) point out, "intersectionality primarily concerns the way things work, rather than who people are."

Given the unfeasibility of capturing all forms of difference and power in Milwaukee, I made strategic choices and sacrifices in order to analyze and theorize some power relations in meaningful ways. For example, this book emphasizes race and gender, perhaps more than class and poverty, in part because the latter is more pervasively explored in dominant urban scholarship, and in part because it follows intersecting material patterns of inequality in Milwaukee. My empirical work focuses specifically on the experiences of African Americans in Milwaukee, particularly in contrast to the experiences of whites. I therefore do not capture the complex realities of all racial difference in Milwaukee. This was a strategic choice in that black-white relations are particularly stark with recent poverty, unemployment, incarceration, and infant mortality rates three to eight times higher for African Americans than for whites (also see Holland 2012). However, my decision was also a product of the spaces and subjects with which I engaged.

Similarly, although I explore diverse people's lives in Milwaukee, I frequently use concepts like women and men to describe actors, populations, and related exclusions and practices. There is limitation and loss in my own and others' partially intersectional and categorical research strategies. In mapping gender, or sex, inequalities, I sometimes reinscribe categories and dichotomies and erase nuance.[18] Gendered variations, disability, age, ethnicity, sexuality, and certain complexities of the real-life experiences of my research subjects and Milwaukee residents remain underexplored. Yet I highlight, with some detail, temporally and spatially specific raced and gendered power relations that persist in Milwaukee and manifest elsewhere. However imperfectly, I articulate some black women's lives, experiences, and perspectives (often erased and obscured), with some integrity and detail. To push against my white privilege and limits to self-reflexivity, I draw heavily upon the words of my interviewees and black feminist theory for assistance.[19] I engage with pressing realities where poor black women experience complex, cumulative oppressions via the state, misogyny, neoliberal capitalism, racialized violence, and more, yet contest and carry on in spatially complex ways.[20] Rather than knowing in advance that any event is just more of the same old story, more of the same patriarchy, the same racism, the same form of class exploitation (Morris 1998, 199), I examine specific practices and how they are being challenged, remade, and reworked over time (see also Gibson-Graham 2006).

This book uncovers and examines affinities, alliances, or contradictions among particular strands and processes of power and resistance, an important agenda for urban research.[21] I consider, for example, whether neoliberal markets are reinvigorating white masculinities and question whether progressive and Socialist practices in Milwaukee were free of raced and gendered power relations. Affinities, relationships, and contradictions related to patriarchy, racism, heteronormativity, and global capitalism in cities need further examination, in part because they reveal openings for activist intervention and offer more thorough forms of explanation. While limited by empirical work focused on a particular place and moment in time, this book engages with and fosters broader conversations about such connections.

CAN FEMINISTS SEE BEYOND THE CITY? PARTIAL MATERIALIST KNOWLEDGES AND RESEARCH

If trying to study complex power relations raises epistemological and methodological questions, so too does thinking in and beyond place. An FPEP approach to knowledge is partial. It challenges epistemic violences, where, for example, all city stories are the same, certain lives are erased or reduced, or all futures already known. Partial approaches to knowledge grounded *in place* are essential. There is value in conscious if imperfect reflexivity, sustained contact with research subjects, and contextualized feminist empirical work, as many feminist scholars have articulated. In this book, I tried to carefully and justly represent my research subjects and sites, not breathlessly characterize them with a sweep of a hand. As such, I sat in homes and coffee shops and attended events. I listened to experiences of exclusion and activists' hopes for better neighborhoods. Elected officials shared with me aspirations and visions of Milwaukee. I sat in "creative-class" events to understand what was silent and what was spoken. As some low-income African American women moved slowly with the aid of walkers, wheezed with asthma, and feared panic attacks on buses, I came to understand how overlapping and sustained power inequalities and traumas related to and outside of neoliberalism became burdens on their bodies. I also observed how these women created spaces of connections and care. I couldn't convey or comprehend these complex experiences by dropping in from above or without engaging with black feminist and other critical frameworks.

But these experiences are threaded to and repeated in places beyond Milwaukee. Thus, my FPEP approach challenges an overly situated approach, drawing on materialist theories and arguing with Ruth Fincher (2006, 23) that feminist geography should move beyond its "clear aversion to generalizing causes beyond the particular context." I argue that neoliberal capitalism, working through and with other inequalities, has wreaked much devastation. Gendered heteronormative structures produce violence and uneven work burdens. Racism in the United States is insidiously embedded in all social, cultural, and economic life (Omi and Winant 2014); and relational violences continue to produce a condition of being black that is predicated on struggle (McKittrick 2011). In Milwaukee and elsewhere, whiteness serves as a marker of privilege by which multiple conceptions of race are situated and constructed as "others" and gendered and racial violence is legitimated and sustained (Pulido 2000; Richie 2012; Wilson 2009). African American women in Milwaukee and throughout the United States are currently the most likely group to be poor, die from intimate violence, and experience precarities related to housing and health (e.g., Hill Collins 2001; Jones 2009; Richie 2012). As black queer feminists articulate, such inequalities are deeply rooted in slave history and not simply about racism or capital accumulation, but also eroticism, colonial imaginations, and histories (e.g., Holland 2012). We might engage a "black sense of place" that materially and imaginatively situates "historical and contemporary practices of domination and the difficult entanglements of racial encounter" (McKittrick 2011, 950).

It might take more than a "situated" view to contest and comprehend such power relations. If situated knowledge seeks to produce, as Gillian Rose (1997, 318) suggested, "non-generalizing knowledges that can learn from other knowledges," then my FPEP approach may be more *partial* than situated. It is also materialist. Deep structures—albeit malleable—related to gender, race, class, and sexuality critically shape urban life, and we might try to understand these systemically unequal and common, if nebulous and contested, power relations.[22] We might make claims and connections in order to contest. Here, a feminist and culturally informed critical political economy has a primary role in contributing to politically enabling understandings of the entanglements of power (Sharp et al. 2000; Springer 2012). As sociologist Michaela di Leonardo (1993) has argued with regard to political economy, "feminists should not leave home without it" (see also McDowell 1991; Wright 2013). In my research, partial and critically interrogated political economic frames helped me ask important questions about urban politics and relationships; to "place" my ethnographic encounters; and to explore how neoliberal, racist, heteronormative, and patriarchal policies and structures continue to create uneven geographies and amplify poverty, difference, and despair in Milwaukee and beyond, although sometimes in clever and new ways.[23] Understanding these relations requires a partial view, as I have suggested, but also a relational analysis, as I explain in the next section.

RELATIONAL RESEARCH: MAKING CONNECTIONS AND SITE SELECTIONS

Without aiming for goddess tricks of generalizability or totalizing theory, my FPEP approach uses relationality to think beyond place and particularities. Using varied terms and metaphors, feminists have argued for relational research that maps links across different sites and scales to recognize difference, common oppressions, and opportunities for activist interventions.[24] In this way, one can recognize the politics of location and power of agency but not be trapped in "defeatism and isolationalism of forever partial and situated knowledges" (Walby 2000, 194). Relational research, for example, makes it possible to understand how inequalities are both locally and globally constructed and contested, and how experiences are connected across space. Relationality takes seriously "spaces of encounter" (McKittrick 2011). Long used by feminists to critique overly economistic, individualist, and rational theories and practices, relationality as a concept reminds us of the connected nature of the human and the nonhuman, and of places, practices, and power, and can emphasize life and possibility (see also Gilmore 2007).

Urbanists (feminist and otherwise), too, draw on relational thinking. Urbanists have called for multiscalar analysis of various phenomena and for a fluid, evolving process produced through contestation rather than a fixed category (e.g., Brenner 2001; Ward 2010). We can see cities not as a stable geography but as assemblages, as unbounded sites and processes organized with and through broader social and political practices and institutions, and as sites of broader subject formation.[25] Cities, experiences, and all relations are ultimately "embeddedness in multiple elsewheres" (Mbembé and Nuttall 2004, 348). Via relationality and relational comparative urban research, one might analyze distinct but not isolated causal phenomena and social relations surrounding cities and urban politics.

However, how to conduct relational feminist urban analysis and make connections in scales, times, and places is not always clear. Feminists and feminist geographers have experimented with varied metaphors and techniques, such as Cindi Katz's (2004) topographies based on thick descriptions of social relations, material practices, and constructions of meaning in different geographical contexts, and Pratt and Rosner's (2006) explorations of the global intimate. Within a broader study of local and national heteropatriarchal urban politics, Isoke (2013) explores subjectivities and social spaces produced or claimed by black women, including homescapes of caring and connection.[26]

These feminist geographic analyses formed a pathway for my own research, which was also informed by Michael Burawoy's (2009) *extended case method* and the *institutional ethnography*, and discourse analysis strategies of Dorothy Smith (1990, 1999) and Nancy Naples (2003). According to Smith (1999), empirical research of marginalized women's daily lives is a critical endeavor that provides questions, answers, and explanations about broader policies, power, and institutions. Institutional ethnography provides insight into how dominant relations of ruling (in knowledge production, texts, policies, and acts) help structure the "everyday worlds" and perceptions of individuals living with them. Thus, these relational ethnographies of lives can reveal how people in one place are aligned with activities and relevances elsewhere (Smith 2005). I also drew on Burawoy's extended case method, which suggests four extensions to produce reflexive understandings of social processes and power and improve theory. In Milwaukee, I extended into the lifeworlds of my participants, visiting their homes, sharing conversations and coffee with them, and attending meetings and protests beside them. (Feminists' ample insights about power and praxis in feminist ethnography and qualitative research, too numerous to cite here, provide useful guidance on this matter.) I also extended my observations across time and space, exploring Milwaukee's history as a Socialist city and its transitions in light of broader national and global trends, including deindustrialization and backlashes against feminism (see Roy 2015 on the importance of history to urban analyses). I extended conceptually, thinking about how the micropolitics of exclusion in City Hall meetings or caring for a sick child are connected to macro processes like sexism and neoliberalism. And in the end, as Burawoy recommends, I inform and perhaps reorient current theories about urban politics based on the findings revealed in the pages ahead.

Perhaps unexpectedly, I chose a single, entire city as my primary research site. On one hand, there has been a recent call among urban theorists (feminist and other) for reinvigorated and even relational comparative urban research, especially spanning supposed North/South divides (e.g., Peake and Rieker 2013; Robinson 2011; Ward 2010). Single case studies of cities might be seen as *too* particular and *too* local, or reinforce divides like Global North and Global South. On the other hand, some feminists might counter that a study of Milwaukee, understood in unbounded ways, could not be partial or situated enough. Feminist urban research has often focused on neighborhood scales or only on households or particular groups of women, a valuable strategy. However, I would argue that there is currently a place and a need for feminist citywide analysis, and even deep single (though relational and embedded) case studies. Cities have too often been built, theorized, and narrated by nonfeminists.[27] Foundational monographs of cities and urban politics (in diverse geographies and from varied theoretical persuasions) may give the impression that raced, gendered, or other power relations are irrelevant. Many obscure a variety of scales and encounters of urban life, and they may be entirely devoid of subjects (Peake 2015). Feminist studies of cities that are deep, wide, and relational, if not strictly comparative, have been and continue to be valuable additions to the literature. These relational contributions might counter a tendency to produce ahistorical or overly synthetic renderings in strictly comparative analysis (e.g., Robinson 2011), and might later be joined or converted into contextualized, multiscalar, relational, intersectional comparative analyses.

In this book, I explore how gendered, raced, heteronormative, and capitalist power relations might *pervade* urban politics and practices, and simultaneously operate in multiple and connected sites and material-discursive ways across time in one city. I sought to understand how discourses and global materialities surrounding urban development were connected to daily and embodied lives of women and to specific practices of elite actors. This was in part a strategy to map gendered, raced, and classed practices and *unfix* synthetic notions about where and how they operate and matter.

I selected Milwaukee because of its status as an "ordinary" city. It also had a unique history of experimentation in urban politics, including an early, eager embrace of neoliberal politics like school privatization and welfare reform under an ideological mayor. Milwaukee was also home to progressive urban politics, including labor and feminist activism. But I struggled with what and who to study and where to locate myself as a researcher in the city. Guided by my FPEP approach, I have tried to select sites, or embedded cases, that would not reproduce or dichotomize gendered concepts (e.g., the global as masculine, the local as feminine, the household as the place where gendered practices happen, "activism" as only predefined public acts). I wanted to see how power relations were historically and are currently present in multiple, connected sites across the city and in extended sociospatial relations beyond Milwaukee.

THEORETICAL TOOLKITS: SEEING POWER MANY WAYS FROM MANY DIRECTIONS

The chapters and stories in this book emphasize not only diverse actors, sites, and scales, but also complex and polyvalent material-discursive processes of power. Drawing inspiration from scholars like Melissa Wright (2006), I used a hybridized "toolkit" that drew on different epistemological traditions and methods, including feminist materialism, political economy, black feminist theory, and governmentality studies. As Springer (2012) recently noted, there is a need for analyses of neoliberalism that enjoin political economy and poststructural or governmentality approaches.

The theoretical toolkit in my FPEP approach is essential to this book in at least three ways. First, it might persuade you, the readers of this book, that pernicious gendered, raced, capitalist, and other power practices continue to shape cities. In a U.S. climate of antifeminism and amid academic antipathy about gendered power, perhaps using different registers and theories can speak to broader audiences. Second, in Milwaukee, my theoretical toolkit helped produce sharper, fuller observations of gendered and other power relations, which can be subterranean and tricky to capture in detail. People often underestimate or are unable to see gendered, raced, and other power-exerting behaviors, biases, and patterns. For example, in one study, employers reported via an anonymous survey that they did not discriminate by race. However, when confronted with white and black applicants with identical backgrounds, they were more likely to call back white applicants with a criminal record than black applicants (Pager and Quillian 2005). Furthermore, as feminists argue, those with power and privilege are often unable to see how their agendas and activities constrain and limit those without power (Harding 1993; Naples 2003; Smith 2005). Patterns of willingly "unseeing" can be connected to practices that undermine opposition, and to aversions to feminism in urban politics and planning and elsewhere. Feminists, antiracists, queer theorists, and others are sometimes seen as "killjoys" who take the solidarity and even fun away from social relations, social movements, and scholarship (see Ahmed 2010; Parker 2016). Thus, one often has to use multiple techniques of observation, analysis, interpretation, and communication to study and engage audiences with topics like feminism, heterosexism, and racism.[28]

This book shows variously located and intersecting material-discursive activities that coordinate and reproduce oppressive neoliberal, gendered, raced, and other systems. Feminists like Liz Bondi (2005) note that gender operates in several ways in cities, including embodied experiences related to perceived identity attributes; a social relation and organizing element in which the structures, functions, and regulations of cities are shaped; and a performance of behaviors or scripts that are often taken for granted and routinely enacted. Racism also operates in these and other ways, shaping resource allocation, urban form, and urban narratives and materialities of life and death (Bonds and Inwood 2015; Holland 2012; McKittrick 2011).

Using feminist materialism, governmentality, and black feminist theories and different emphases in each chapter (described below) helped me reveal these varied modes of power relations. Responding to calls for more integrative analysis of neoliberalism (Springer 2012), this book demonstrates how gendered, heteronormative, raced, and neoliberal practices operate in intertwined material-discursive manners: through *subjectivities*, *texts*, and *discourses* that valorize neoliberalism, masculinities, whiteness, notions of competition, markets, efficiency, and specific autonomy and that impose associated rules and practices. These same discourses, texts, and policies devalorize care, connection, femininities, social reproduction, feminism, and racialized women and other practices. These relations of rule also work through structures like the state and neoliberal capitalism and the *oppression of females, female-identifying and racialized bodies, and neighborhoods* via exclusion, silencing, dispossession, microaggressions, violence, incarceration, and failure to allocate resources or enforce equity.

My theoretical toolkit helped me observe and articulate these different practices and relations without assuming the hegemony of neoliberalism and revealed some possibilities for activist interventions. While researching this book, I stayed open to learning from and engaging with other theories, knowledges, and encounters in the field.[29] My research started with flexible points of entry (e.g., organizations and individual actors in Milwaukee), but I did not imagine they would manifest as neatly organized cases. Thus, like most books, this one ended up somewhere rather distant from its starting point, and there are perhaps many threads to grasp. However, I have tried to map, match, and challenge the mutating and wily ways that power operates in Milwaukee.

Conclusion and Organization of This Book

The content and organization of this book reflect the FPEP approach. Using different theories, I provide an analysis of how gendered, raced, neoliberal, and other power relations unfold and operate in U.S. urban politics, especially in

Milwaukee. For the reader, there may be many paths to follow. However, I have infused variety and stripped theoretical jargon within chapters so as to make this book accessible and sufficiently engaging to readers of varied persuasions and backgrounds. Therefore each chapter is slightly unique in tone, intent, and empirical focus; draws on specific theoretical traditions; and reveals different facets of gendered, raced, neoliberal, and other power relations in Milwaukee.

Chapter 2 complicates the dominant narratives of urban neoliberalism in the United States. Drawing on diverse feminist scholarship, it provides an intersectional and nuanced rendering of the evolution of urban neoliberalism that gives more equal footing to projects like patriarchy and racism. It articulates several gendered, raced, and capitalist discourses and values that have forged and continue to shape urban politics, including competition and autonomy. It then explores contemporary related inequalities and practices in governance, urban development and housing, and everyday lives and labors in cities.

Chapter 3 shifts the focus back to Milwaukee. Relationally, it describes Milwaukee's history as a Socialist city and its shift toward neoliberalism. It explores tenacity and transformation in raced, gendered, capitalist, and other power relations in the city's urban politics (and the broader United States) over a period of more than one hundred years. Drawing on feminist materialism, it shows how racism, sexism, and uneven capitalism persisted throughout this period, with periods of progress often followed by a backlash. This happened in temporally specific but patterned ways, even as different governing regimes were more or less egalitarian and/or attentive to social reproduction.

Chapter 4 explores uneven urban governances via specific practices, discourses, and policies, including new urbanism. It articulates the same gendered and raced dimensions of new urbanism—a nostalgic urban design and planning movement promoting walkability and sustainability. Drawing from antiracist feminist materialism informed by poststructuralism, it describes new urbanism as a rationality that reinforced and supported neoliberal, raced, and gendered inequalities through texts and discourse and related resource allocation. Somewhat more straightforwardly and using new urbanism as a lens, it also explores gendered neoliberal governance in terms of who composes city leadership and associated consequences for urban discourses, decision making, policy and resource allocation, democracy, and specific raced and gendered inequalities.

Chapter 5 analyzes creative-class policies and discourses, whereby cities like Milwaukee sought to attract young, creative elites as a strategy to boost economic development. Using antiracist feminist materialism, governmentality, and embodiment approaches, the chapter examines the subjectivities, performances, and institutions surrounding creative-class politics in the city, considering who and what they valued, for example. The chapter focuses briefly on Richard Florida as the national and then global purveyor of creative-class theories. However, using qualitative interviews and observations, it then focuses on an organization, Young Professionals of Milwaukee, that embodied and espoused idealized creative-class subjects.

Chapter 6 is intentionally feminist in its exploration of households and everyday life in a book about urban politics. It is the most explicitly ethnographic chapter, foregrounding the voices of low-income African American women. It draws from feminist materialism, black feminism, and social reproduction theories to explore women's daily lives and labors, surrounding policies (like welfare reform), and power relations and contestations.

Chapter 7 focuses on activism and urban development in Milwaukee, including the intersectional and material-discursive power relations that surround them. It describes the constrained context for community organizing—especially for feminist and black organizations—beginning in the late 1980s. It then explores Milwaukee's plan for a signature, neoliberal downtown development project in the early 2000s and the protracted activist effort to include "community benefits" like affordable housing in the development. I show how gendered and raced inequalities of exclusion were threaded through conventional politics and places like City Hall, but also manifested in progressive institutions and practices.

Collectively, these chapters allow a complicated and somewhat novel story to unfold about gendered, raced, and neoliberal urban politics in Milwaukee. Rather than provide one more case of new and nefarious neoliberalism, this story connects and explores a wider range of urban power relations and practices over time, including but not limited to patriarchy and racism. It does not erase history and geography. It bridges the material experiences of poor women of color and wealthy creative elites in Milwaukee to each other and to discourses about what cities should be and whom they are for. Collectively, the chapters frame a feminist rendering of urban neoliberalism in Milwaukee and beyond—a version that reinforces some existing conceptions, but dismantles and challenges others.

CHAPTER TWO

Reconsidering History

Gender, Race, and Neoliberal
Narratives in U.S. Cities

Mayors must rid themselves of the self-pity that focuses on urban pathology and
ignores the advantages and virtues of cities—thus undermining the ability of cities
to compete in the marketplace.

MILWAUKEE MAYOR JOHN NORQUIST, 1998

An emphasis on a city's ability to "compete in the marketplace," at any social
cost, has grown to prominence among many U.S. mayors, urban power brokers,
and federal policy makers. These views parallel reductions in federal funding
for cities; sharp cuts to urban services and privatization of others; decreases in
the size and scope of governments; intensified focus on downtown development, cultivation of capital, and revenue-generating activities; and abdication
of investment in minority neighborhoods, poor residents, and social welfare
more broadly. The role of cities is now to aid and abet business growth, with
benefits gradually trickling down to citizens. These practices, along with their
ideological emphasis on markets, competition, unfettered capitalism, and individualism, are commonly labeled "neoliberalism" by scholars and activists.

In this chapter, I first explore how these perspectives, policies, and practices
came to prevail in U.S. cities. Disrupting some mainstream narratives, I argue that shifts toward neoliberalism in Milwaukee were more contiguous than
abrupt. I also suggest that gendered and raced power relations were essential to
and integrated with the increased prominence of these neoliberal urban policies and practices. Importantly, uneven gendered and raced relations were *also*
fundamental features of the political regimes and policies that preceded neoliberalism, including Keynesianism. In fact, intersecting and imbalanced power
relations have been a consistent component of the discourses and practices of
U.S. urban politics. It remains a critical task for urban researchers to understand
complex gendered, raced, capitalist, and other power relations, which manifest
uniquely and interact differently in varied moments of time.

In this vein, I turn to extant urban inequalities in the second section of this chapter. I first argue that there are dominant discourses and values surrounding U.S. politics that are neoliberal capitalist, gendered, and racist. Related uneven material conditions for women, the poor, and nonwhite individuals persist in cities, in governance, in urban development and housing, and in everyday life and labors. These inequalities contribute to disparate earnings and poverty rates, among other things. Finally, I briefly consider how feminist and other "resistance" projects have fared in challenging uneven power relations in cities.

This chapter lays the groundwork to support the central aim of this book: to provide a feminist intersectional narrative of urban politics, and to empirically explore gendered, raced, neoliberal, and other power relations and their contestation in U.S. cities like Milwaukee. Subsequent chapters deepen and expand this argument.

Gendering and Racing Narratives of Urban Politics

Many scholarly narratives suggest that neoliberalism, as a philosophy and a set of policies and practices, emerged in the late 1970s in the United States, and contrast it with the reigning political and economic practices that preceded it, often labeled "Keynesianism." Named after economist Maynard Keynes, Keynesianism dominated U.S. policy and ideology from the late 1940s to the early 1970s. Among other things, Keynes argued that government had a role in stimulating and balancing capitalism, counteracting its crudest effects. In this vein, the U.S. government provided direct economic stimulus and investment, workplace and wage regulation, protections for some workers and consumers, and a basic "safety net" for some citizens, consisting of cash assistance, food stamps, and other social entitlements. The rationale for these latter practices was not entirely altruistic. An underlying assumption of this model was that economically stable workers and citizens were good consumers, would drive "demand," and thus would help maintain a robust economy.

During the Keynesian period, financial resources were channeled to distressed cities in the forms of subsidies and grants, providing safety nets in some places. For example, severely troubled cities like Detroit and Newark received funds for planning, job development, and social services during the 1960s and 1970s under an effort titled the Model Cities Program. On some occasions and for short periods, urban crises, and the resources targeted to address them, were defined in holistic ways that addressed not only economic problems, but also racial exclusion, social inequality, and community disintegration (Sites 2003, 37). There was some federal commitment to addressing poverty and troubled cities. However, feminist scholars have shown that Keynesian urban investments and policies surrounding housing, social welfare, and urban renewal were often laced with gendered, classist, and racist practices.[1]

Not unrelated, cities experienced high levels of social activism related to civil rights, women's rights, and broader social equality during the Keynesian era. This activism both influenced and was influenced by the broader political climate and Keynesian policies. Activism connected to discriminatory housing practices, school racial segregation, and violence against women, to name a few, touched many cities, and municipalities began to have African Americans and minority leaders (and to a lesser extent, women) on their city councils. In 1967, Carl Stokes became the first African American to be elected mayor of a major American city, Cleveland. Second-wave feminist activism in cities peaked in the 1970s. For example, over twenty thousand women gathered in New York City in 1970 for the Women's Strike for Equality, demanding equal political and work opportunities for women (Gourley 2008). In the 1970s, several Milwaukee charter chapters of the National Organization for Women, a women's rights organization, were founded. So too was the organization "9 to 5," which focused on race and gender inequality and the rights of working women.

This activism produced substantial legal and political achievements for women, workers, and minorities, including but not limited to the Civil Rights Acts of 1964 and 1968, the establishment of the Equal Employment Opportunities Commission, and the illegalization of marital rape (Dierenfield 2008; Gourley 2008). Thus, while the Keynesian era was marked by discrimination and inequality produced by the state and society, government also played a role in mitigating some of these oppressions through specific policies. Furthermore, new forms of feminist and community organizing emerged, focusing on collectivity, inclusion, care, community-driven activism, and democracy. During the 1960s and 1970s, there was public appreciation for these new ideas and the necessity of collective action and investment (not withdrawal) to counter inequalities and create more livable communities. Public investments in shared goods like libraries, universities, and even the arts reflected and cemented these beliefs (Bourdieu 1998; Brodie 2007; Walby 2011).

By the late 1970s, as the U.S. economy was floundering, U.S. cities were awash in vivid unrest. Capital flight, deindustrialization, oil crises, declining profits for businesses, and an associated decrease in national welfare funding at a time of increasing immigration, need, and social conflict plagued U.S. cities. In some cities, the decade's gains by public labor unions and activists had increased the city's financial obligations. In New York, these issues came to a head with the infamous budget crisis. Extensive tax exemptions for real estate and generous benefits and contracts for city workers had strained the city budget, and short-term borrowing of up to three billion dollars annually to finance mortgages on risky downtown development pushed it over the edge (see Greenberg 2008, 125; Sites 2003, 37–39).[2] The New York fiscal crisis was eventually "resolved," with severe cuts to local government, social services, public infrastructure, and worker benefits. New urban regeneration strategies were put into place, focusing on incentivizing business attraction and growth and downtown development via subsidies and tax breaks.

Some scholars have argued that the resolution of the fiscal crisis in New York and the surrounding discourses and policies ushered in and epitomized the shift toward neoliberalism in the United States, which had largely replaced Keynesianism by the 1980s.[3] Other cities embraced New York's strategies, redefining good urban government as the "ability of formal government to assist, collaborate with, or function like the corporate community" (Hackworth 2007, 11).

The narration of the New York crisis and its resolution was important to the increasing popularity of neoliberalism. The crisis was not described as a failure of capital. Foundations, media, and other commentators argued that the city's crisis erupted because of excessive demands from the poor, minorities, community groups, and liberal politicians. Much less blame accrued to developers and financial institutions (led by elite white men) who had overbuilt and profited, or the city's risky mortgage investments. This framing, enabled by a broader backlash against labor, feminist, and civil rights movements, helped justify reduced social services (such as transportation, housing, and hospital services), most intensively relied on by women and minorities (see Greenberg 2008; Sites 2003).

Many scholars agree that urban neoliberal policies became an intractable reality in U.S. cities by the mid-1980s, although fewer have explored how and why they were blended with raced and gendered ideologies, discourses, and practices.[4] These power configurations (locally tailored but fueled in part by global changes and the Reagan administration) have continued to shape U.S. urban landscapes, especially through norms, subjectivities, and governing discourses (e.g., Brown 2015; Dardot and Laval 2013; Hackworth 2008; Larner 2003). Their seeming dominance actually helps obscure the fact that "welfare queens" emerged as a social threat almost out of thin air, that racial and gender equality have not been achieved through markets, and that concepts other than competition, entrepreneurialism, and autonomy might shape our collective understanding of urban governance.

By the late 1980s, pervasive neoliberal policies emphasized urban growth and downtown urban development, privatization, interurban competition, reductions in taxes and social services, and cuts in social welfare spending, among others (Peck and Tickell 2002). Unmoored from federal supports, cities were expected to compete with each other for economic development and even for residents. It was a "sink-or-swim" environment, with cities blamed for their own economic fates. Social welfare spending and protections were increasingly seen as an inefficient impediment to the market.

Cuts in social welfare affected women and people of color the most, and often deepened inequalities. Even as welfare spending had been constructed and delivered in raced and gendered ways, its reductions disproportionately targeted programs that were staffed by and served African Americans. Diminished social services hurt poor residents, usually women and minorities, in cities across the United States. Nonprofit organizations and churches, often staffed by women, were also affected. For example, a dramatic cut in food stamps left churches and other charitable organizations in cities around the country hard-pressed to feed hungry residents and homelessness as a social phenomenon emerged and persisted. Emergency service needs related to health, food, and housing intensified around the country.[5] Direct federal welfare cuts were combined with other excisions and rescaling where responsibility for social welfare and other social assistance was downloaded to local governments, but with insufficient and ever declining resources. Local governments then contracted with nonprofit, for-profit, and religious organizations to deliver social services, again with inadequate funds to meet community needs.

New kinds of actors and organizations emerged in urban governance under neoliberal policies, and "old" actors (e.g., developers, real estate professionals, corporate leaders) often claimed more influence. New private and nonprofit entities emerged to deliver urban services, and public-private partnerships increased. Emerging arrangements like business improvement districts allowed public tax dollars to be allocated (temporarily or permanently) to the private sector for economic development purposes.[6] Foundations and think tanks, including some based in Milwaukee, seriously influenced urban policies and governance (see chapters 3 and 7; Peck 2006b; Springer 2010).

Milwaukee embraced neoliberal practices. Belying its history of "Sewer Socialism," it infamously privatized the city's sewer system, along with museums, electric power plants, hospitals, and welfare services for low-income women. Other cities acted similarly: Chicago has privatized a wide range of services and infrastructure projects since the 1980s, from janitorial work to engineering, parking enforcement, tollways, and, to residents' dismay, even parking meters (Ashton, Doussard, and Weber 2012; Janega 2009; Thornton 2007). Cities such as Philadelphia and Indianapolis privatized more than 50 percent of their services in the 1990s. In some areas, such as garbage services, privatization has doubled in cities. The town of Maywood, California, made headlines in 2010 because it no longer employed a single worker. These trends suggest a "new normal" for cities with regard to urban governance and engagement and the influence of private actors. However, these findings ought to be considered in context. In 2007, over 50 percent of urban service delivery remained public, according to the Reason Foundation's Annual Privatization Report (Warner and Hefitz 2007). Recent data hint at a backlash against privatization, with cities and states reclaiming previously outsourced or privatized services or implementing responsible contracting requirements (Ball 2014; In the Public Interest 2014).

Scholars sometimes suggest that the harsh economic dogma of neoliberalism replaced a softer, socially oriented Keynesianism. While this argument hints at the austerity entailed in neoliberal reforms and policies, it belies the fact that both Keynesianism and neoliberalism, in pure form, are based on instrumental economic logics and principles, and were largely produced and purveyed by a narrow body of elite, Western, white male economists. In the United States, economists and economic theories are often construed as rational, scientific, and incontrovertible. However, economic rationalities are socially produced and often work with or actively disguise racist, sexist, or other ideologies, practices, and motives. For example, welfare reform, seen as a quintessential "neoliberal" reform and couched in discourses about markets and efficiency, was also fueled by racist attitudes and anxiety about the 1960s erosion of racial and sexual control.[7] As legal scholar Margaret McCluskey (2003, 815) argues, "In 1977, Nobel Laureate economist James Buchanan and coauthor Richard Wagner warned that the Keynesian policies favoring inflation over unemployment contributed to 'increasingly liberalized attitudes toward sexual activities, a declining vitality of the Puritan work ethic . . . [and the] explosion of the welfare rolls.' Anti-Keynesian economic rhetoric about the failures of 'big government' took root in a sociopolitical context that linked a strong federal government with equal protection for African Americans." "Economic" claims about the expense and inefficiency of welfare were attached to racist attitudes. For example, as more people of color enrolled in welfare programs, public support declined. Reforms and reductions in welfare programs also became more popular when they were attached to media stereotypes about racialized poor mothers and urban narratives of decline (Fraser and Gordon 1994; Williams 1995). According to geographer David Wilson (2009, 142), "The Reagan years featured stunning pronouncements about a supposed reality in these cities and beyond: the rise of spiraling, out-of-control black and Hispanic populations and communities. These narrations widely featured politically charged terms like 'Welfare Queens,' 'Welfare Kings,' 'the malignancy of welfarism' and the 'pretending disadvantaged.'"

The city of Milwaukee and Wisconsin as a whole were first in line with welfare reform experiments, at the urging of then-mayor John Norquist. Milwaukee eventually adopted some of the strictest work requirements for welfare recipients in the country. As in other cities, white women received more job training and better jobs, and women of color were penalized more times and for greater amounts when they missed work or committed some other infraction in Milwaukee (Collins and Mayer 2010).

Other assaults and inequities helped produce and were part of the shifting raced, gendered, and neoliberal political climate in Milwaukee and the United States. In the years leading up to 1980, during periods of high activism, nearly 70 percent of legal and political outcomes in equal rights, family law, choice and reproduction, violence against women, and employment rights were profeminist. This dropped to 47 percent during the Reagan years and to 20 percent in the 1990s (Bashevkin 1998). As Susan Faludi (2006) describes, this occurred amid a broader backlash against women and feminism. In this backlash, women's rights were attacked, while simultaneously feminism was blamed for the problems that these attacks produced. This gradually gave way to a supposedly "postfeminism" moment.[8] In the urban planning and policy arena, actors argued that we had already "done women," and more radical feminist visions of urban transformation were often translated into bland and elite visions of new urbanism and livability.[9]

While feminist and antiracist influences and activism persisted in various forms, a similar backlash occurred against civil rights. White people "tired" of rights rhetoric and policies. Discursive aggression toward minorities in cities became amplified, and a quiet assault on black people occurred through rapidly rising incarceration rates (Alexander 2012). A 1993 research study, seldom cited by mainstream neoliberal theorists, suggested that racial attitudes were the most important source of opposition to welfare among whites, more so than economic self-interest or individualism (Gilens 1995).

These processes suggest that shifting power relations in cities were and are more contiguous and complex than the template narrative of urban neoliberalism might entail. Insights from feminists, antiracists, and other scholars and empirical scrutiny of one locality (Milwaukee) help fill in gaps and shift the story to include historical continuities and hybridities. As much feminist research has done, intersectional analyses give more equal footing to a range of power relations, projects, motivations, and assemblages connected to and beyond neoliberalism (see Larner 2011; Larner et al. 2013). They can disrupt a sometimes synthetic tale where a romanticized Keynesianism was trumped by evil neoliberalism, at the peril of all minorities, women, and poor people. This is certainly not the full story in Milwaukee. As feminists have argued, particular and contradictory power configurations exist in specific spaces and at particular moments in time. In this way, both the Keynesian state and the neoliberal state were and are racist, sexist, heteronormative, classist, and perhaps occasionally liberating.[10] Different regimes might unhinge particular gendered and raced inequalities while ensconcing others. Similarly, it is possible for there to be perverse alliances between both neoliberalism and masculinities *and* neoliberalism and feminism, for example.[11]

In summary, dominant narratives of urban neoliberalism and its histories tend to simplify and erase gendered and raced power relations and historical continuities between the Keynesian state and the neoliberal state. Feminist research reminds us that cities and daily urban life have historically been shaped not only by capitalism or neoliberalism, but also by varied manifestations of heteronormative masculine power and white privilege, and that these power relations are interlinked.

In the following section, I discuss some contemporary gendered, raced, and capitalist/neoliberal power relations in U.S. cities. Using feminist perspectives,

I briefly probe concepts (which are elevated as values) and discourses that tend to dominate in U.S. urban politics. Some of these values, such as autonomy, are framed as *newish* and *neoliberal* in the literature. Certainly they have evolved and in some cases intensified in recent years. However, as I suggest below, they have been historically salient in the development and propagation of U.S. cities, emanating from distinct but intertwined power relations like capitalism, racism, and patriarchy.

Gendered, Raced, and Capitalist: Dominant Discourses and Values in U.S. Cities

Uneven power relations in U.S. cities manifest themselves not just through material practices such as paying women lower wages for the same work as men, but also through dominant discourses and values and the subjects, spaces, and practices to which they are attached. In other words, what we value, what problems we highlight, and how we talk about them have important implications for justice and equality in cities.[12] In the section below, I focus on the discourses surrounding three salient values/concepts in U.S. urban politics: autonomy, competition, and work. These discourses rationalize and promote certain policies and practices, and are gendered, raced, and capitalistic in their constitution and effects. They often ensconce certain forms of power as well. Throughout the book, I return to these concepts to explore the intersectional dimensions of creative class, new urbanism, and other development discourses and governance practices in Milwaukee.

AUTONOMY

In U.S. cities, autonomy is an oft-touted value that underpins neoliberal policies and shapes everyday life and cities.[13] Autonomy is often linked to or serves as a code word for individualism, independence, personal or local responsibility, and entrepreneurialism. For example, cities valorize and try desperately to attract urban elites who can autonomously move from city to city, doing as they please. New urbanism and downtown development projects target women as condominium owners or apartment dwellers, offering security and selling the "autonomy" of home ownership and urban life (see chapter 4; Kern 2010a). With the expansion of privatized schools in cities, parents, especially mothers, have the autonomy to choose their children's schools. City leaders argue that "the market" and urban developers in Milwaukee should have autonomy that is unimpeded by regulations (see chapter 7). Low-income mothers are supposed to desire and acquire autonomy through paid jobs or heteronormative marriage dependency rather than welfare support.[14]

Urban and neoliberal discourses surrounding autonomy are often narrow.

They focus on "market citizenship," where individuals are supposed to satisfy all their needs autonomously through the market (e.g., Bakker and Gill 2003; Brown 2006, 2015; Gill 1995; Roberts 2013). Autonomy means freedom from the state and jettisons notions of political autonomy that advocate political participation, protest, or shared governance for a type of autonomy that focuses on individual rational calculations and self-interest (see Brown 2006). These discourses are also wrapped up with raced and gendered notions and often perpetuate white male privilege. For example, feminists and antiracists have noted that historical liberal discourses about autonomy are based on a "white, wealthy, mythical masculine norm" (Lorde 1984; McKittrick 2011) and have always been hypocritical in that they were propagated while slavery fueled the economy. According to feminist sociologists Ferree and Mueller (2003, 28), "'Rights of man' [liberal ideologies] are premised on exercise of formal rights and a social position as head of the household, one who is autonomously able to enter into contracts, participate in labor markets, and exercise free choice. Anchoring of concepts of modernity and democracy in a marketized and gendered vision of autonomy (freedom from family dependency and rejection of moral claims that would interfere with self-interest) made it inconceivable that women could or should be included as appropriate actors." In the United States, people of color have been denied autonomy through slavery and reformulations of plantation life in cities and society. Not without contestation, race has structured mobility and citizenship rights, segregation, housing, possession and dispossession, and who lives with criminal records and/or behind bars (e.g., Alexander 2012; Gilmore 2007; McKittrick 2011). Women's unpaid labors in the home also created the foundation for wealth accumulation for white men and entire societies. Even today, women of all races and ethnicities still conduct the vast majority of caring labors in U.S. cities, often relinquishing jobs, promotions, and moves due to these labors and caring relationships. When caring labor is devalued and recklessly marketized via neoliberalism, it has consequences for not only low-wage workers but also entire communities and countries (e.g., England and Folbre 1999; McDowell 2004). While women have many rights in the United States, they earn less than men, are more likely to be poor, and are often subjects of violence and domination. Thus, there is a serious problem with the valorization of a type of autonomy that erases inequities and related differentiated capacities to exercise it, while blaming individuals for their circumstances.

A second concern is whether the kind of autonomy touted in urban policies is what individuals want, at what cost one must acquire it, and whether it helps foster socially just cities. For many urban residents, neoliberal policies often involve a small degree of autonomy or choice that is accompanied by burdensome consequences and increasing regimes of control (see Mirowski 2013). For example, an African American mother can now *choose* an autonomous, privately run "charter" school, rather than send her child to the neighborhood public school. However, this "choice" involves substantial testing and tricky enrollment processes, increased monitoring and surveillance, and heightened travel and expenses for her and her child. Her participation also results in subtle undermining of the broader system of public education. What might be preferable to the mother, in fact, is a nonracist and excellent neighborhood public school, but that is not among her choices. Similarly, cities can autonomously choose how to execute their "entrepreneurial" capacities to lure industries, the creative class, or other resources, but an atmosphere of interurban cooperation or freedom from capitalist bond markets is outside the realm of reality (Hackworth 2007).

Critically, in neoliberal urban discourse, autonomy comes with blame and responsibilities for one's history, present, and past. Those who confront constrained choices or experience structural problems like racism and poverty are told to "find a biographic solution to systemic contradictions" (Beckis 2001; Brodie 2007; Lawson 2007; Mirowski 2013; Peck 2005). Workers who can't find jobs are construed as not creative enough; working mothers who quit their jobs in the absence of decent maternity leave in cities are labeled as not having a strong work ethic or as returning to their biological destiny via choice. Women with deep and present histories of domestic violence are presented as failed mothers when distress or abuse causes them to miss a shift at work. Home owners whose homes are foreclosed are framed as irresponsible spenders who borrowed more than they could afford, even if they had limited capital and few housing options due to years of racist housing policies and were racially targeted for subprime loans (see, e.g., Gottesdiener 2013; Satter 2009).

Of course autonomy, in the sense of authentic freedom, often resonates with people as an important value in society, and feminists and civil rights activists have mobilized this concept against domestic violence, segregation, and other oppressions. However, the dominant urban discourses surrounding autonomy erase differentiated practices and access surrounding it. Instead, they emphasize individualism, entrepreneurialism, and self-commodification, while obscuring equity, connection, collectivity, and ethics of care, for example.

Although not specific to women, these latter values have often been associated with women because of their social roles as caregivers and nurturers. These values have also been promoted by feminists (e.g., Held 2002; Lawson 2007; McDowell 2004). Feminists have argued that greater attention by the state to caregiving and other shifts are necessary for gender equality and to foster fairer cities. However, this has never been achieved in the United States, especially for women of color, and has been especially discouraged via neoliberal and other policies.[15] While some other states have witnessed "postneoliberal" discourses and state investments in social inclusion and caring (see Simon-Kumar 2011), this has not happened to any great degree in the United States, and certainly not in cities. Collectivity and connection remain undervalued in cities, and aspirations for justice and "care" remain underrealized, while autonomy persists as a foil that erases material interdependence, inequality, and exploitation. For example, elite women's labor often depends on poor women's labor, and one city achieves wealth or secures a new global company at the expense of others.

WORK AND PRODUCTION

"Work" in a U.S. context has nearly always been construed as paid labor, and good "workers" are still seen as good citizens in U.S. cities. Historically and contemporarily, unpaid labor and other unpaid contributions to society remain undervalued and undersupported.[16] Related to this, U.S. city leaders have long focused on economic priorities rather than the social. In contemporary cities, certain types of paid work, usually in sectors dominated by men like law and real estate, are elevated over others, as are the global cities attached to these industries. National and urban neoliberal discourses—including popular creative city discourses—suggest that individuals who work hard (and exert creativity) can succeed and be rewarded in the marketplace, regardless of race, class, gender, disability, sexual preference, and so on.[17] These discourses obscure the raced and gender inequalities that structure paid labor markets and the difficulties faced by workers. In addition, benefits such as social security, food assistance, and welfare payments are supposedly made more virtuous if they are "earned" through work. Even though real wages have not increased in over twenty-five years, welfare reform discourses in cities suggest that those recipients who show self-discipline and a willingness to work will be able to pull themselves out of poverty.

Conversely, the unpaid labors of *social reproduction* remain less visible and less valued in cities, even as they are increasingly commodified. Originally coined by Karl Marx, but reworked by feminists, social reproduction refers to the labors, practices, and social relations that surround and sustain households, cities, and, more generally, human life.[18] These relations include, but are not limited to, caring for, feeding, and clothing children, meeting education, health, and social needs of urban residents, and creating community networks. This labor is often unsupported by the state and disconnected from the economic benefits of citizenship, such as employment insurance or social security.[19] For brief and faltering moments, notions of a "mother-citizen" role made inroads with early labor legislation and mothers' pension proposals. A 1946 government handbook on the welfare program at the time (Aid for Families with Dependent Children) emphasized the social value of giving an impoverished (white) mother the opportunity to reject wage work in favor of "staying at home with the children," touting the benefits for children who will become "citizens capable of contributing to society" (quoted in McCluskey 2003). These patriarchal and paradoxical policies toward poor women offered aid, but established a distinction between paid women workers who "earned" social benefits and women who received simple handouts from the government (e.g., Fraser 1989; Pateman 1989).

Sometimes shaped by white, middle-class women, historical welfare programs entailed racial exclusions, class biases, and moralist undertones (e.g., Fraser 2013; Fraser and Gordon 1994; Mink 1990; Orloff 1996; Williams 1995). Until legal equity mandates were put in place in 1970, states were allowed "discretion" to exclude poor African American women from benefits (Williams 1995). As more people of color received benefits, the image of welfare recipients began to change at that time from "worthy white widow to lazy African-American breeder" (see Jones 2009; Maranville 1990; Williams 1995). Moralizing policies began to bar recipients from watching television and fathers from having contact with families, conflating the inability to provide financially with moral corruption and inadequate parenting. Work requirements became a part of welfare for the first time.

The reform of welfare that came about in the 1990s was no less sexist or racist. It completely dismantled the idea of the mother-citizen, especially for women of color. Racial resentments, media stereotypes about unwed mothers, and ideologies about work and motherhood fueled strict work requirements.[20] In 1990, poor women with children in Milwaukee were mandated to work thirty to forty paid hours per week in order to receive financial support from the government, facing sanctions if they did not. In 1991, Wisconsin Governor Tommy Thompson stated, "Our welfare reform initiatives are geared to help individuals help themselves. Some people think they are very harsh, and some are. They are tough love" (*Time* 1991). As Peck (2001), Simon-Kumar (2011), and others have noted, such neoliberal discourses about care were used to push women into low-wage labor markets that benefitted employers and caring into the private sector and home, regardless of quality.

Thus, notions of work, caring, and motherhood in Keynesian and neoliberal times are construed in (differently) patriarchal and racialized ways that devalue "feminine" and social reproduction labor. These are issues that I explore in more detail in chapter 6. In addition, as detailed through the book, cities continue to disinvest in social reproduction (especially for the poor) and prioritize the economic over the social (see Katz 2001, 2008; Meehan and Strauss 2015).

COMPETITION

In U.S. cities, especially in urban planning, policy, and economic development arenas, discourses and practices of competition are ubiquitous. The colonization of the United States and resulting urbanization were a product of Western competition and often greed. Early speculators and boosters in Boston, New York, and Chicago competed with one another for land purchasers, residents, businesses, railroad lines, world fairs, and specialized industries in the late

1800s and early 1900s (e.g., Abu-Lughod 1999; Cronon 2009). Around this time, Milwaukee touted its own specialized expertise as the "machine shop of the world." Among urban elites, this sense of competition hardly abated, as U.S. cities vied for the grandest boulevards and the tallest skyscrapers from the early 1900s. This competition reached new heights under neoliberalism, as cities received less federal aid, encountered declining revenue, and were encouraged to be fiercely entrepreneurial. In the late 1980s and after, Milwaukee's Mayor Norquist continually pushed this concept, arguing that it was a "natural" process for cities to compete as marketplaces (see Norquist 1994).

Now entrepreneurial cities compete not only for Olympic events and exclusive developments, but also for the elusive creative class and "coolness."[21] Cities that fail to thrive are framed as not being sufficiently entrepreneurial or having failed to market their amenities to lure the creative class. This perception of flailing cities persists, regardless of cities' situatedness in broader processes like deindustrialization, migration, and environmental degradation. These rationales underpin the almost ludicrous suggestion that Richard Florida made to Milwaukee's urban policy makers: "You need to really tout the fact that the Violent Femmes [a rock band] came from Milwaukee."

Competition is often culturally associated with norms of dominant white Western masculinity, where aggression, power, and dominance, however subtle, have been prized. Not the same thing but not unrelated, white, elite men have been the unequivocal victors in a global capitalism that was built on slavery and women's unpaid labor, and city leadership is dominated by this same group (Bonds and Inwood 2015; Connell 2013). In urban politics and development, competition normalizes some cities as "winners" and others as "losers," with economic performance, growth, and visibility used as measures. In the 1990s, the *Economist* heralded Milwaukee Mayor John Norquist as a national role model, even as infants of color in the city were dying at three times the rate of white infants, women of color had poverty rates hovering around 40 percent, and African American men were sent to prison at alarming rates. Historically, competition has contributed to oppressive practices like slavery and segregation in cities. Competition continues to push governments toward growth and to subsidize developers and businesses rather than transform education, heath, or social services. This is true even as black and Latino families experience a vanishingly small portion of the much touted prosperity, as I explore in chapter 7.

Like the cultural constructions of "autonomy" and "work," urban competition discourses emphasize individualism (among residents and among cities). They often erase, delegitimize, or dichotomize other priorities and values like care, collectivity, collaboration, and cooperation. In small ways, some dimensions of these latter values, advocated often by feminists and other progressive activists, have made inroads into government practices by way of interagency collaboration and occasionally more "feminized" agencies, but remain over-shadowed in dominant urban development discourses and practices.

Overall, the framing and valuation of concepts like "autonomy," "work," and "competition" in U.S. cities have helped align with and bolster capitalist, masculinist, and racist power and privilege, also revealing affinities among them. Importantly, "masculine" discourses do not map perfectly onto men's lives or male-identifying bodies. Rather, they represent "regulatory fictions" (Roy 2003) that shape what and who is valued in cities and how idealized cities and subjects ought to behave. They signal what is supposed to be important. White elite men have historically had the power to shape these discourses and priorities, and simultaneously acquire power in part because of their cultural association with masculinity (Hooper 2001). Conversely, women have historically held less social, political, and economic power in the United Sates. As the discourses imply, women and the "feminine" have often been associated with the devalued opposite of masculinity in cities (e.g., if masculine equals aggressive, economic, scientific, and productive, then feminine equals passive, social, intuitive, and unproductive). Similar kinds of valuations and stereotypes exist related to race in the United States. Those who are racialized nonwhite and don't fit neatly into categories like men and women and don't ascribe to related norms and performances have often been particularly marginalized.

Resource allocation is related. In cities, white male developers, investors, and leaders have favored economic markets (in which they held power) and architectural design over "social" interventions and attending to complex human needs and experiences (e.g., Hayden 2002; Metzger 2010; Spain 2004; Wirka 1998;). When governments invest in "care" and "social reproduction," resources are redistributed from men and a general taxpayer base toward women (often as caregivers) and those with less economic and social privilege. When governments retract from "care" and "equality" investments and regulation, women and people of color disproportionately suffer.[22] This argument is of course made more complicated when those investments push caring into the private sector. Overall, the diminishment of values like care and collectivity and surrounding policies and practices helps produce unbalanced and unjust societies and cities, often contributes to the lower status of women and minorities while obscuring the reasons for their status, and helps maintain power for elite white men, an issue I turn to in the next section.

Practices and Power: Persistent Patriarchy, Racism, and Capitalism in U.S. Cities

In this section, I shift the focus from values and discourses to connected practices and power related to gender, race, and neoliberal capitalism in contemporary U.S. cities. Like other feminists, I argue that it is time to (re)notice sexism and patriarchy and to examine complex intersections of power in cities.[23] As I argued in chapter 1, these power relations should not be seen as fixed, and categories like women and race are unstable and problematic. Sexual and gender identities are fluid; female-identifying persons' lives are diverse due to class, race/ethnicity, sexuality, age, geography, age, and other variables. Racial categories are socially constructed and not related to genetic characteristics, yet racism based on skin color is real. Thus, gender and race remain lived and uneven realities in cities.

The chapters that unfold next offer more specificity about different experiences and actors in Milwaukee, from low-income African American women to female- or male-identifying elected officials to creative-class members. These specific experiences can be contextualized by general trends that suggest that gendered and raced inequality persists in urban governance, women's everyday lives and labors, and urban development and housing.

It is important to consider the historical roots, persistence, and new formulations of these inequalities, beginning with urban governance. U.S. cities were constructed through colonial domination, racist exploitation, tumultuous capitalism, and patriarchal practices.[24] In the late 1800s, female reformers (racially segregated and often motivated by moral anxieties) called for more "homelike" cities, addressing poverty, neighborhood development, and community and social needs. But as women made important advances as a group and for cities, gaining the right to vote and some political power, gendered anxieties and exclusions heightened. Male leaders simultaneously pushed women out of formal leadership positions and degraded their "city social" agenda (Hayden 2002; Parker 2011; Spain 2004). As Daphne Spain (2004, 12–13) argued, "Male professionals built grand boulevards and civic monuments in search of the City Beautiful. Female volunteers built the places of everyday life, the neighborhood institutions without which the city is not a city," but even these spaces were often marked with raced, classed, and moralistic bias.

Feminists, women, and activists have continued to transform cities in multiple dimensions in the twentieth and twenty-first centuries, pushing for women's suffrage, reshaping labor movements, contesting domestic violence, advocating for better urban services, and reshaping neighborhoods and urban development practices. However, wave after wave of such activism has encountered backlashes, and urban governance and policy making have generally remained a masculine and white affair.

Women, especially minority women, remain vastly underrepresented among elected officials, developers, and business leaders, and urban landscapes and development projects often reflect the (not always cohesive) interests of elite white men.[25] Currently, women hold less than 20 percent of all city council and mayoral seats in the United States. For women of color, the numbers are much lower (Center for American Women and Politics 2014). There is no steady up-ward trajectory in these rates, but lots of flat lines and occasional blips. This is not inconsequential. As Isoke (2013) argues, heteropatriarchy persists even in cities like Newark, where African American men dominate local elected office. In a recent study, Alec Brownlow (2009) found that city leaders in Baltimore actively manipulated data about rapes, potentially endangering women in order to preserve and promote economic development.

In the United States, some efforts at participatory planning and inclusive urban governance exist, but they seldom attend to gendered exclusions. Mean-while, women are often adversely affected by urban development and related re-source priorities and distributions, via displacement, lack of access to affordable housing, and abdication of social infrastructure, social services, and welfare provisions, which women benefit from in greater numbers (e.g., Campbell 2014; Nagar et al. 2002; Simon-Kumar 2011; Wekerle 2005b). Thus, urban governance patterns reveal problems with democracy, representation, and resource alloca-tion, as well as a disproportionate influence of the private sector, issues explored in chapter 4. As suggested above, not only are women, especially minority women, and feminist practices marginalized in cities, but urban development and city building are often rendered masculine and central, while the "social" realm and everyday lives are tertiary—the work of "frustrated housewives," ac-cording to one city councilor (Beck 2001; see also Brownlow 2009; Hubbard 2004; Isoke 2013; Kern 2010b).

Neoliberal, patriarchal, and racist configurations may be reinforcing each other in cities, as neoliberalism privileges increased private-sector influence (generally male) on local politics and development and "informal" and elitist decision making rather than deep democracy, as chapters 4, 5, and 7 explore. Changes in urban governance mean that private foundations (often funded by corporations), private businesses, and developers (often white, conservative, and male) shape important decisions about urban development, politics, and the allocation of public resources. In a somewhat uncommon analysis of urban neoliberalism and masculinity, Phil Hubbard (2004, 682) argues, "Neoliberal policies are also about asserting the primacy of virile masculinity. Accordingly, neoliberal urbanism is not just about the recentralisation of capital; it is also about the re-assertion of the authority of the father figure in Western consumer society." At a different scale, Beatrix Campbell (2014) argues for a "neoliberal neo-patriarchy" label. In other words, the "man" has not disappeared from the urban state. Not all men are faring well or benefitting from current power con-figurations in urban governance and beyond, but many are.[26]

Gendered, raced, and other inequalities persist not only in governance and urban development, but also in the paid and unpaid labors of residents, espe-cially women. In the past thirty years, the labor force has become more stratified, casualized, and globalized. Feminists have long argued that economic and other independence (not necessarily through the market) is essential for women's equity (e.g., Fraser 2013; Lister 1990; Orloff 1996). For some women and certain categories of workers, waged labor before and after neoliberalism has enhanced economic privileges, independence, and quality of life, increasing differences *among* women. There has been tremendous growth in women-owned small businesses in Milwaukee and elsewhere, with such businesses contributing three trillion dollars to the U.S. GDP. In some cities, young, single, and childless female workers outearn their counterparts (Hindman 2010), mainly due to increased college graduation rates for women and declining wages for men. In Milwaukee, the gendered wage gap has narrowed, but it persists. In the United States, full-time female workers earn seventy-seven cents for every dollar earned by full-time male workers. Importantly, irrespective of gender and race, the vast majority of people in cities labored for *more* hours and for *lower* real wages in 2005 than they did in 1975.

Furthermore, many female-identifying people in cities do not work full-time, but form the most precarious part-time or contingent workforce, due to historical patterns, gender discrimination, and social reproductive duties that still largely fall on women's shoulders. Regardless of part-time or full-time status, women and racial minorities remain segmented in low-wage "feminized" jobs, including the ever growing service economy. In fact, new workers filling low-paid service jobs in the 1990s were almost all unmarried mothers with a high school degree or less, and women constituted two-thirds of the minimum wage workforce in 2014 (Collins and Mayer 2010; Shriver and Center for American Progress 2014).

Critically, racial and ethnic disparities in urban job markets are especially pronounced. Full-time African American female workers are still more likely to live in poverty than white women in the same situation, and African American women earn fifty-five to seventy cents to every dollar earned by white men for full-time work in Milwaukee, depending on the neighborhood or region. Only 4 percent of African American female workers earn more than seventy-five thousand dollars per year, and the majority earn less than twenty-five thousand (Bertrand and Mullainathan 2003; Biernat 2003; Jones 2009; Levine 2013a; Williams and Hegewisch 2011). In the fractured, casual, and decentralized economy, companies capitalize on inequalities and stereotypes to justify poor wages and working conditions, and discriminate based on age, race, gender, sexual preference, and motherhood status.[27]

The United States has never experienced its current level of income inequality before, with some wealthy families earning 288 times more than poor families (Shriver and Center for American Progress 2014). Such inequality is raced and gendered and often dependent on citizenship status. This inequality has always been particularly visible in cities, where the richest and poorest sometimes labor in the same spaces. Law offices and public relations firms close at night for the janitorial shift filled by low-income immigrants, and the homes of the wealthiest employ an array of precarious workers to clean, care for children, garden, and provide security. Despite rhetoric to the contrary and the fact that some men have certainly fallen behind and some white women have gained, white men in the United States retain the most advantaged positions in the paid economy, in terms of salary, wealth, power, and job categories.

In cities and elsewhere, social reproduction labors, usually unpaid work that sustains children, households, and communities, still predominantly fall to women. Poor women are particularly likely to be single parents, with single parenthood growing across all demographics. Women in all kinds of custody arrangements, as well as women without children, conduct caring labors at high rates, with women in heterosexual marriages conducting 1.9 times more housework and child care than men in 2010 (Bianchi et al. 2012). Meanwhile, cultures of "intensive mothering" and "new momism" have emerged that raise expectations of maternal perfection and time and resources parents are expected to devote to their children.[28] With increasing withdrawal of the state from welfare and regulation, more responsibilities have been "downloaded" to homes and women, who may then outsource some labors to poorly paid women of color and/or migrant workers.[29] Most female parents, and increasingly male parents, report anxiety and stress about meeting their multiple responsibilities.

Meanwhile, as described above, the economic, social, and political environment in the United States has never been supportive of social reproduction labor, expecting that it invisibly and quietly occurs in households or is outsourced to private markets. Governmental support for food security, child care, housing, and social welfare has generally been declining since the 1980s (Bashevkin 1998; Brown 2006; Kingfisher 2002), while usage of emergency services skyrocketed in Milwaukee during the 1990s (Fendt, Mulligan-Hansel, and White 2001). Much responsibility for helping families get by has fallen to urban churches and the nonprofit sector, with insufficient resources and complicated results.

In addition, as cities and neighborhoods and especially marginalized communities have been hit by neoliberal austerity and a recession, "informal" community labors have intensified. By this, I refer to the various forms of support that family members, neighbors, and friends provide to each other.[30] Women often care for each other's children, bring their relatives to live with them, provide emotional support to friends and family, and participate in church- or neighborhood-based activism and support networks. Neoliberal politics, rapidly increasing incarceration rates, and other issues are producing new and intensifying community burdens for low-income African American women and households.

At the same time, feminism, social and family changes, and declining real wages have sent more women into the paid workforce for longer hours. Labor protections, wages, and job stability have become precarious with economic restructuring, neoliberal deregulation, and the demise of labor organizations (e.g., Collins and Mayer 2010). Paid employment rarely provides benefits like sick days or maternity leave. Of minimum wage workers, 60 percent have no paid sick days (Shriver and Center for American Progress 2014). Community and care activities are often constrained or compromised, especially for low-income women. For example, it is very hard to find quality, affordable child care, so mothers rely on fragile friend or family networks that collapse when the provider experiences an illness, a personal crisis, or a move. Unpredictable schedules for low-wage workers heighten the problem (Dodson and Bravo 2005; Williams and Boushey 2010). For this and other reasons, a recent study found that 42 percent of low-income women experience high stress, compared to 22 percent of low-income men (Shriver and Center for American Progress 2014).

In this way, women's triple burdens of reproduction, production, and community work have intensified (Gilmore 2007; Nagar et al. 2002; Simon-Kumar 2011). Race, ethnicity, class, and citizenship status make this more true for some women than for others. In chapter 6, I explore everyday life and labors of low-income African American women, shedding light on complicated stories of resistance, power relations, and survival strategies.

Affordable and adequate housing remains a critical need in cities for many residents, even as urban development has often focused on elite and downtown development. Low- and moderate-income women, women with children, and those who have experienced domestic violence and/or incarceration often struggle to meet housing needs. In Milwaukee, up to 40 percent of poor families do not have affordable housing, an issue I explore in chapter 4. Inadequate housing affects nearly every dimension of family life, including children's health, education and job possibilities, and mental health.

In the United States, home ownership in cities has historically been seen as a path to economic and social security and a way for women to help accomplish some of their paid and unpaid labors. However, in cities this has been a mixed experience for women, in part because of the way that homes, property, and mortgages are bound up in capitalist practices and neoliberal growth strategies. New urbanism has given material and discursive fuel to such strategies in Milwaukee, drawing on nostalgic narratives about community and women's emancipation through independent urban living (see Kern 2010a, 2010b). Racialized low-income women and families have historically been denied secure housing, mobility, and home ownership. Over many decades after slavery, African American families were stripped of their wealth through theft, blockbusting, evictions, and neighborhood demolition. For years they were denied access to mortgages. Nearly the only way they could buy houses was through land contracts with sketchy terms, exorbitant markups and fees, and likely eviction, thus losing their entire investment. Historian Beryl Satter (2009) estimated the wealth lost to African Americans in Chicago in this way in the 1950s at one million dollars per day. Conversely, at the same time white families accumulated wealth through government-backed mortgages and access to suburban housing and wealthier neighborhoods.

In recent years, housing needs have persisted. A combination of conservative, progressive, capitalist, sexist, and racist neoliberal practices led to increased home ownership in poor neighborhoods and communities in the 1990s. By the 2000s, single women were the fastest growing group of home owners (Baker 2014; Roberts 2013). However, an economic and foreclosure crisis followed. Capitalist narratives and practices built on masculine notions of competition and risk and executed mainly by elite white males in the finance industry fueled a housing and economic bubble. Amid neoliberal policy shifts, new types of lenders, competition, and mortgage tools were created that were not covered by protective housing legislation or federal protection (Ashton 2009; Baker 2014; Kern 2010b; Roberts 2013). A flood of subprime mortgages ensued. Female homebuyers, regardless of ethnicity or income, were far more likely than men to be classified as subprime borrowers. African American women of all income groups fared the worst: they were 256 percent more likely to receive subprime loans than men of any race, and more than 50 percent of all subprime loans went to African American families (Gottesdiener 2013). Gendered relations of social reproduction also mattered, as pregnant women and women on pregnancy-related leave were denied mortgages. Lenders perceived them to be risky borrowers because of the inferred job interruptions and lower wages associated with motherhood (Roberts 2013).

Because of this situation, wealth and housing security eroded for women and women of color. Owners with subprime mortgages were six to nine times more likely to go into foreclosure, and over ten million families were evicted from 2007 to 2013, not least because subprime mortgages carry costs such as ballooning payments and high insurance premiums that regular mortgages do not. Entire neighborhoods, many black and poor, were decimated, and security for women dissipated (see Baker 2014; Roberts 2013).

Even prior to the housing bubble and as new urbanist developments flourished, a lack of affordable housing troubled thousands of poor households in Milwaukee, as two and three families doubled up in apartments and many went homeless (see chapter 4). The problems persist. In cities like Milwaukee, most poor people spend over half of their income on housing, and nearly 20 percent of renters were forcibly evicted between 2009 and 2011. While black women constitute 9 percent of Milwaukee's population, they compose 30 percent of eviction cases, and discrimination in rental searches against women of color remains rampant (see Desmond 2016). Despite this, the city has rarely made affordable housing a priority.

In summary, data suggest that contemporary uneven and intersecting power relations related to governance, urban development, everyday lives and labors, housing, and other issues like uneven incarceration and violence rates persist in cities, especially for poor people, women, those without citizenship, and people of color. These inequalities have deep roots sowed in the soil of unfree labors, coercion, violence, and accumulation by dispossession, to name a few. Liberal and neoliberal discourses often obscure these injustices (that fuel uneven wealth accumulation) while promoting an "autonomous" subject who purportedly chooses his life path. Over the years, some uneven power relations have softened, and others have taken new forms, subtle and insidious. In some cases, contemporary raced, gendered, neoliberal policies and discourses have stalled slow marches toward equality or exacerbated inequalities.

Challenging Urban Inequalities: Feminist and Other Projects of Resistance

Historically, feminist and progressive movements have been key features of cities and urban politics. Importantly, there are multiple feminisms, and not all women are feminists. However, women and feminists have helped push against gendered, raced/ethnic, capitalist, heteronormative, and other inequalities in cities. Progressive movements have often done the same. At their best, these types of efforts have articulated alternative and inclusive visions for cities that improved material conditions and processes. Some research has documented and analyzed these movements. There is a useful contemporary literature that explores how feminism has fared under neoliberalism in the United States and in other geographies, although it does not often focus on cities.[31] Additional research has explored urban social movements that contest neoliberal politics in the United States.[32] Notably, several authors have argued that feminism, antiracist movements, and community-based efforts have been diffused and in some cases co-opted by U.S. neoliberal urban politics and the emergence of a shadow state.[33]

It is not the intent of this book to examine feminist, antineoliberal, or other forms of resistance in full detail or in multiple geographic contexts. However, I do briefly explore the ways that backlashes toward feminism and civil rights organizing shaped urban governance, everyday life and labors, especially for women, and urban development and housing in Milwaukee. Throughout the book I also touch on "resistance" and progressive politics in Milwaukee, most explicitly exploring urban contestations in chapter 7. I argue that the terrain for activism, antiracism, and feminism has become more difficult in cities like Milwaukee, although neoliberalism is not solely to blame. A wicked cocktail of sexism, neoliberalism, racism, and other power relations (sometimes at odds but often in collusion) has dampened but not eliminated feminist and other projects of resistance.

Even within activist or progressive movements, feminist voices are sometimes marginalized, and racist practices persist (see Parker 2016b). This reminds us that intersecting power relations related to gender, race, etc., are not always cumulative and aligned, and complex subjectivities related to "progressivism" and "feminism" persist. For example, white elite developers might embrace certain feminist projects, and progressive labor activists might express racist behavior and exclusions.

Nonetheless, individual and intersecting power relations related to neoliberal capitalism, heteronormativity, gender, and race/ethnicity (among others) are open to challenge and alternative imaginations. They rely on multiple and sometimes tenuous strategies, including cultural consent, discursive centrality, institutionalization, and marginalization of alternatives. As Janet Newman (2013) has argued, feminist projects have influenced capitalism, the state, and communities in important ways over the years, and many activist endeavors remain vibrant in cities like Milwaukee. In this way, a stacked deck might rarefy transformative and just urban politics, but it does not preclude them.

Conclusion

Standard narratives of urban politics and about the emergence of neoliberalism in the United States pay insufficient attention to gender, race, and other intersecting urban power relations. They also tend to submerge related complex historical specificities and continuities in the practice and discourses of urban politics. For example, the racist underpinnings of the delivery and restructuring of welfare services during both the Keynesian and neoliberal eras are important. Likewise, early experiments with Socialist urban government, the presumed antithesis of neoliberalism, were marked by gendered and raced exclusions in Milwaukee. Thus, reappraisals of historical and contemporary urban politics informed by antiracist feminist research and epistemology are needed.

A feminist partial political economy of place lens requires that we document and challenge complex and uneven power relations and material inequalities in cities, as well as the dominant discourses and values that help sustain them. These material-discursive inequalities are persistent, but not stagnant. They mutate over time, as do the affinities and alliances among them. In this chapter, I have pointed to some critical gendered and raced inequalities related to urban governance, everyday life and labors of women and other residents, and urban development and housing. For example, women constitute less than 10 percent of the Milwaukee City Council and local African American women earn less than 70 percent of white men's wages. I have also suggested that dominant values and discourses in Milwaukee and other cities are built on and often invigorate gendered, raced, and neoliberal inequalities. The discourses valorize competition, certain forms of autonomy, paid labor, and "economic" activities while eschewing alternative and feminist ethics of care, connection, and collectivity, among others. In Milwaukee, the celebration of values like autonomy and competition were epitomized in discourses and policies related to downtown development, new urbanism, and the creative class.

It is also valuable to assess the varied terrain and practices that resist and challenge urban inequalities and systems like racism, patriarchy, and neoliberalism. These include but are not limited to feminism, antiracist efforts, and progressive social movements and organizations. In Milwaukee, many vibrant and justice-oriented endeavors remain visible and have secured important advances for women, the poor, workers, and people of color. Nonetheless, these movements have faced formidable challenges and internal struggles that hinder a more egalitarian and progressive urban politics, especially in these recent decades of raced, gendered, neoliberal policy.

This chapter has necessarily been brief and skeletal, referring to scholarship, practices, and data from Milwaukee and cities around the United States. The following chapters add empirical flesh to the arguments presented here, providing sustained stories about real people and events in Milwaukee. I introduce important characters such as a new urbanist-neoliberal mayor; Milwaukee-based conservative think tanks with the financial resources and ideological zeal to frame welfare mothers as cheats and community activists as radical Socialists; African American women carrying and resisting the burdens of racism, violence, and poverty literally in their bodies; and a Greater Milwaukee Committee described by the press in 2004 as still "dominated by white male powerbrokers" (Miner 2004).

CHAPTER THREE

From Sewer Socialism to "Sewers for Sale"

Milwaukee's Journey toward Neoliberalism

> Some eastern smarties called ours a "Sewer Socialism." . . . But we wanted
> much oh—so very much more than sewers. We wanted our workers to have pure
> air; we wanted them to have sunshine; we wanted planned homes; we wanted
> living wages; we wanted recreation for young and old; we wanted vocational
> education; we wanted a chance for every human being to be strong and live a life
> of happiness. And we wanted everything that was necessary to give them that;
> playgrounds, parks, lakes, beaches, clean creeks and rivers, swimming and wading
> pools, social centers, reading rooms, clean fun, music, dance, song and joy for all.
> **MILWAUKEE MAYOR EMIL SEIDEL, 1910–12**

> The best role of the city is to create pro-urban zoning and otherwise get out of the
> way, letting the markets work to create the setting for an attractive urban life style.
> **MILWAUKEE MAYOR JOHN NORQUIST, 1988–2004**

As the epigraphs to this chapter imply, markedly different visions have shaped
urban politics in Milwaukee over time, occasionally to national acclaim. Leading
periodicals like *Time* and the *Economist* have twice praised Milwaukee as the best
governed city in the United States, once featuring Socialist Mayor Dan Hoan,
and later featuring neoliberal Mayor John Norquist. Locally and beyond, praise
for public sewers and services gave way to commendations for privatization,
as Milwaukee politicians pursued Socialist and neoliberal agendas with vigor.
These agendas, and the social relations in which they were embedded, were
both distinctive and continuous. Importantly, they were each shaped by a historically unique blend of capitalist, gendered, raced, and other power relations.

Milwaukee has always influenced and reflected changes rippling through
Wisconsin, the United States, and the world. These include intense immigration,
industrialization, world wars, the civil rights movements, women's mass entry
into the labor force, and deindustrialization, to name a few. As geographers have
argued, these are not static, unidirectional processes—the global, national, and

local are constituted together. Several times over, Milwaukee has been held up as a national model, inspiring other cities and inciting national commentary on issues such as socialism, financing government, social service provision during the Depression, welfare reform, privatization, and "new urbanism."

Milwaukee's mayors have not been alone in garnering fame. The city's progressive activists are also known for producing a tenacious labor town, helping charter chapters of the National Organization for Women, forming a committee on human rights to challenge antigay hate campaigns, lobbying for open housing legislation, securing one of the nation's first urban "living wage" ordinances, and recently trying to negotiate the first legislative-based community benefits agreement on a downtown development project.

Milwaukee is distinctive for other reasons as well. For example, a historically unique pattern of African American immigration and the city's racialized response helped create the sociospatial segregation that marks Milwaukee. Because of this, Milwaukee consistently ranks among the top three most segregated cities in the United States. Similarly, an interesting combination of conservative politics, suburbanization, and moralism congealed with a track record of progressive feminist activism to shape contemporary gender relations in the city.

In this way, Milwaukee's journey toward neoliberalism provides both locally specific and broader insights into urban politics in the United States and intersecting power relations. As is the case in many other places, Milwaukee's gendered and raced relations and its path toward neoliberalism involve more contextualized continuity and change than abrupt breaks in order. After introducing present-day Milwaukee and historical roots of its stark inequalities, I explore Milwaukee's complex raced, gendered, and capitalist history via five phases of urban politics, beginning with Sewer Socialism and ending with Norquist's neoliberalism. While focusing on urban governance, urban development and housing, and everyday life and labors in Milwaukee, I situate them in national and global trends and processes.

Overview of Milwaukee

Milwaukee sits on the southwestern shore of Lake Michigan, approximately ninety miles northwest of Chicago, with a population of nearly six hundred thousand residents. The city is surrounded by some of the wealthiest and whitest suburbs in the country, many founded decades ago. The Milwaukee and Menominee Rivers trisect the city, composed of three main areas and several neighborhoods with distinct character and ethnic composition. The East Side of Milwaukee, bordering Lake Michigan, boasts the city's oldest and wealthiest neighborhoods, including the historic Yankee Hill and newer Whitefish Bay.

The South Side of Milwaukee, once home to Polish immigrants, is now largely populated by Asian and Hispanic immigrants. The North Side of Milwaukee, once a site for German settlers, has been nearly exclusively home to African Americans since just after World War I. Downtown Milwaukee, until the past twenty years, had been the site of primarily commercial activity. However, condominium development and upscale residential living have blossomed since the 1990s. Tourism, festivals, and associated consumptive activities have also flourished in the past two decades.

Milwaukee's urban population is racially diverse, while the suburbs remain lily white. The metropolitan area is the most segregated region in the United States, with black and white segregation particularly intense. Fewer than 10 percent of black Milwaukee-area residents live in the suburbs, compared to 70 percent of whites (Levine 2003b, 2013b). Even affluent African American residents tend to live in high-poverty, segregated neighborhoods. These demographics are shaped by historic and contemporary racism, persistent inequalities between black and white residents, and a relatively light and late touch of national and international immigration in Milwaukee. African Americans moved to Milwaukee in large numbers only toward the end of the World War II boom. Promptly segregated, they consistently found economic and spatial integration to be elusive. In recent years, over 95 percent of residents have been born in the United States, and 66 percent have been born in Wisconsin (U.S. Census Bureau 2010; see table 1 and figure 1).

Racial and income disparities align in Milwaukee. Black neighborhoods are the poorest in the city, and African American poverty rates in metropolitan Milwaukee are nearly five times higher than white poverty rates (Levine 2013b). While the black poverty rate in the city of Milwaukee hovers around 40 percent, it is only around 6 percent in several adjoining counties. Ten years ago, the *Black Commentator* declared, "Wisconsin, and Milwaukee in particular, justly

TABLE 1. The changing racial composition of Milwaukee, 1970–2010 (percentages)

	1970	1980	1990	2000	2010
White	84	73	64	50	45
Black or African American	15	23	31	37	40
American Indian/Alaska Native	1	1	1	1	1
Asian and Pacific Islander	<1	1	2	3	4
Native Hawaiian and Pacific Islander				<1	<1
Other	<1	2	3	6	1
Two races	N/A	N/A	N/A	3	3
Hispanic population (any race)	1	4	6	12	17

SOURCE: U.S. Census Bureau (2010).

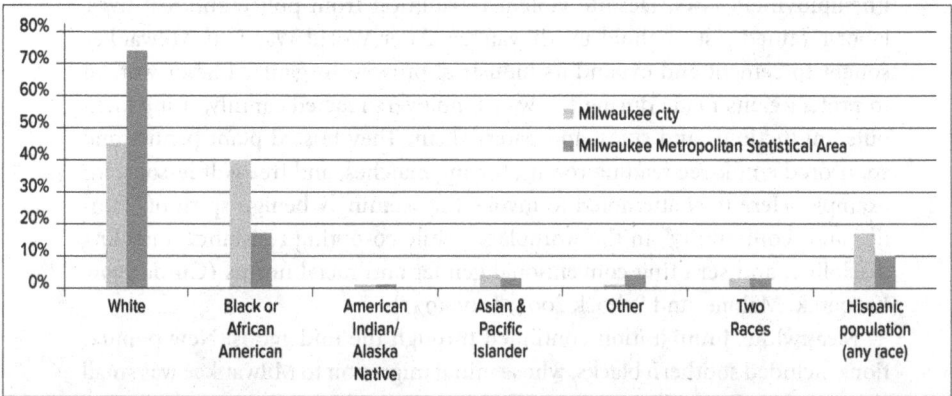

FIGURE 1. Comparative race composition in Milwaukee and in the Milwaukee metropolitan area, 2010.

merit the invidious distinction of being the worst place in America to be black" (Dixon 2005). This quote still rang true over ten years later. Four out of five black children live in poverty in Wisconsin, a state that incarcerates the most black men in the country and holds the highest education achievement gap between black and white children.

These inequalities and Milwaukee's current economy are embedded in a long history of colonialization, racism, and capitalism. Milwaukee was originally home to communities of Native Americans, who traveled by canoe, fished, and cultivated rice in the wetlands of Lake Michigan. European settlers and fur traders drove out or killed off Native American communities, and speculators invested in Milwaukee. By the mid-1800s, swamps had turned to streets. German immigrants, arriving en masse in the 1840s, brought cultural and political institutions and strong Socialist beliefs. They were followed by immigrants from Ireland, Poland, and elsewhere in Eastern Europe.

Immigration and industry marked Milwaukee politics and markets for the next century. With a continual supply of immigrant labor, Milwaukee gradually left its trading and transportation roots. The city's manufacturing establishments quadrupled between 1870 and 1900, with meatpacking, tanning, brewing, and machinery forming the major industries. In 1880, the city billed itself as "Milwaukee: The Machine Shop of the World." At this time, nearly 86 percent of Milwaukee residents were immigrants, and over half of adult males were industrial workers, a percentage rivaled only by Detroit, Michigan (Gurda 1999).

With this growth came the organized Labor movement. Organizations like the Knights of Labor and the Eight Hour League agitated for eight-hour workdays and child labor laws, holding massive strikes in Milwaukee. They led Wisconsin to pass the first workers' compensation law in the country, and later unemployment laws. Despite violent retribution from police and lost lives, labor retained a stronghold in Milwaukee. After World War I, as Milwaukee sought to cement and expand its industrial prowess, organized labor worked to protect gains made during the war. Employers reacted cannily, using lock-outs, injunctions, and spies, and paternalism. They hosted plant picnics and sponsored employee reading rooms, boxing matches, and free golf lessons, for example. Here they attempted to invoke the seemingly benign spirit of "family" and "community" in the workplace, while co-opting resistance, instilling discipline, and scripting conventional gender and racial norms (Gurda 1999; Kasparek, Malone, and Schock 2004; Tone 1997).

Meanwhile, immigration continued through the mid-1900s. New populations included southern blacks, whose initial migration to Milwaukee was small compared to cities like Chicago. The World War II increase in manufacturing hastened this migration, but more African Americans landed in Chicago than Milwaukee. As Milwaukee factories worked to produce war weaponry, including nuclear equipment, they were strained for employees. Women joined the factory lines in record numbers, and some remained after the war. African Americans migrated to Milwaukee in their largest numbers after the World War II boom. In some cases they found good-paying industrial jobs. However, there was little time for blacks to gain economic security or for a black middle class to emerge.

By the 1970s and 1980s, the industrial bases of Milwaukee began to erode. A city that had long relied on stable working-class jobs was fundamentally changed. Due to increasing international competition, declining profits, and the shifting of manufacturing operations overseas and to the suburbs, Milwaukee manufacturing jobs declined nearly 30 percent between 1970 and 1990.[1] Many of Milwaukee's major employers, including Allis-Chalmers, Schlitz, and Pabst, were bankrupt or closed by the 1990s. In the 1960s, almost 60 percent of metro Milwaukee's industrial jobs were located in the city; today, less than 19 percent of regional manufacturing takes place in the city (Levine 2013a). Like most cities, Milwaukee began to see an expansion of jobs and firms in the service sector, including health care, insurance, and food and beverage (see table 2). These service jobs generally paid substantively less than declining unionized jobs.

The dramatic shift in jobs was sharply epitomized in the ascendant growth of Manpower, a Milwaukee-based temporary employment agency that ranked 138 among the *Fortune* 500 companies in 2010. A Milwaukee machinist might have earned eighteen dollars per hour, whereas a temporary employee through Manpower often earned less than eight. In addition, Manpower and other agencies were the largest employers of welfare-to-work participants. In 2005, 42 percent of welfare-to-work participants worked for temporary agencies. Most were African American women (Wisconsin Legislative Audit Bureau 2005). In addition to their low wages, temporary jobs usually come without benefits and with

TABLE 2. Trends in employment by industry in metropolitan Milwaukee, 1970–2010 (percentages)

	1970	1980	1990	2000	2010
Agriculture, forestry, fishing and hunting, and mining	0	0	1	0	1
Construction	3	3	4	4	3
Manufacturing	35	31	22	19	14
Wholesale trade	5	4	4	3	2
Retail trade	16	16	17	10	11
Transportation and warehousing, utilities	6	4	4	5	4
Information	N/A	3	2	3	2
Finance, insurance, and real estate	5	6	8	7	6
Professional, scientific, management, administrative, and waste management services	18	5	7	9	11
Educational, health, and social services	N/A	17	19	23	28
Arts, entertainment, recreation, and accommodation and food services	4	3	4	9	10
Other services (except public administration)	4	4	5	4	4
Public administration	4	4	3	4	4
TOTAL	100	100	100	100	100

SOURCE: Bureau of Labor Statistics (2010) and U.S. Census Bureau (2010).

limited advancement options, underscoring problems with both welfare reform and Milwaukee's economy.

The majority of job growth in Milwaukee occurred primarily in the suburbs in the 1990s, with suburban white residents taking many well-paid jobs in downtown Milwaukee (Levine 2003a; Levine and Zipp 1994). In recent years, there has been small growth in higher-paying jobs in central Milwaukee, secured primarily by a burgeoning population of young white residents. Within and outside of the city, jobs and earnings remained distributed by gender and race, as is evident in tables 3 and 4.

These demographic and economic trends in Milwaukee have been shaped by global processes as well as the shifting historical political context. This history, beginning with Milwaukee's long-running experiment with Socialism helps explicate the city's gradual shift toward neoliberalism, which largely defines its situation one hundred years later.

The Rise of the Sewer Socialists (1900–1945)

In the early twentieth century, Milwaukee established a Socialist presence in city government and cemented its reputation as a tenacious labor town. Largely German immigrants, Milwaukee's original Socialists were dubbed "Sewer Socialists"

TABLE 3. Gendered employment patterns in metropolitan Milwaukee, 2010 (percentages)

Industry	Men	Women
Agriculture, forestry, fishing and hunting, and mining	1	0.2
Construction	6	0.3
Manufacturing	19	9
Wholesale trade	2	1
Retail trade	11	11
Transportation and warehousing, utilities	6	3
Information	2	2
Finance, insurance, and real estate	6	5.5
Professional, scientific, management, administrative, and waste management services	13	10
Educational, health, and social services	13	41
Arts, entertainment, recreation, accommodation, and food services	11	9
Other services (except public administration)	5	4
Public administration	5	4
TOTAL	100	100

SOURCE: U.S. Census Bureau (2010)

TABLE 4. Earnings and unemployment by race and gender in metropolitan Milwaukee for full-time workers (2007–11)

	White male	White female	African American male	African American female	Hispanic male	Hispanic female
Median earnings ($)	55,457	42,133	36,546	30,631	29,651	26,611
Percentage of white male earnings (%)	—	76	66	55	54	48

SOURCE: U.S. Census Bureau, American Community Survey. Only the majority racial/ethnic populations in the metropolitan Milwaukee region are provided in this table.

because of their interest in enhanced water and sewer systems in the city. But as Socialist Mayor Emil Seidel (1910–12) articulated in the epigraph, the party agenda extended far beyond sewers and sanitation and included issues like labor protections and living wages for workers and a commitment to parks and community and social services.

Achieving a majority on the Common Council in 1910, some Milwaukee Socialists forwarded radical ideas for the time like abolishing the U.S. Senate, creating old-age pensions, and granting women suffrage (Beck and Zeidler 1982). These ideas were unpopular and failed. However, Milwaukee Socialists transformed government and upgraded many city services, in part by pressuring private companies to improve city transit and pave streets. Socialists believed that citizens owned the government. Mayor Seidel declared that "any citizen coming to an office occupied by a socialist has been received with courtesy" (Seidel n.d.).

Moreover, according to historian John Gurda (1999, 215), Socialists also pursued efficiency with "a zeal that would have warmed the heart of any red-blooded capitalist." A Bureau of Economy and Efficiency was formed, with the goal of improving governance and services to poor and working-class residents. The early Socialist regime inventoried all city property, tightened voting procedures, increased health inspections of factories, and established and reformed schools. Housing and fire commissions and public health and city planning programs were founded. In addition, the city limited deficit financing, establishing a debt amortization fund and a civic savings account meant to erase indebtedness (Beck and Zeidler 1982; Gurda 1999; Miller 1981).

Despite these accomplishments, Milwaukee's Socialism suffered during World War I in part due to nationalist fervor related to the war, its pacifist platform, and associations between Socialism and German politics. Socialists and unionists began to split, as Woodrow Wilson's Democratic Party offered prolabor policies, such as the eight-hour workday (Beck and Zeidler 1982). Yet Milwaukee clung to some of its Socialist roots: Daniel Hoan, a Socialist, was elected mayor in 1916 and governed for twenty-four years, including during the Great Depression. He implemented several measures to mitigate the effects of the Depression, which earned him national recognition. In contrast to later neoliberal policies, he maintained municipal spending and services even during crisis. Mayor Hoan imposed shorter working hours to address unemployment and supported local job creation efforts, using local milkmen to distribute cards soliciting odd jobs, for example. The Milwaukee Common Council launched a work relief program funded in part by a voluntary 10 percent reduction in city workers' paychecks, including the mayor's. Milwaukee also introduced "baby bonds," notes secured by delinquent tax certificates that holders could use to pay city obligations or redeem at Milwaukee stores or professional offices. In 1933, the city began to pay its employees with a mix of baby bonds and cash. Such measures were unique during the Depression, as were Milwaukee's status as a deficit-free city and its investment in thirty million dollars worth of capital improvements without relying on bonds (Beck and Zeidler 1982).

Milwaukee's governance strategies during the Depression garnered fame. On April 6, 1936, Mayor Hoan graced the cover of *Time* magazine, which declared on page 18 that "Daniel Webster Hoan remains one of the nation's ablest public servants and under him Milwaukee has become perhaps the best-governed city in the U.S." Interestingly, nearly sixty years later, a similar quote in *Financial World* magazine would praise Mayor John Norquist's neoliberal regime, labeling Milwaukee "one of America's best-run cities" in 1994 (Barrett and Greene 1994).

Not all primary or secondary sources agree on the tenor and accomplishments of Socialism. According to *Time*,

Milwaukee's election system insures absolute honesty.... Milwaukee's 107 superbly equipped and managed schools provide ordinary, vocational, and leisure education for every citizen over 4 years of age. It claims the biggest and best part-time vocational school in the world, the nation's largest municipally-owned educational museum, the largest per-capita adult night-school enrollment in the U.S. It has a magnificent system of 67 city parks, 68 city playgrounds, 21 social centers, produces outdoor opera, maintains free bathing beaches, operates dance halls in the parks, and uses 47 of its school buildings every night for drama clubs, bridge games, chess tournaments. (*Time* 1936, 19)

Milwaukee historian John Gurda (1999, 301) agreed that Milwaukee residents could take pride in the performance of their local government in the 1930s for its decision to invest in public services and recreation rather than to slash services. Most guardedly, urban sociologist Anthony Orum (1995) argued that the Socialists had made government run efficiently, but had not accomplished lofty goals of improving life for the mass working class.

Regardless of their enthusiasm about Milwaukee's Socialism, few urban scholars discuss the surrounding gender, ethnic, and racial dynamics. Historian Sally Miller (1981, 1983, 2002) has pointed out that despite policies and rhetoric that endorsed women's and immigrant rights, the national Socialist Party in practice remained largely "for white men only" (2002). Socialists did not substantively promote gender equity policies or attract women in large numbers. When women did join the national Socialist Party beginning in the early 1900s, they were marginalized into a short-lived Woman's Chapter that received limited resources and endorsement from the party as a whole. Women were rarely represented in national leadership positions, such as the National Executive Committee (Miller 2002).

In Milwaukee, these national patterns held to some extent. Historian John Gurda argued in an interview that "Milwaukee was really distinctive in terms of being open to leadership opportunities for women. There seemed to be an intentional inclusiveness." This inclusivity was influenced by German traditions and a family-centered ethos where women were partners. However, the dynamics were also constrained by conventional gender norms of the times.

In Milwaukee, a few women, including some members of the working class, ascended into local and state leadership positions within the Socialist Party. For example, Meta Berger and Elizabeth Thomas both served on the Milwaukee School Board, which the Socialists had helped transform into an elected body (Reese 1981). More common than female leadership within the Socialist Party, and perhaps specific to Milwaukee, was the inclination of Milwaukee Socialists to collaborate with Milwaukee women's groups and other groups committed to issues such as poverty and education. Milwaukee women's clubs were part of a national reformist movement in cities around the country, where middle-class women played a prominent role in addressing and improving the everyday lives of residents, neighborhoods, and communities, although often in racialized and moralizing ways. Milwaukee hosted the 1900 biennial gathering of the General Federation of Women's Clubs (see Hayden 2002; Parker 2011; Spain 2004; Wirka 1996).

Milwaukee women's clubs and the Socialists shaped each other's agenda. Reflecting on the contradictions and power relations in these alliances, historian Reese (1981, 22) writes, "The Socialists, for example, sensed the popularity of many of the social welfare programs already financed or suggested by women's voluntary associations: the playgrounds, vacation schools, lunch programs, and social centers." Just as the Socialists adopted (or co-opted) several of the women's social service programs (and historically received credit), some Milwaukee women came to adopt more Socialist political views or join the party. The Woman's School Alliance, for example, soon had several Socialist members and leaders, including a president who asserted, "We believe it is the right of every child that is born into the world to have enough to eat, and suitable clothes to wear" (cited in Reese 1981, 23).

Despite these strategic cross-alliances around social reproduction and social services, members of the Milwaukee Socialist Party retained ambivalent positions with regard to gender equity. For example, some Socialist leaders, especially females, appeared largely in favor of suffrage. *The Milwaukee Leader*, the Socialist daily newspaper, wrote that Socialist women had shown "the falsity of the contention that women have no concern in affairs outside the immediate circle of the family" and that they "would do their part in the political field for human betterment and labor's emancipation" (Buenker 1981, 131). Yet a 1912 referendum for suffrage was defeated handily in Wisconsin, with many Milwaukee Socialists and sympathizers leaning against the vote for women. White female Socialists were leaders in white women's suffragist efforts and other groups. However, women had far fewer positions in Milwaukee Socialist Party leadership or elected office (except the school board). This was particularly true of immigrant and nonwhite women, who did not always reap benefits of Socialist-sponsored programs.

Female party leaders were often subjected to male chauvinism and were expected to uphold traditional family relations. Despite internal tensions that later led to a divorce, Mayor Hoan's family and wife were carefully depicted as traditional and secure in family life; in 1936, *Time* magazine wrote, "At 5:30 the Mayor drives home, where he and motherly Mrs. Hoan, who he thinks is the world's best cook, usually eat in the kitchen" (1936, 18). Meta Berger, who was an elected school board member, independent career woman, and wife of Victor Berger, privately bemoaned her exclusion from Socialist meetings in her own home (Berger 2001).

As Miller (2002) argues about the national Socialist Party, the assumption remained that to be a "worker" and a "Socialist" was to be a male—a construct that was seldom challenged in Milwaukee's version of Socialism. Ironically, the passage of suffrage may have intensified gendered exclusions. A national backlash against feminism led to a decline in women's leadership and political involvement and a renewed emphasis on traditional family and gender roles, consumption, and leisure (see Faludi 2006; Spain 2004).

Racism also persisted under Milwaukee's Socialist regime, even though there were some progressive views and generalized black electoral support for Socialist Mayor Hoan (Trotter 1985). There was little, if any, concern for African Americans, Native Americans, or Mexican Americans. Victor Berger, a Milwaukee Socialist with national influence, stated frequently that blacks constituted a lower race (Miller 2002), although he later converted some of his views and engaged in an antilynching campaign (Beck and Zeidler 1982). Milwaukee Mayor Daniel Hoan had more egalitarian views, even serving on the Milwaukee NAACP Board, an unusual position for a mayor at this time. At the urging of black leaders and some whites, Hoan also strongly opposed the Ku Klux Klan, closing the Milwaukee auditorium to Klan meetings in 1922. When Klan members offered to help "clean up" Milwaukee and raid speakeasies, Hoan responded vigorously "that if they intruded on law enforcement they would find Milwaukee 'the hottest place this side of hell'" (Beck and Zeidler 1982, 231). In part because of this stance, the Klan never rooted itself as firmly in Milwaukee as in several other northern cities (Trotter 1985, 138), although other forms of racism certainly persisted.

While historian Joe William Trotter (1985, 136) frames Mayor Hoan's motivation as largely political, he notes that blacks and Socialists had some amiable relations and partnerships. Some black union members were Socialists, and occasionally Socialists participated in the socioeconomic and political affairs of the black community. For years, Milwaukee's African Americans stood firmly by Socialists, even when they came under attack by both Republicans and Democrats. The *Blade*, the black daily newspaper, declared, "As for the Socialists, we are yet to be convinced that they are all rascals" (Trotter 1985, 121). However, there remained very few blacks or non-German immigrants in Socialist Party leadership positions and virtually no women of color.

For local and national reasons, racism increased during and after the Depression, even as Socialists governed. Black migration to the city increased to some degree, competition for economic and social resources intensified, and racial hostility and discrimination became more overt. African Americans received limited benefits and protections from Milwaukee's labor unions and campaigns, and did not always benefit from Socialist programs designed to ameliorate the Depression's effects. Similarly, a report by a white social worker in 1929 suggested that "all the charities are open to the Mexicans as well as to other foreigners, which they know well and use freely" (Fenton 1930). However, black Milwaukeeans and Mexicans reported discrimination in accessing relief programs. Exacerbating matters, blacks experienced job losses in the 1930s at a rate much higher than whites in Milwaukee and across the country, and Milwaukee had twice the number of unemployed blacks than Detroit did in 1940, despite its small black population (Sundstrom 1992). In addition, Mayor Hoan told a racist story in 1932 to a crowd of six thousand people. While he later apologized, this incident symbolized an increasingly direct racist climate.

Black women perhaps fared the worst among Milwaukee residents under Socialism, especially with regard to employment (Trotter 1985), a situation that largely persists today (see Jones 2009). Racism and sexism barred black women from most industrial jobs. Not atypically, a Milwaukee business owner argued that black women "should aspire to becoming first class house servants and stop worrying about other types of work because they made the world's finest Mammies" (Trotter 1985, 159; see also Hill Collins 2002). Black women labored intensively as domestic servants, often working for seven or eight families in a single day while their own families remained poor. However, Socialists were often silent regarding the racism, sexism, and social conditions for women of color. Victor Berger, for example, described an optimistic and sexist order in 1921: "As we have Socialism now, it goes without saying that we have no poverty. Only a sick man is considered a poor man" (Muzik, 1960, 13).

In summary, Milwaukee's strongest decades of urban Socialism helped create greater efficiency in urban governance. To some extent, Socialists forwarded the goals of white working-class Milwaukeeans, providing some labor protections, basic infrastructure, necessary services, and even recreation for many residents. Socialists implemented a number of creative urban governance strategies that mitigated some of the potentially disastrous effects of the Depression.[2] Moreover, the Milwaukee Socialists had more female leadership and involvement than was typical for Socialist movements, and governing Socialists formed partnerships with middle-class women's groups, black leadership, and immigrant labor unions. These partnerships, along with female reformers' mobilizations to improve cities, resulted in stronger government investments in *social reproduction*, including community schools and public health. Even if the Socialists received the credit, these partnerships and the salient government emphasis on social reproduction concerns were unique historically and geographically. These partnerships also resulted in a strong Milwaukee NAACP chapter and a government that was less racist than many others at the time.

However, Milwaukee's Socialist leadership and interests were largely dominated by white men, and equity regarding gender and race was a relatively tertiary concern. While Socialist women and nonwhites argued that a better civilization rested on more than just class struggles, such voices were often unheeded (see Buhle 1983). The presumed Socialist citizen and subject was a white male worker, and women and minorities were often excluded from leadership and social service benefits. According to historian Sally Miller (1981, 29), "Narrow racial and gender visions were at the core of the party's consciousness and policies." Of course, Socialist Party attitudes were not separate from broader gendered and raced norms and practices. In Milwaukee and across the United States, the normative, white household model was based on a presumed male "breadwinner" and female "housewife." In covert and overt forms, sexism and racism persisted in urban society and urban labor markets.

In the early 1900s, women's urban reformist movements shifted these roles slightly as some female leaders, club women, and female Socialists imagined urban spaces and lives based on creativity, collectivity, and care. In Milwaukee and elsewhere, these women formed partnerships, instituted policy changes, provided direct services, and helped to establish housing and public health reforms. Such movements—whether mainstream or radical and however successful—were often framed as an extension of maternal and household labor to increase their appeal and deflect resistance. Even without the full support of Socialists, Milwaukee women were at the forefront of women's suffrage. Wisconsin was the first state to ratify suffrage in 1919 and to pass a women's equal rights bill two years later. However, gendered inequalities and anxieties constrained women's political leadership and participation in Milwaukee and elsewhere. As Hayden (2002, 47) argues, women's groups had "asserted a direct political challenge to their seclusion in the home by demanding a homelike city. Yet many men preferred to promote better government by men as defenders of women and children in the home rather than to accept direct female power."

The Winds of War in Milwaukee

During World War II, local and national energies gradually became consumed with war efforts, and a subdued Milwaukee Socialist regime continued under Mayor Daniel Hoan. In the technical sense, Milwaukee was not a war boomtown. The city was already an industrial powerhouse prior to the war. However, production intensified during the war, and weekly wages rose 20 percent between 1941 and 1942 (Pifer 2003). Conservative gender politics in Milwaukee initially restrained women's entry into the war workforce. As late as January 31, 1943, the *Milwaukee Journal Sentinel* wrote, "There is no compelling need for women with minor children to leave their home responsibilities for war work. . . . A housekeeper owes it to those war workers to stay home to prepare food and restful surroundings for her family." However, demand eventually superseded these discourses, so that women composed 57 percent of Milwaukee's workforce by the end of the war; 20 percent of them had children under age fourteen.

With greater autonomy, independence, and employment opportunities, women mobilized their energies. Nationally, women joined unions in droves and protested for equal rights and better day care. Both Republicans and Democrats added the Equal Rights Amendment to their platforms in the early 1940s, and it was voted on the Senate floor three times. However, the tone in Milwaukee was more cautious. City and county leaders resisted federal efforts to expand day care in the Milwaukee region. Social service workers, the press, and Milwaukee labor representatives noted that married women would soon return home and no institutional support was needed. Milwaukee wartime working mothers managed by working a double shift at work and home and relying on friends, family, and paid help. For this reason, when one company proposed a ten-hour day shift six days a week, women opposed, insisting that the company hire black women instead. In addition, they denounced a rumor—allegedly spread by the company—that they would not work with blacks (Pifer 2003, 142).

In spite of this instrumental endorsement of white female workers, the reality for wartime black workers was mixed. Only when pressured by black activists and when white labor was nearly drained (or tired of doing double duty at home and work) did Milwaukee firms began to hire black workers. Allis-Chalmers—whose building turned into a local welfare-to-work office in the 1990s—was one of the first companies to hire black workers (see Collins and Mayer 2010). While the Milwaukee Urban League proudly proclaimed in 1943 that "today there is hardly a Negro Man in Milwaukee who is physically able and willing to work who is not employed," the jobs were often the least desirable and dirtiest, and even during wartime few jobs beyond domestic service were available for black women (Trotter 1985, 165). As I describe in the next section, black women's participation in the labor force and wage-earning needs were often subordinated to those of black men. The industrial foothold for women of all races and ethnicities was a short-lived, wartime experience, as a backlash against working women and feminism ensued (Faludi 2006; Fure-Slocum 2000; Trotter 1985, 171).

Milwaukee after the War: Markets, Modernity, and White Masculinities

Debates, discourses, and patterns of governance following World War II shifted gradually but saliently away from Socialism in Milwaukee. While Socialists retained the mayor's office until 1960, the party's platform weakened as business interests strengthened their positions and competing values resonated with the public. It is also possible to discern many roots of Milwaukee's neoliberalism at this time, including the reascent of white markets and masculinities. While labor interests retained a strong presence in Milwaukee, the intertwined politics around gender, sexuality, race, bonds, public housing, and suburbanization demonstrated a movement away from Socialism toward "modern, enterprising," and deeply divided urban politics in the second half of the century.

The shift away from Socialism and the emerging tendrils of neoliberalism are perhaps best exemplified in the discourses and debates around debt and redevelopment after World War II in Milwaukee. The perceived physical and social degeneration of postwar Milwaukee became a major concern, as in many other large U.S. cities. In a powerfully gendered discursive act, a *Milwaukee Journal Sentinel* writer nicknamed postwar Milwaukee "Old Lady Thrift" and described her as "a plump and smiling city . . . [sitting] in complacent shabbiness on the west shore of Lake Michigan like a wealthy old lady in black alpaca taking her ease on the beach. . . . All her slips are showing, but she doesn't mind a bit" (cited in Fure-Slocum 2000, 258). Drawing on gendered, raced, and classed metaphors, this imagery reflected and reinforced fears among Milwaukee's elite about the future of the city. These fears were related not only to the physical state of Milwaukee, but also to local and national anxiety surrounding perceived disruptions of sexual, class, gender, and racial norms (Berube 1990; Cuordileone 2000; Fure-Slocum 2000).

As several scholars have explored, the postwar U.S. society was shaken by a feeling of vulnerability and unease. The country had seen its national security threatened; economic and social changes had come quickly, especially in cities; and women's autonomy and sexuality had become less restrained as they flooded the workforce, reshaped communities, and managed households while their husbands were fighting overseas. Black immigration had intensified, and black workers had accrued some wealth and status in certain communities. The cultural responses in the United States were to exalt a nuclear, white, heteronormative family, particular versions of domesticity steeped in racialized and gendered geographies and consumption patterns, and a vision of a modern and masculine city. While 75 percent of surveyed women wanted to keep their jobs after the war, two million female workers were displaced from heavy industry by 1945. As Susan Faludi (2006, 80) describes, they encountered a backlash that was material, political, and rhetorical:

> With the close of World War II, efforts by industry, government and media converged to force a female retreat. Employers revived prohibitions against hiring married women and imposed caps on female salaries, the government shut down its day care services and defended rights of veterans to displace women. Employers who had applauded women's work now accused working women of incompetence and bad attitudes. Advice experts filled bookstores with usual warnings; education and jobs were stripping women of their femininity and denying them marriage and motherhood; women were suffering fatigue and mental instability from employment; women who used day care were selfish fur-coated mothers.

Child-care authorities, most notably Dr. Benjamin Spock, demanded that wives stay home. Advertisers reversed messages and claimed woman must choose, and choose only home. (Faludi 2006, 80)

This backlash was against not just women, but also lesbian and gay communities and cultures that had grown during the war. Antigay rhetoric was visible in cities like Milwaukee. New laws were passed against homosexuality, and there was a purge of gay and lesbian government workers and elected officials, led in part by Wisconsin senator Joseph McCarthy. Under President Eisenhower, "sexual perversion" was listed as sufficient and necessary grounds for dismissal from the federal government in 1953.

Amid the strongest national assault on feminism and careerism since 1905 and hostility toward homosexuality, a group of Milwaukee executives formed the 1948 Corporation. This enterprise, later becoming the Greater Milwaukee Committee, advocated for civic improvement projects and soon forwarded a vision of a masculine, marketized, modern city. The Greater Milwaukee Committee was dominated by business interests, and not a single woman or person of color was included. Its membership of 150 people owned or managed 25 percent of the business property in the city (Gurda 1999). The corporation's initial marketing messages and ensuing politics drew on and reinforced discourses of rational planning, efficiency, and masculine power. As a national *Time* article fed into the worry that American men were becoming passive and irresponsible because women were not fulfilling their feminine duties, the Greater Milwaukee Committee's development program helped to reestablish gender hierarchies that had been unsettled during the war (see Faludi 2006; Fure-Slocum 2000). Now, advertisements for downtown shopping along Milwaukee's magnificent mile targeted middle-class women as shoppers and cultural consumers at a time when white families were increasingly fleeing to the suburbs. Milwaukee historian John Gurda describes this as a "bigger, better, and blander" Milwaukee: "I think that Milwaukee was largely right in step with national trends, including suburbanization and somewhat traditional roles for women. Milwaukee was not particularly exceptional. Suburbanization was on the rise, there was a national tendency toward conformity and modernity. . . . After the war, women largely slipped back into traditional roles" (Gurda, interview, 2004).

The new Greater Milwaukee Committee played a critical role in shaping the debates and spatial layout of Milwaukee's postwar future. Conveying the Socialists' no-debt policy as backward, "passive," and feminized, the committee's pro-bond campaign described an orderly, rational, and enterprising city in which financial markets, bonds, and suburbs had a fundamental role. This prodevelopment movement gained the support of some working-class people, minorities, and women activists by promising improved affordable housing (which never materialized) after "blighted areas" had been removed. Mayoral candidate

Frank Zeidler argued against bonds, appealing to organized labor. In the end, voters tried to choose both, reflecting changing norms and gendered and raced tensions. They authorized debt bonds for expressways, blight removal, veteran housing, parking, and a sports arena (Norman 1989), but shortly after, voters elected Socialist candidate Zeidler (Fure-Slocum 2000).

Zeidler's victory was propelled by a primarily white, working-class majority but came amid attacks on socialism as a communist philosophy that undermined American capitalism (see Smith 2003). During this time, radicals and communists (real or perceived) were purged from the Milwaukee labor community. A climate of fear of appearing anticapitalist decreased much opposition to the new Greater Milwaukee Committee and its development agenda. The Zeidler administration clashed with the committee over several issues, including public housing and redevelopment. In this way, the committee was able to execute only smaller-scale projects during the 1950s (see Rast 2006). However, business leaders were often in unison and the influence of the raced, gendered, and classed Greater Milwaukee Committee would continue to grow, setting the course for Milwaukee's future development and the growth of neoliberal urban policies. Urban scholar Jack Norman (1989, 178–79) argued that "the Greater Milwaukee Committee was the leading voice of the private sector" and that once the Zeidler administration ended, city government became more passive in allowing the committee to set the agenda for development. In this way, some dimensions of neoliberalism, including but not limited to the strong influence of the private sector, a weakened state that caters to business interests, and emphasis on downtown development, have long been in place Milwaukee.

Intense white flight and subtle and overt racism were also reflected in the "modern" and "masculine" Milwaukee and related debates about public housing. Like other urban centers, Milwaukee experienced a postwar explosion in suburban development and white flight, after two world wars, a Depression, and disinvestment created crowded inner-city neighborhoods. This pattern combined with soaring rates of African American immigration and racist practices to cement and deepen sociospatial inequality in Milwaukee. Milwaukee's suburbanization, like the process across the country, was fueled by discourses of a dying, declining city; racist attitudes; low-interest loans provided by the Federal Housing Administration and Veterans Administration to whites; federal and local investments in expressways; and pernicious real estate and governance practices that confined African Americans to segregated neighborhoods in the city (e.g., Kruse 2013; Massey 1993; Orum 1995; Satter 2009). Nationally, the Federal Housing Authority financed eleven million suburban homes between 1945 and 1972. According to the FHA guidebook of 1936, desirable housing locations for loan applications were "in the middle of an area well developed with a uniform type of residential properties." Furthermore, nearby schools should not be attended by pupils from "inharmonious racial groups." Boosted by these lending guidelines, suburban housing units doubled between 1940 and 1950 in Milwaukee and many other cities and white flight accelerated, creating a profound and lasting divide in the city.

African American neighborhoods in the city were pressed by segregation, crowding, and a lack of investment. A 1946 study found that more than 67 percent of African Americans lived in homes that were unfit for habitation or in need of major repair (Gurda 1999, 359). According to a 1952 Mayor's Commission report, segregation was "widely and openly practiced" and "had resulted in a ghetto pattern" in which African Americans found it "almost impossible to move out of Milwaukee's worst housing area" (*Milwaukee Journal Sentinel*, March 20, 1952). Making matters worse, the building of freeways uprooted, displaced, and further concentrated African American communities in Milwaukee. White working-class Milwaukeeans, many of whom benefited from racialized federal housing loans and suburbanization, did not experience similar housing crises. They either remained in "white" areas of the city or moved to the suburbs.

Meanwhile, with some exceptions, efforts to improve inner-city housing, integrate neighborhoods, and create public housing in Milwaukee were stonewalled by coalitions of urban land elites, such as the Milwaukee Board of Realtors and the Milwaukee Property Owners Association, as well as some elected politicians and white residents (see Rast 2006; Smith 2003).

As historian Kevin Smith argues, the framing of urban debates around housing, bonds, and other issues in anticommunist, proenterprise, promodernity rhetoric by urban leaders minimized overtly racist appeals while achieving racist outcomes (see Smith 2003). While attempting to preserve Milwaukee's reputation for tolerance and sounding remarkably like contemporary neoliberals, opponents to public housing labeled public housing "un-American."[3] Elected officials and business leaders blamed Socialists and black residents for decay and problems in the city. Milwaukee residents were more direct. At a meeting of four hundred South Side residents, the majority cheered when one resident declared, "we do not want the colored people on the south side, and believe me, that is the whole thing" (*Milwaukee Journal Sentinel*, September 1, 1960).

Racism was even more amplified in the suburbs, and an increasingly antiurban attitude emerged and hardened in Milwaukee's iron ring of white suburbs with overt hostility toward black, poor residents. As Milwaukee historian John Gurda (1999, 341) describes, "Most galling was the suburbs' obvious desire for city resources, particularly water, and their equally transparent unwillingness to share responsibility for city problems, especially those associated with poverty."

To stem this impending bifurcation and retain a strong tax base, the city of Milwaukee pursued suburban annexation in the 1950s with the support of business leadership and elected officials (see Rast 2006). While it experienced some initial success, this effort was undermined by a conservative movement and related Wisconsin State law in 1955 that allowed any town adjoining Milwaukee with at least five thousand residents and property valued at twenty million dollars to incorporate. Such conflicts intensified and worked in concert with racist ideologies and lifestyle differences to shift both power and white populations to the suburbs. They also sharpened the equality gap between city and suburban residents.

This situation was further problematized by the early 1930s split between the Milwaukee County and Milwaukee City governments. In this unusual and shifting arrangement, Milwaukee County draws its tax base from the entire county and assumes certain responsibilities, such as social service provision, while Milwaukee City controls the urban water supply and a number of other services. As the suburbs rapidly grew, the Milwaukee County government ballooned. Initially, candidates with strong ties to Milwaukee city neighborhoods filled these leadership positions. However, gradually this pattern gave way, and county and city leadership reflected a true divide between suburb and city.

Just as white residents persistently resisted integration, Milwaukee's business community and conservative elected officials increasingly argued that private enterprise—primarily white, heteronormative, and male—should oversee postwar urban renewal (Norman 1989). At the same time, white women, who had previously been activists on housing issues for residents of all races, began to withdrawal their involvement (L'Aberge 1995). In these ways, "whiteness" framed a limited convergence among Milwaukeeans of different class and gender backgrounds in the late 1950s.

This convergence, along with gender norms and rapid and uneven wealth accumulation, enabled a merger of white masculinities and markets that helped usher in and preserve politics that were later labeled "neoliberal." Racism trumped, and many blacks lost jobs, savings, and wealth through urban renewal and other forms of dispossession. Mayor Zeidler's support (lukewarm as it may have been) for racial integration nearly cost him a reelection bid in 1956 and bolstered conservative opposition movements. Milwaukee's white elites benefitted through expanded financial markets and urban development projects, and others gained housing and wealth through subsidized suburban development. Facing pressing heteronormative, gendered norms and amid a climate of racism, white women largely disinvested in equity projects and were not united across race lines. Although many white and black women worked outside of their homes, they labored in the lowest paying and least prestigious jobs, especially the latter group.

Situated in a cultural climate antipathetic to feminism and female leadership, women remained mostly invisible in elected politics. Vel Phillips was voted in 1958 as the first African American female City Council member, an event that historian John Gurda called "anomalous," noting that "the fact that she was elected had much more to do with her being an African American than with her being a woman" (interview, June 2006). In fact, it was nearly twenty years before another woman joined the City Council.

Business as Usual in Milwaukee under Mayor Maier (1960–88)?

The time period from 1960 to 1988, overseen by outspoken, probusiness Mayor Henry Maier, witnessed the growth of overt racial unrest in Milwaukee and across the country, accompanied by growing black political power and increasing feminist and gay and lesbian activism. At the same time, elite business and political insiders, mostly white and male, gained increased influence over formal Milwaukee politics, and lingering Socialist politics all but dissipated. Socialist mayor Zeidler was no longer in office to contest or balance the business community, clearing the way for increased private influence over development (Rast 2006).

By the 1970s and 1980s, many American cities, including New York, Baltimore, Houston, and Atlanta, began slashing urban services and support for the poor. Amid deindustrialization, stagnating growth, and declining federal aid, cities also began orienting their policies toward public incentives and subsidies intended to animate downtown business districts (Sites 2003, 43). With the Greater Milwaukee Committee firmly in place and decades of conservative, racist, and masculinist leadership, Milwaukee was ahead of the game.

Henry Maier was elected in 1960 with an agenda that eliminated Socialist appointees and called for more private influence in urban development. Maier's largest majorities came from Milwaukee's white South Side. Black leadership had been growing in the city, and Vel Phillips and others pushed Maier and the city for open housing legislation and greater inclusion of African Americans in city government. Maier and the Common Council resisted such efforts so fully that a cadre of black leaders wrote, "It is disappointing that the mayor of our city has beclouded the hopes and aspirations of Milwaukee Negroes" (Norman 1989, 114). Eventually, dissatisfaction over housing turned into sustained public demonstrations by the black community with some support of white Catholics, in some cases becoming violent. While ultimately bowing to some housing reforms, the Maier administration was never an ally for the black community, and integration stalled.

Like many mayors and in contrast to later Mayor Norquist, Maier actively pursued federal funding for urban renewal. New federal and state laws allowed the city to take control of private land "threatened" by blight and redevelop it as long as housing replacement was planned. During the 1960s and 1970s, 266 acres of Milwaukee (including intact neighborhoods and houses) were cleared for new development with federal urban renewal funds. Of this land, 56 percent was used for residential development, 30 percent for business development, and 14 percent for expansion of a private university west of downtown.

For the most part, these projects maintained segregation and ignored Milwaukee's neediest neighborhoods. They did not reflect the desires of the broader black community. Renewal projects, including road and expressway projects, destroyed some black neighborhoods and eliminated more housing than they created. Relocation efforts simply shoved blacks into already crowded neighborhoods, concomitantly worsening race relations and not ameliorating poverty.

Urban renewal also contributed to uneven raced and gendered wealth accumulation, in part through dispossession of land, neighborhoods, businesses, and homes owned by African Americans (Maskovsky 2001; Massey 2008; Norman 1989; Satter 2009; Venkatesh 2000). White men and their families fared particularly well, as they built wealth through home ownership and profits gained through real estate, development, and business generation. Married white women benefited under this arrangement as well, although their control of family resources was more constrained. Many scholars argue that this historical moment was critical in cementing current income disparities between whites and African Americans, as the latter population lost homes, wealth, small businesses, job opportunities, and sometimes entire communities (Massey 2008; Satter 2009).

In Milwaukee, urban renewal funds were used for downtown office space and high-rise, high-rent apartments, as well as an indoor shopping mall. These downtown projects were hotly contested by black leadership, who argued that neighborhoods were badly in need of repair and investment (Norman 1989, 187). In fact, in the 1970s, some black aldermen threatened to block the Common Council's application for federal funding for the mall unless the city ceased building a planned freeway through black neighborhoods and applied for federal funds to rebuild demolished black neighborhoods. These threats failed in the face of solid public support for the mall. The media helped garner that support, writing that "inner city alderman, especially, should remember that their constituents have much to gain for the downtown mall-hotel proposal jobs, improved shopping opportunities, and an enhanced city tax base" (*Milwaukee Journal Sentinel*, December 28, 1977).

This contention persists in Milwaukee, despite local evidence showing that downtown development rarely benefits inner-city residents and neighborhoods (see Levine and Zipp 1994), an issue explored in chapter 7. As urban anthropologist Jeff Maskovsky (2001, 221) explains, downtown development is rarely a winning strategy for poor people: "It runs on public subsidies and therefore takes previous public resources away from poor and working class neighborhoods in which redlining, industrial withdrawal and job loss already have produced downward mobility, decay of housing stock, population turnover and the weakening of local civic and community organizations."

In concert with the Greater Milwaukee Committee, Mayor Maier consolidated the city's urban development efforts by combining three departments into the new Department of City Development (Orum 1995). He endorsed the creation of the Milwaukee Redevelopment Corporation—a for-profit spin-off of the Greater Milwaukee Committee. This public-private partnership flourished in the 1980s, epitomized by the collaborations between the Department of City Development and the Milwaukee Redevelopment Corporation (Norman 1989, 198). While some neighborhood groups were included in the partnership to a limited extent in the 1980s, business interests dominated the Milwaukee Redevelopment Authority and the city administration did not press for democracy or inclusion. Urban scholar Anthony Orum (1995, 136) argued that the Greater Milwaukee Committee had "a blind spot for social issues.... They appeared to have little interest in helping to overcome the vast social division that had grown up in the city; the composition of their own membership testified to their impatience with social differences."

Largely excluded from decision making, neighborhood groups began to form their own alliances. Thus, while ties between Milwaukee's male political and business elites deepened under Maier, the 1960s and 1970s was also a time of expanding political power and engagement for neighborhood, as well as feminist, gay and lesbian, and black and ethnic organizations in Milwaukee. In the 1960s, the number of neighborhood groups grew from eight to thirty-three, and many were located in the inner urban core. These organizations were active at City Hall in defending community interests, including housing issues and the development and revitalization of urban neighborhoods (Orum 1995).

Feminist and gay and lesbian activism grew during this time as well, and Milwaukee was a place "where women's political participation was extensive and relatively effective," according to feminist urban scholar Janet Boles (2001, see also Boles 1992). A gay and lesbian community center was established in Milwaukee in 1975, the Milwaukee Committee on Human Rights was formed to combat antigay discrimination soon after, Milwaukee activists introduced the first antigay discrimination legislation, and a feminist bookstore opened for business. While there was almost a twenty-year gap between the first female elected to a city office in 1956 and the next, more minorities and women gradually were elected to the City Council during this period. In the 1980s, women composed 28 percent of the Milwaukee County Board, 29 percent of the Milwaukee City Council, and 55 percent of the Milwaukee School Board (Boles 1992).[4] While not necessarily claiming a causal relationship, historian John Gurda argued in a personal interview that there were powerful women and strong progressive impulses in the 1980s within the City Council: "There were several outspoken, powerful women at that time on common council.

'Sally' came from a community organizing background. 'Mary' had been involved in a campaign. And it wasn't like they necessarily voiced an agenda that was evidently feminist, but definitely a progressive agenda. And Milwaukee was really no different than any other Northern cities at the time. . . . This was a time when women were ascending in political power over much of the country" (interview, June 2006).

Milwaukee women were also critically engaged in feminist activism, locally and nationally. Several Milwaukee charter chapters of the National Organization for Women were founded, as was 9 to 5, an organization focused on the rights of working women and gender and race inequality. In 1972, the Milwaukee Women's Coalition was founded as an umbrella organization to link more than thirty feminist groups that had formed locally (see Boles 1992; Dombeck 1987). Its mission at the time was "to form a coalition of feminist groups . . . to combat sex discrimination . . . to provide assistance to new feminist groups and create alternative institutions within the women's movement" (Dombeck 1987, 17).

For over sixteen years, the Women's Coalition used social service delivery, direct action, advocacy, lobbying, and personal relationships with elected officials to improve the status of Milwaukee women. Lesbian women and organizations participated and ensured a focus on people with varying sexual and gender identities. The coalition integrated family violence awareness curriculum into schools, instituted a mandatory arrest policy for domestic violence calls, established special prosecution and sexual assault counseling units within the District Attorney's office and police department, and improved direct services to women. The coalition also helped establish day care centers in county facilities, created a loan fund to increase the supply of private day care services, changed the system for delivering means-tested day care subsidies, and implemented city zoning changes to facilitate the creation of new urban day care centers (see Dombeck 1987).

Finally, the Women's Coalition, in conjunction with local leaders, helped form the Women's Crisis Line, the Task Force on Battered Women, the Displaced Homemaker Project/Network, the Take Back the Night campaign, and the short-lived Task Forces on Prostitution and Pornography. Some of these groups still existed when Norquist was elected in 1988. However, by 1990, city leaders were complaining that feminist activism had declined. According to several elected officials, women's groups were "dormant," "on the wane," and "dying on the vine" (cited in Boles 2001, 80). This decline was partially fueled by a pernicious feminist and civil rights backlash and the related rise of neoliberal policies and practices, as I explore in detail in chapter 7.

In summary, during the twenty-eight-year Maier administration, there were tremendous political and social changes and substantive increases in neighborhood, minority, gay and lesbian, and feminist activism. While Mayor Maier adeptly secured federal funds for urban renewal projects, his administration failed to address racial and political divides or support burgeoning activist movements. According to urban sociologist Anthony Orum (1995, 134), "[Maier] was a very cautious and conservative politician who had no desire to move forward to promote greater equality for all Milwaukee residents. In this regard, Maier simply reflected the general abilities and attitude of leading figures in Milwaukee: good at finances and efficient in keeping the machine running, but reluctant to take heroic action. Moreover, none were willing to seriously address issues of fairness and justice in the city." Indeed, under Maier, more and more development decisions fell under the control of urban and business elites, including the race- and gender-exclusive Greater Milwaukee Committee (see Orum 1995). This happened even amid local activism, an increase in services that improved everyday life for gay and lesbian residents and women and families (like a visiting nurse program for families with new babies), and the presence of more women on the City Council.

Norquist, New Urbanism, and Neoliberalism (1988–2004+)

It was in this context and amid a national shift in local politics that Mayor Norquist was elected in 1988. Successful in securing large campaign funds (mainly from suburban residents and businesses), Norquist campaigned on a probusiness, change-oriented platform. In an interview, one Milwaukee scholar described the election in this way: "[Norquist] essentially told the business community, 'I'm your guy. I will be the most probusiness mayor that you have ever seen.' . . . So he came in with a mandate of sorts to be their mayor—to implement this kind of neoliberal corporatist agenda—to be a developer's mayor" (academic, white, male).

Trying to appeal to progressives, Norquist also presented himself as an experimental, progressive mayor, even a "fiscally conservative socialist." As I explore in chapter 7, Norquist's articulations and policies gradually revealed a more hardened market fundamentalism. Perhaps in resistance to percolating activism, Milwaukee pursued a neoliberal policy platform that would further cement Milwaukee's elite power relations and marginalize many feminist, antiracist, and progressive voices.

There was plenty of local precedence and national inspiration for this effort. Milwaukee had shown its capacity for municipal experimentation before. Men and market rationalities cemented after the war still largely dominated the city, via the Greater Milwaukee Committee and dominant conservative discourses and leadership, segregation, limited minority and female leadership that would decline, and uneven wealth accumulation in the city. National and local backlashes against feminism and civil rights activism were fully brewing, and had helped subvert more radical, collective agendas and garner popularity for reforms. Several Milwaukee-based conservative foundations were waiting in the wings to take action. Cities like New York, Baltimore, and Atlanta offered models, vigorously slashing urban services for women, minorities, and the poor, focusing on business development and expansion (Hackworth 2007; Sites 2003, 43).

Faced with industrial erosion and other problems, Milwaukee took up the national discourses that privileged the private sector, individualism, and competition, which had been percolating locally since the postwar period. While the intensifying coherence of a neoliberal agenda was perhaps slow to dawn on Milwaukee residents at the time, several shifts in urban governance and development are retrospectively evident: increasing privatization of urban services; increased private-sector influence (including by foundations); reduced government support and services, including welfare reform; and a focus on downtown development, business-friendly policies, and the attraction of urban elites. While some of these shifts (such as welfare reform) occurred at multiple scales of governance, they were endorsed and sometimes spearheaded by local urban leadership (see Gurda 1999; Mead 2004). As I have suggested, these policies and priorities were not all new but often reflected extensions of previous practices and values in Milwaukee. Similarly, as is explored throughout this book, many of these trends like privatization were not only neoliberal but also gendered and raced in their ideological constitution and execution, affecting daily lives and labors of Milwaukee residents.

PRIVATIZING AND SHRINKING GOVERNMENT

Beginning in the 1980s, both the Milwaukee City and Milwaukee County governments privatized a significant number of facilities and services, a trend followed by cities like Indianapolis and Philadelphia in the early 1990s (Blackstone and Hakim 1997). For example, the formerly county-owned stadium was sold to the Milwaukee Brewers baseball team in 1992, a county-owned electrical plant was sold to Wisconsin Electric Power, and control of the Milwaukee County Public Museum was transferred to a private board soon after (Held 2002). More substantively, by the late 1990s, Milwaukee County completely abdicated its role in hospital management and ownership, selling its county-owned hospitals and contracting with private facilities to provide care for Milwaukee's low-income residents (Gurda 1999, 431–32). Importantly, many of privatization efforts benefitted local and national elites and shaped gendered and raced accumulation, as the majority of large corporations and urban development companies in Milwaukee are owned and led by white men.

Mayor Norquist touted privatization. He targeted the Milwaukee Public School System, which experienced dramatic transformations and partial privatization through the use of school vouchers (Miner 2002a). In addition, in a crucial political and symbolic move, the city that was once known for its "Sewer Socialists" transferred city sewer services to a private company, United Water Services, in 1998 under prodding from Mayor Norquist (Schultze 2005). Challenging Milwaukee's unique socialist history and civic pride, the sale of sewers helped cement the change in tenor toward a more neoliberal urban government.

"Softer" and contiguous forms of privatization and public-private partnerships, several formed decades earlier, flourished under Mayor Norquist. The Milwaukee Redevelopment Authority remained populated by private-sector representatives and had increased authority over development projects during the 1980s and 1990s. Scholars and critics of Mayor Norquist argued that the Department of City Development became increasingly focused on serving private developers and on design and physical infrastructure rather than citizen and community needs. In addition, there was a boom in business improvement districts—privately run collectives of businesses that use government-collected taxes to execute "business improvement projects" in geographically defined public and private spaces (see Ward 2007a, 2007b). By 2007, the business improvement districts in Milwaukee numbered thirty-nine, a remarkably high total for a city of such size (Milwaukee Department of City Development 2007). These moves enhanced the influence of Milwaukee's already concentrated masculine and raced business community.

A tight emphasis on tax reform and fiscal austerity accompanied the increases in privatization. For nearly a decade after his election in 1988, Mayor Norquist reduced taxes, shrinking the overall tax levy by 21.4 percent. In line with the Socialist rhetoric of nearly a decade before, Norquist described these cuts as a form of social justice: "We need to shrink government to help our cities become better places to live. There are few surer ways of helping people than by leaving more money in their hands. Cutting taxes, like educational choice, can be a form of social justice" (Norquist 1998a, 34).

Such rhetoric emboldened reductions in urban services and city employment. In his first six years, Norquist proudly reduced 250 city positions, a number that climbed to 1,118 by the end of his sixteen-year term (Norquist 2003). Milwaukee County, in combination with directives from the Wisconsin state government, also substantively scaled back social services. It eliminated its general assistance program in 1996, reduced mental health and child welfare services, and slashed its total financial assistance budget for poor families by 28.7 million dollars over nine years. In addition, between 1992 and 2002, the number of full-time county employees fell by 21 percent (Held 2002). According to Norquist, these cuts resulted in improved benefits for citizens and workers, such as lower insurance copays and lower costs for the city (Norquist 1994).

However, Norquist's zeal for cuts did not come without costs. As was discussed in chapter 2, racist motivations in Milwaukee and elsewhere often shaped antipathy toward welfare and social services. Women and families are the most direct beneficiaries of social services, so the cuts affected them deeply (see Brodie 2007; Campbell 2014; Walby 2011; see also chapters 2 and 7). In Wisconsin, the poorest citizens are African American (nearly four of five black children are poor), so reductions in aid were racialized in effect. Employment cutbacks in government had gendered and raced effects as well. Due in part to civil rights and feminist gains, many women and minorities had found good jobs in local government. They were able to insert feminist influences into these positions and occasionally to use these jobs as a stepping stone to local elected office (see Boles 1991; Newman 2013). Some of these opportunities compressed or disappeared as government jobs were reduced and eliminated.

In addition, urban service delivery and infrastructure suffered. In the same year that the city ranked thirteenth out of forty-four in a national survey on urban efficiency, the City Council faced a seven-million-dollar shortfall and the council's president argued, "I think we are already slipping to a lower level of services. Each year it takes us longer to repair and fix things that historically we have always been good at" (Borowski 2001).

One of the most dramatic gendered, raced, and neoliberal policies to reverberate through Milwaukee was welfare reform, in a program known as Wisconsin Works, or w-2. Welfare reform was shaped by ideological rhetoric and policy at the local, regional, state, and national levels. Mayor Norquist was among the first and most vocal mayors to advocate for welfare reform. In 1994, he wrote, "Welfare pays millions of people not to enter the labor market. If they do enter it, they are punished if they make more than a certain amount, not only by getting kicked off welfare, but in some cases by having to repay their earnings. Abolishing welfare is key to the health of cities" (Norquist 1994).

Wisconsin led the United States in creating an experimental welfare program based on "work participation and personal responsibility" in the 1980s. By 1997, this program was fully enacted and replaced other forms of welfare support that included cash payments (Wisconsin DWD 2005). w-2 sought not to "end poverty" or provide transformative "poverty relief," but to increase and maintain labor force participation among poor families. In fact, Wisconsin's welfare programs remained the most work-focused in the nation into the next century. Families could receive no cash benefits unless they participated in at least thirty hours of work or work-like activities, and their labor was provided to private and nonprofit companies like Manpower at below minimum wage (see Collins and Mayer 2010).

Although Wisconsin's welfare reforms were distinctive and especially austere, they were built around and bolstered generalized neoliberal rationalities, including autonomy, new paternalism (the idea that citizenship rights should be contingent on the performance of responsibilities), service delivery privatization, flexibilization, and the control of labor supply (Collins and Mayer 2010; Mead 2004; Peck 2001). For example, w-2 was administered in Milwaukee County by several private and nonprofit entities that had to compete for welfare contracts. This structure was supposed to improve efficiency in service delivery, but also placed nonprofits in a position to compete for these dollars. Furthermore, as an intentional strategy to discourage "dependence on the state" and reduce expenses, participants were not offered all of the services for which they were eligible, only those requested. In addition, strict work requirements and term and lifetime limits on support were instituted. Finally, welfare reform served a broader neoliberal goal of maintaining a low-wage labor force, benefitting corporations (see Naples 1997; Peck 2001). This is evident in the quote by Pierce Quinlan, executive vice president of the National Alliance of Business: "the training of welfare recipients in the private sector is not only good social policy; it is good economic policy" (cited in Naples 1997, 926; also see Peck 2001).

As discussed throughout this book, the motivations, discourses, and effects of welfare reform and its previous manifestations were racialized and gendered. These effects were produced and experienced intensely in Milwaukee. Welfare caseloads dropped dramatically after reforms in Milwaukee, in part because of strict mandates and deterrence practices and the "disappearance" of former participants.[5] However, the program has not mitigated poverty and has been plagued by administrative problems and racist service delivery.[6] Rigorous studies have shown that participation in low-wage jobs for w-2 participants actually led to a "downward spiral in the labor market" and Milwaukee "participants left the program no better off than before" (Collins and Mayer 2010; Courtney and Dworsky 2006). Welfare reform did, however, help provide flexible workers, often at below minimum wages, to several Milwaukee companies, including Manpower, adding to patterns of elite, white wealth accumulation. As described earlier, in the early 2000s, while over 50 percent of African American female workers in Milwaukee earned less than twenty-five thousand dollars per year, the CEOs of Milwaukee's four largest companies (all male) received nearly thirty million dollars in compensation (Levine 2013a). The reform's implementation also coincided with an increased demand for emergency services, as poor people overwhelmed hospitals and nonprofit agencies with health, housing, and social service needs. As I explore in chapter 6, welfare reform, along with other uneven power relations, negatively amplified the lives and labors of many poor African American women in Milwaukee.

Welfare reform and other neoliberal policies were shaped by private think tanks and foundations in Milwaukee. They molded the nature of reforms, influenced public opinion, and helped dispel community-based resistance. The Milwaukee-based Bradley Foundation, among the largest conservative think tanks in the United States, was a leader in this regard. The *National Review* once called Michael Joyce, who oversaw the foundation for over fifteen years, the "chief operating officer of the conservative movement" (*Milwaukee Journal*

Sentinel, February 27, 2006; see also Miner 2001). In 2004, the foundation had over seven hundred million dollars in assets and provided over thirty-three million annually in grant funding, twelve million of which stayed in Wisconsin (see Bradley Foundation 2004). Beginning in the 1980s, its board of primarily conservative white men made welfare reform and educational privatization the prime components of its agenda (Bradley Foundation 2006).

During the 1980s and 1990s, the Bradley Foundation spent millions on marketing, funding, and designing welfare reform projects in Milwaukee and the country. The organization invested heavily in national neoliberal reforms, in part by supporting several conservative research foundations, such as the Hudson Institute, the Heritage Foundation, and the Manhattan Institute. These entities produced publications demeaning public assistance and touting welfare reform during the 1980s and 1990s. The Manhattan Institute produced conservative books such as George Gilder's *Wealth and Poverty* and Charles Murray's *Losing Ground*, significant publications in shifting public and political opinion against "traditional" welfare.

As part of a larger movement of conservative intellectuals and as a specialist in urban policy, the Manhattan Institute was a potent neoliberal and neoconservative force in shaping public and policy debates. As geographer Jamie Peck (2006b) argues, "Being right has been the Manhattan Institute's method and mission for almost 30 years now, a period that has witnessed a dramatic shift in both the character and the content of the urban policy debate in the United States. If cities began this period as a policy category-cum-beneficiary, they ended it as an often-maligned political target; if urban policy once designated a set of programs *for* cities, conceived as centers of progressive reform and policy innovation, today the dominant view is that it is cities *themselves* that must be reformed" (Peck 2006b, 682–83). In fact, the Manhattan Institute, located in New York but with financial linkages to the Wisconsin-based Bradley Foundation, often used Milwaukee as an example of a city "being right." In the early 1990s, the Bradley Foundation awarded funds to the Hudson Institute "to support a study of welfare reform in Wisconsin," a grant that was used to create the Welfare Policy Center in Madison, Wisconsin (Bradley Foundation 2005). Then-governor Thompson was invited to participate, and this center helped shape the Wisconsin welfare reform program. These foundations later promoted the effects of welfare reform in Wisconsin. In 1997, a Heritage Foundation research report described "Wisconsin's Welfare Miracle." The report described "Dependence and idleness as harmful to the welfare recipient and insists that he perform useful labor in exchange for benefits he receives. Thus a serious work requirement provides not only a sound moral foundation, but also performs a crucial gate keeping function" (Rector 1997).

The Bradley Foundation also promulgated and funded school privatization and educational vouchers in Milwaukee. Former Wisconsin superintendent John Benson called Joyce, the former CEO of the Bradley Foundation, the firepower behind the voucher initiative: "He's the one who fired up and then convinced then-Governor Thompson," Benson said. "And he did that with the power and finances of the Bradley Foundation. Without them, we wouldn't have school vouchers" (Miner 2001). The Bradley Foundation spent over ten million dollars on pro-voucher research, organizations, public relations, and advocacy in Milwaukee, and several million more at a national scale.[7] As I explore in chapter 7, the foundation made investments in researching and countering progressive movements in Milwaukee, and their campaigns and funding strategies often divided African American communities that were starved for resources. Milwaukee journalist Barbara Miner (2001) also argues that the Bradley Foundation "funded many projects with sexist and racist overtones."[8]

The presence and influence of powerful neoliberal, neoconservative foundations in Milwaukee and associated actors was somewhat unique. However, foundations and think tanks are a crucial and often invisible way that the (masculinized and raced) private sector acquires more influence over cities and shapes governance (see Peck 2006b).[9] Milwaukee was one of several urban exemplars—including New York City—at the front lines of experimentation funded by foundations. Through its model status and relations with cities and intellectual think tanks, Milwaukee was simultaneously learning from and contributing to a national raced, gendered, and neoliberal project and network.

DOWNTOWN DEVELOPMENT FOR THE FEW, NOT THE MANY

Urban politics in Milwaukee from 1988 to the early 2000s, which I have largely characterized as gendered, raced, and neoliberal, were affected by previous decades of private-led development and accompanied by newish sociospatial imaginations and effects. In particular, new urbanism ascended as a philosophy and practice, as did a commitment to attracting young professionals and the "creative class" to Milwaukee. These approaches reinforced an ongoing focus on downtown development and growth. New urbanist and creative-class practices and discourses often helped legitimate gendered, raced, and neoliberal ideologies, policies, and inequalities. They extracted value from low-income communities and land through dispossession and redevelopment, transformed space in and through competition, (re)spatialized inequality, and articulated and reified particular subjectivities.[10] Imaginatively and practically, these strategies and priorities constructed cities for the few, not the many.

As I have suggested, some of the specific rationalities, projects, and techniques of raced and gendered neoliberalism took inventive forms, like new urbanism and creative class, in the 1990s and 2000s. However, the associated practices, policies, and outcomes—including gentrification, segregation, and persistent poverty—were connected to previous local and national policies and the legacies of racism in Milwaukee. Notions of modern and masculine cities fueled by private leadership and urban elites that emerged after World War II are generally consistent with these current policies, as are the patterns of wealth accumulation.

New urbanism, for example, is a specific set of neotraditional design principles related to housing, streets, and commercial districts in cities endorsed by architects and urban planners, now part of a well-financed political and professional movement (Al-Hindi 2001; Talen 1999). Mayor Norquist was a staunch advocate of new urbanism, and Milwaukee was an exemplar in implementing new urbanist design. New urbanism was connected to creative-class policies and discourses in Milwaukee, as Mayor Norquist argued that a market-driven, new urbanist city could attract the creative class to Milwaukee. In a retrospective analysis of his term as mayor, he concluded, "Downtown needed people living, working, shopping and dining close-by to come alive. In neighborhoods, the emphasis turned from destroying tax-generating buildings to create suburban-style right turn lanes and wider streets to bring back traditional main streets. The best role for the city was to create pro-urban zoning and otherwise get out of the way, letting the markets work to create the setting for an attractive lifestyle" (Norquist 2003).

This type of new urbanist and creative-class downtown renewal was a cornerstone of policy in Milwaukee and elsewhere, and transforming the city this way is still seen as a harbinger of broader and better urban changes in the United States (Wyly and Hammel 2004). As Rachel Weber (2002) argues, this redevelopment has served symbolic and economic purposes, helping reorient cities around the commodification of land in part through discourses of obsolescence and decay. It was also led by the private sector; the Greater Milwaukee Committee and its private subsidiary helped set the agenda and provide the funds for a number of downtown development projects, including the Grand Avenue Mall, Riverwalk, Milwaukee Art Museum, and several condominium projects.

Many residents and external commentators trumpeted the benefits of these types of development and new urban subjects. Milwaukee received national media acclaim for the aesthetic and economic "turnaround" of downtown in the 1990s (see *Economist* 2004; Gould 2003). Proponents pointed to increased tourism, more downtown residents, and the economic generation made possible by creative-class residents. New organizations like the Young Professionals of Milwaukee arose specifically to attract more young professionals, and the members believed they were making a better city.

Critics countered that creative-class politics had wasted vital resources, gentrification was rising, and neighborhood development had suffered.[11] These issues are explored more in chapters 4 and 5, but an uneven pattern was evident in Milwaukee's 1999 Downtown Plan and the sizable projects funded and subsidized by the city and the Greater Milwaukee Committee in the downtown area and Third Ward. In contrast, neighborhoods received substantially less city and private investment dollars during this period, and the amount of community development block grant funds going to African American districts and organizations for economic development and housing substantially declined in the 1990s (Bonds 2007). Described fully in chapter 7, the Park East Development Plan in Milwaukee and the community contestation thereof reflect this dilemma and demonstrate how race, gender, economic privilege, and other relations are bound up in urban development in Milwaukee.

Conclusion

Milwaukee's history of urban politics and power relations is marked by continuity, change, and a little radical experimentation. It is striking to note that white masculinities and markets were persistent and powerful forces beginning with the colonization of the city. Notably, a series of local and national backlashes against women, civil rights, and feminism have coincided with intensifications of privatized urban power and white patriarchal capitalist accumulation. Racism and segregation, with roots a hundred years deep, remain rampant. Tendrils of contemporary neoliberalism, such as private influence on development, grew first in colonial Milwaukee and flourished after World War II. However, gendered, raced, capitalist, and other urban power relations manifested and combined uniquely during different periods in Milwaukee, including Sewer Socialism and Norquist's neoliberalism. Different actors, practices, and governance strategies emerged, often connected to broader social, cultural, and political practices and ideologies in the United States. In this way, the Milwaukee case reminds us of the importance of rendering deep, local histories to understand and challenge diverse urban inequalities and avoid synthetic stories about new and nefarious neoliberalism.

Practically, Milwaukee's Sewer Socialism provides a historical model that challenges current constructions of what is possible and what might be valued by cities. As Matthew Sparke (2013) reminds us, thinking about alternatives to neoliberalism is a critical responsibility of "non-neoliberals." Under the leadership of the Socialist Party, Milwaukee built a comparatively comprehensive government that increased safety, transparency, services, and labor protections for many citizens. While Socialists had a zeal for efficiency that matches neoliberalism, the associated dividends were circulated to citizens perhaps more than private capital. Even during the Great Depression, Socialists did not choose austerity (today's ubiquitous urban governance solution). Innovatively, they kept services available, funded in part by a voluntary 10 percent reduction in city workers' pay. Importantly, an emphasis on social reproduction—from education to playgrounds—was central to the city's agenda. Conversely, social

reproduction is often abdicated or selectively supported for the elite in contemporary versions of urban politics (e.g., Katz 2001, 2008; Parker 2008). The
social reproduction agenda of the Socialist era was shaped by classed, raced,
and often heteronormative women's groups, as female reformers in Milwaukee
and around the country lobbied for a "city social" agenda that addressed not
only infrastructure like sewers but also the broader needs of citizens, families,
and communities.

However, despite equity rhetoric and policies, Socialist Party Milwaukee
reflected and upheld broader gendered and raced inequalities. Women had
greater influence in Milwaukee than in some other cities through leadership positions, national visibility, and partnerships among women's clubs and Socialists. However, there were marginalizations and contradictions often obscured
in historical literature. For example, Milwaukee's Socialists were lukewarm in
support of suffrage, even as Wisconsin was the first state to ratify the women's
vote. White women's clubs collaborated with Socialist city officials to include
social reproduction concerns in the city agenda. However, women did so from
marginalized political positions and within a conservative, racist, and sexist
climate that privileged white male wage earners and middle-class wives. In addition, a feminist backlash after suffrage (the first of many) ensured that female
activists did not gain strong footholds in local or national politics (e.g., Faludi
2006; Spain 2002).

Similarly, while African Americans often supported Socialists and Mayor
Hoan took an active stance against the Ku Klux Klan, rarely did nonwhite men
or women assume leadership positions within the party. Racist rhetoric was
not uncommon among some Milwaukee Socialist mayors. Furthermore, while
Milwaukee built an efficient and comparatively comprehensive government
that increased safety, service delivery, labor protections, and social programs,
such generosities extended rarely to people of color. Especially as black migration increased, the tone toward African Americans turned harsh. Throughout
the period of Socialist Party control, African American women had important
roles in establishing black women's clubs and to some degree in the Milwaukee
labor movement. However, they remained in some of the most marginalized
positions in the labor market (often as domestic workers) and were excluded
from many leadership positions. Thus, Milwaukee's history demonstrates how
"progressive" regimes and politics can still perpetuate sexism and racism and
how elitist masculinist tendencies might saturate local urban politics. In fact,
similar exclusions were manifest in more recent labor and progressive politics
in Milwaukee, as depicted in chapter 7. These are important lessons for social
justice advocates who keep their steely gaze on neoliberalism alone.

Milwaukee's urban politics gradually shifted away from Socialism as World
War II approached. During the war, women worked in factories while also
maintaining homes and caring for children. White women in particular experi-

enced new forms of autonomy, freedom, and leadership, and a feminist agenda percolated nationally and in small ways in conservative Milwaukee. Lesbian and gay communities began to emerge as well. African American women attained industrial jobs in much smaller numbers. Nationally, women joined unions in droves and protested for equal rights and better day care. Both Republicans and Democrats added the Equal Rights Amendment for women to their platforms in the early 1940s.

However, reflecting continuous local conservative gendered norms and national patterns of insecurity after the war, Milwaukee asserted a white, heteronormative, modernized, masculine vision of urbanism. Milwaukee business leaders (white and male) assumed a greater role in development through the formation of the Greater Milwaukee Committee and continued to exert strong influence for more than sixty years. Socialist leaders were unable to improve housing and social services or achieve greater integration, and another national backlash against women constrained their progress and political leadership.

Amid increasing black migration toward the war's end, racist hostility also grew. A campaign by property elites framed progressives and prohousing reformists as "communists" (a pattern that persisted in recent Milwaukee politics), helping weaken their campaigns and remove existing Socialists from elected positions. Within this climate and the intensification of suburbanization, many of Milwaukee's leadership and citizens converged around shared "whiteness." Racial segregation solidified, so much so that Milwaukee remains one of the most segregated cities in the country today.

Probusiness Mayor Maier stepped into this climate in the early 1960s, embracing features of contemporary neoliberalism. Under his leadership, the private sector consolidated influence over city resources and development through organizations like the Greater Milwaukee Committee and its redevelopment arm, the Milwaukee Redevelopment Authority. While Maier secured many federal resources for the city, he was generally antipathetic to the African American community and to progressive politics. Most federal funding went to urban renewal projects that further displaced and then concentrated the black community or to downtown development projects facilitated by the Milwaukee Redevelopment Authority. In this way, neoliberal practices that emphasized downtown development, individualism, and public-private partnerships had a strong foothold in Milwaukee long before the 1980s.

In spite of this, civil rights, labor, gay and lesbian, and feminist activism retained or gained momentum in Milwaukee and across the country from the 1960s to the 1980s. These efforts led once again to greater attention to social reproduction concerns within city government, including child care, social services, and domestic violence protections. As feminists argued that the private is political and more women joined the City Council and the workforce, Milwaukee's domestic violence protections and services increased, as did labor protections for some women. More women, minorities, gays and lesbians, and feminists became elected officials and staff members in city government, influencing both the processes and focus of government. The city and state became a testing ground for policies and programs that protected against sexual discrimination. African American groups made some gains in housing legislation and neighborhood groups in some cases effectively lobbied city government for more resources and greater equity. Nonetheless, heteropatriarchal leadership persisted, and the private-sector influence on development remained salient.

Neoliberal Mayor John Norquist entered this arena in the late 1980s, in a campaign funded and ushered in by the business community. Norquist linked himself to Milwaukee's past by labeling himself a socialist and efficiency expert. Such labels quickly gave way to a hardened support of market fundamentalism. Norquist's brand of neoliberalism became a national exemplar, as had Sewer Socialism a hundred years before him. While white masculinities and markets already had a deep footprint in Milwaukee, Norquist's leadership helped impress it further. This occurred within the context of a third backlash against feminism and civil rights in the United States and associated fears that fed a concentrated white, patriarchal, and capitalist development agenda.

The deepening of gendered and raced neoliberalism in Milwaukee beginning in the 1980s expanded capital markets and power into more and new domains, including schools, health services, and the sewer system. Milwaukee's neoliberal urban politics were hybrid, experimental, and ideological. Existing inequalities and power relations combined with new practices and policies in ways that were similar to and different from the past. Powerful Milwaukee-based foundations, mainly led by whites and men, funded and promoted experimental welfare-to-work programs and education privatization. These programs had divisive and often negative effects on African American communities and the daily life of poor women.

As described in the chapters ahead, Milwaukee Mayor Norquist connected neoliberal ideologies to neoconservatism and new urbanism through specific discourses about history, community, gender, race, and markets. As in many other cities, in Milwaukee the spatial logics of downtown renewal and attraction of the creative class were also rationalities for neoliberal platforms, which worked in concert with and amplified gendered, raced, and classed inequalities, as chapters 4 and 5 reveal. Chapters 6 and 7 shed light on other dimensions of power and inequality in Milwaukee's urban politics. For example, there was some dampening of feminism, antiracist, and progressive politics and a decline in women's leadership, ongoing sociospatial segregation in the city, and precarious lives and labors for the city's racialized poor women, even as the city's downtown "boomed."

CHAPTER FOUR

Rationalities of Rule

New Urbanism, Neoliberalism, and Gendered Governance

We should neither try to bury nor rescue cities. We need to unlock the potential of cities through a series of changes in transportation, welfare spending, housing and budget policies that will result in less spending, a smaller, less intrusive federal government . . . and the restoration of the wealth generating abilities of cities.

JOHN NORQUIST, 1999

The desire for traditional districts has steadily gained popularity. Demographic and consumer-preference changes over the last decade have created greater demand for walkable urban real estate in communities with mixed residential and commercial uses. New development has not served this demand because federal policies and practices discourage it.

JOHN NORQUIST, 2014

"New urbanism" and the surrounding philosophies of Mayor John Norquist (1988–2004) became a cornerstone of his agenda for Milwaukee, pushing the city into the national spotlight in the 1990s. New urbanism was seen as both the ideal spatial habitat for the creative class (discussed in chapter 5) and a "design and development fix" for Milwaukee's economic and social woes. As a practice and discourse, new urbanism helped reinforce gendered, raced, and neoliberal ideologies and inequalities, although sometimes in contradictory ways. In particular, new urbanist development strategies were supported by and bolstered patriarchal governance structures and urban development practices.

"New urbanism" refers to a specific set of neotraditional design principles endorsed by architects, urban planners, and others, now part of an extremely popular and well-financed political and professional movement (Al-Hindi 2001; Talen 1999). At the heart of new urbanist philosophy, which first rose to popularity in the 1990s, is a polycentric critique of modernist and government-centric urban planning. In particular, adherents of new urbanism critique post–World War II zoning regulations that separated cities from suburbs, eliminated mixed land use, created sprawl, and fostered automobile-centric lifestyles and associated pollution problems. New urbanists also criticize architectural forms that discourage pedestrian use and neighbor interaction, lack public and green space, waste real estate, and constrain those who lack access to automobiles, for example (Al-Hindi 2001; Congress for New Urbanism 2001; Markovich and Hendler 2006). Central to new urbanism thought is the notion that close-knit communities of the past can be "regenerated" in part through proper design principles (see Katz, Scully, and Bressi 1994; Talen 1999).

In the media, Milwaukee was labeled a "hotbed of new urbanism" (see Gould 1999b), and Mayor Norquist was a central figure in Milwaukee's new urbanist efforts. The national Congress for New Urbanism praised Milwaukee in 1999 for "proving the principles of new urbanism in a tough real estate market—a rust belt city" (Congress for New Urbanism 1999). Milwaukee's mayor was perhaps the most vocal advocate of new urbanist planning and design in the United States. Norquist delivered frequent speeches on the topic, and his administration prioritized new urbanist design in the redevelopment of downtown. When Norquist resigned from his position as mayor in 2003, he became director of the Congress for New Urbanism, an organization he helped found.

Mayor Norquist began purveying the benefits of new urbanism upon election in 1988. Soon thereafter, he hired Peter Park, a head planner who ascribed to a new urbanist vision. Under Park, Milwaukee implemented changes related to aesthetic regulations, zoning, and the developer-permitting process (Voigt 2006). Park also spearheaded the redevelopment of a gentrifying urban neighborhood, Beerline B, providing new urbanist design regulations and restrictions and encouraging competition among developers. Private investment of over $200 million ensued, property values escalated (some up to $1.5 million), and the Beerline neighborhood became a national model (Langdon 2007).

Milwaukee's 1999 plan for downtown articulated the city's new urbanist vision and was spearheaded by Park. One journalist described the plan as "a virtual textbook of compact, walkable development" (Gould 1999b). The plan is also an exemplar of how various neoliberal sociospatial imaginaries—including new urbanism, neoliberalism, and creative-class concepts—came together and reinforced each other in Milwaukee. The goal was to add value to Milwaukee, primarily through commercial and upscale residential development, and to guide development to create "a more vibrant, active, and exciting place to live, work, learn and play" (Milwaukee Department of City Development 1999, 8). The plan identified desired downtown residents as young professionals and empty-nesters. This sentiment was echoed by developers and architects who helped construct the plan. One firm described Norquist's new urbanism as a plan "to create a downtown with urban sex appeal and to attract the coveted 'creative class'" (Schmid 2007a). The plan did not include low-income housing, and condos in planned developments ranged from $240,000 to $1 million.[1]

Framing the Problem and the Fix: New Urbanism as a Rationality of Rule

It can be argued that new urbanism reflected and bolstered raced and gendered neoliberalism in Milwaukee, as one of many *rationalities of rule*. As scholars have argued, rationalities of rule work to manage social conduct and secure conformity around specific principles (see Ilcan, Oliver, and O'Connor 2007; Larner 2000; Rigakos and Greener 2000; Rose 1999). New urbanism functioned as a rationality of rule in several ways. First, it mirrored the ideologies of neoliberalism, such as free market principles and emphasis on private property, limited roles for government, emphasis on pleasing business and luring elites to urban communities, and the importance of extracting value and construing cities as marketplaces (also see Kenny and Zimmerman 2004; Weber 2002). Norquist wrote in 1999 that "new urbanism is about getting more value out of real estate by rediscovering some time-tested rules of planning" (Gould 1999b); and residents generally view new urbanist property as a commodity (Cabrera and Najarian 2013; Johnson and Talen 2008; Talen 1999). New urbanist developments have generally served affluent populations, and Mayor Norquist and local firms presumed that new urbanist developments would be filled with young creative-class members who could "breathe new life into old urban centers" (Schmid 2007a). New urbanist developments in Milwaukee and elsewhere have attempted to center social life around commercial centers and consumption (Cabrera and Najarian 2013; Goetz 2003; Hay 2003; Johnson and Talen 2008; Talen 1999).

Importantly, new urbanism helped rationalize gendered and raced neoliberalism by framing Milwaukee's urban problems and presenting naturalized solutions. Mayor Norquist argued that Milwaukee's poverty, segregation, stagnant downtown, and sluggish economy were not a result of capitalism, racism, or structural problems. Rather, according to him, they had been created by poor physical planning, government heavy-handedness, cultures of dependency, and individual moral failure. His assertions created a "backward linkage" that reinforced key features of neoliberal policy and discourse: "After World War II, communities with porches, side-walks, streets, blocks, neighborhoods, and grand public spaces were largely abandoned and replaced with the now-familiar collection of strip malls, cul-de-sacs, and sprawl. But it wasn't only design that hurt U.S. cities. . . . Instead of being rescued, U.S. cities were victimized by federal interference" (Norquist 1998a). Poisoned by poor planning and government oversight, cities had been emptied of their true roles as natural marketplaces, according to Norquist. Urban citizens were now seeking "something more from life . . . a sense of belonging, of community." As many new urbanists claimed, this community could be developed through neotraditional design, neoliberal prescriptions, and communities built around common consumption practices (Norquist 1994; see also Talen 1999).

In this way, Mayor Norquist argued for a *neoliberal economic fix and a new urbanist design fix* for Milwaukee's woes. Scholars have noted that the framing of problems in these specific neoliberal and new urbanist ways often facilitates ideological objectives, limits alternative perspectives, and points to naturalized solutions (see Bacchi 1999; Lakoff 2002; Peck 2006b; Sparke 2013). Problems rooted in poor planning, design, and government inefficiencies and interference implied a neoliberal, new urbanist antidote, whereas problems labeled as racist dispossession or parasitic suburbanism might have called for redistribution or policy transformations.[2] According to Norquist, cities as well as individuals stood to benefit from neoliberal remedies like self-reliance and a narrowly defined "autonomy": "One prescription for urban success is the free market. Cities are *places* and *markets* more than they are government entities. State and federal interference with markets, though sometimes well-intentioned, has on balance hurt cities. Much of what is necessary to ensure urban success amounts to no more than removing baggage and setting cities free" (Norquist 1998a, emphasis original).

Like much neoliberal rhetoric, these statements exaggerated and romanticized local responsibility and autonomy for creating and solving problems like poverty. Meanwhile, they demeaned the role of state and federal investments, which were, in fact, desperately needed (see Rodriguez 2014). Such rhetoric was used to justify not only new urbanist development and an emphasis on downtown and elitist developments, but also cuts in government, welfare, and urban services, as well as reduced regulation. Norquist's ideas circulated widely and were reinforced by think tanks such as the Manhattan Institute and the national Congress for New Urbanism. In these sites, promarket and antigovernment new urbanist and neoliberal discourses swirled together and gained momentum through networks of urban policy makers, well-financed projects, and conservative publications such as *City Journal* and *Civic Bulletin*.[3] These networks helped establish Milwaukee's role as a national exemplar and popularized initially fringe ideas like welfare reform and new urbanism across the United States (see Peck 2006b).

Importantly, the new urbanist toolkit mainly contained simplified design solutions for urban ills. As new urbanist scholar Kristen Day (2003, 88), points out, "physical problems are often easier to improve than the entrenched issues of poor schools and chronic unemployment." Milwaukee consciously evaded stickier urban problems like racism, segregation, unemployment, and the needs of the poor, focusing on design details and high-end developments. According to a Milwaukee activist,

[They don't ask] is the development of a Walmart a good or bad thing but where is the parking lot going to be located? What kind of wrought iron fencing will be around it? The way new urbanism had been applied here—the planning and architecture side of new urbanism has been stressed. And then they've had Richard Florida here a few times and what is our "coffee shop quotient" are we "cool enough" so this idea that we need more young urban professionals and it is all about high-end condos and new urbanism and a playground for the rich. (activist, white, female)

Gendering and Racing New Urbanism

As a rationality of rule, new urbanism not only bolstered neoliberalism, but also animated gendered and raced norms. It did so in at least three ways, not without contradictions. First, new urbanism romanticized a racist and sexist past in Milwaukee. Second, it erased structural gendered and raced inequalities or realigned them to market solutions and subjectivities embedded in physical design. Third, it often downplayed social reproductive labors and institutions as a crucial component of everyday life and equality in cities. Importantly, as I discuss below, the theoretically feminist and transformative elements of new urbanism that did exist failed to materialize in Milwaukee.

As many critics have argued, new urbanism is often moralistic and nostalgic. It romanticized a particular raced and gendered moment in Milwaukee when streets were vibrant and community-oriented because of walkable streets and porches, people were self-reliant, and civic-minded progress dominated urban politics. As Milwaukee scholars Kenny and Zimmerman (2004, 93) argued, "Missing from this picture of Milwaukee's social life after World War II [is the fact that] the city's small African-American population was restricted to a tightly bound ghetto, where overcrowded housing and restricted participation in the local labor market were the order of the day."

As described in chapter 2, a feminist backlash was also in full swing after World War II. Many white women were pushed out of labor markets, excluded from many dimensions of social and political life, and encouraged to simply shop and provide happy homes. While women's lives were in reality more diverse, nonheterosexual and nontraditional sexual and social relations were largely prohibited. Meanwhile, women of all races and ethnicities conducted most of the household and community labors that sustained "vibrant" streets invoked by new urbanists. While black women were part of the labor force, their work was often low-paid, precarious domestic service at the behest of white families.

Meanwhile, the masculinist celebration and interpretation of "self-reliance" and "autonomy" ignored the fact that the city was built by and benefitted from colonialism and slave labor, that men and entire communities relied on women's unpaid labor, and that white families have often relied on the work of women of color (see chapter 2). Ironically, this community life after World War II was also made possible for some white families by preneoliberalism wages that allowed one worker to financially support a household. As discussed elsewhere in this book, the neoliberal "free markets" celebrated by Norquist resulted in longer work hours, multiple jobs, and lower wages for many households, impeding on community life and leisure time that were celebrated in new urbanist rhetoric.

In addition, this rhetoric in Milwaukee strategically and selectively remembered and reimagined African American neighborhoods. Norquist bemoaned the federal freeway projects that had decimated African American neighborhoods (like Bronzeville and Park East). While presenting slide shows he would point out, "This is the African American community in Milwaukee in the late 1950s. You can see the Buick Special there. [This is the] Regal Theater where Duke Ellington played after hours." Then he would show a slide of a freeway and how it had wiped out the community (Norquist, 1999b). Such stories helped reinforce self-help narratives that suggested bad design had caused inequalities and poverty and good design could solve them (see Rodriguez 2014).

However, the city was selective about its design remedies. City leaders tried to reconstruct a new historic Bronzeville (the old one had been demolished by a freeway) by promoting a walkable commercial and entertainment district in a black neighborhood. Using Harvard business professor Michael Porter's rationale and new urbanist discourses about autonomy and competition, they argued that revitalizing commercial activity in an inner-city neighborhood would solve its woes. Ironically for new urbanists, they decided big-box stores like Walmart were needed in the "ghetto" (Rodriguez 2014).

However, the city had a different plan for a prime downtown area (Park East) that had housed an African American community prior to freeway construction. After the freeway spur was torn down, the city imagined a market-led, walkable development of high-end condominiums and shopping districts, as described in chapter 7. Mayor Norquist and new urbanist supporters opposed a community benefits agreement that would have ensured affordable housing (and therefore economic and racial inclusion) in the neighborhood and requirements that would have created African American employment opportunities.

Gender inequalities were nearly absent in Milwaukee's new urbanist discourse or were seen as resolvable through design and markets. For example, as geographer Leslie Kern (2010a) found in Toronto, Milwaukee's new urbanist developments targeted single, middle-class women to live in condominiums and apartments downtown. These developments drew on gendered and raced discourses of fear by providing and advertising ample security and safety. Women's presence as autonomous consumers and new urbanist dwellers was lauded as both feminist progress and urban revitalization.

These geographically concentrated opportunities for some elite women helped mask the reality that new urbanism did not serve many, especially low-income, women in Milwaukee. They also happened alongside a retreat from redistribution, social investments, and urban services that have proven to benefit women and low-income people. One activist commented on new urbanist and downtown developments: "I think the city has benefited as far as the beautification and the projects, the bridge downtown—I think it makes the city look good. It looks great. But those projects didn't really benefit our community. There weren't more jobs. There weren't better jobs. They built more houses, but for people who really couldn't afford those houses it didn't happen" (activist, African American, male). Two low-income African American women echoed this sentiment with regard to new urbanist retail developments: "You know they make it so high so that you can't afford to shop there. Nobody around here needs to buy bed sheets. They need a bed" (activists, African American, female).

As a national discourse, new urbanism asserted racial inequality and asserts the need for affordable housing and access to reliable and affordable public transportation (Congress for New Urbanism 2001). Feminist urban planners have raised these same concerns. In particular, they have noted that affordable housing and proximity to multiple services and sources of employment are important to and supportive of women's multiple household and societal roles. These issues are particularly critical for low-income women. However, feminist planning in theory and practice has been substantially less popular than new urbanism. Furthermore, new urbanism in practice has rarely addressed these issues or upheld feminist principles. Instead it has catered to affluent residents.[4] Feminist architect Dolores Hayden (2002, 187) critiques the failures of market-centered new urbanism:

> Could new urbanism be seen as a new neighborhood strategy for women? The neighborhood strategy depends on a social and economic program of mutual accountability, not merely on swimming pools, sidewalks, or porches as symbols of community. It requires interdependencies of a more fundamental kind. . . . A nation with more cars than children, and no child-care policy, will have a hard time shoe-horning itself into new urbanist housing based on the image of a small town of the 1920s. Some additional attempts to reconnect housing with social services and economic activity are necessary to improve neighborhoods for women, yet these are the very decisions large real estate developers are often unwilling to make, since they involve non-market as well as market activity.

Hayden (2002, 10), among others and after decades of research in this area, notes that "a feminist critique of housing policy still points to the interlocked disadvantages of class, race, and gender." Poor women of color and their children remain those with the most minimal access to decent housing in Milwaukee and elsewhere. This shortage worsened under neoliberal policies and after the housing crisis they created. During the 1990s, 3,314 low-income housing units in Milwaukee were demolished, with only 185 new units built (Norman and

Borowski 1999). A study of seventy-eight low-income female-headed families found that 45 percent of participants were essentially homeless, living with family or friends or in shelters. Another 9 percent reported that their eviction was imminent (Women and Poverty Public Education Initiative 2003). The number of families living in crowded conditions increased 114 percent between 1980 and 2004. One-fifth of renting families paid over 50 percent of their income toward rent around that time (Interfaith Conference of Milwaukee 2006). My interviews confirmed that housing was a critical need for many poor women.

> Housing is the most important part because you've got to have housing. If people have jobs and they haven't got housing, they still aren't going to be able to make it. It's not good for a kid to be bouncing from place to place. It doesn't give them the sense of security. They're here today. They're there tomorrow. It's not good for a kid. So if more people had affordable housing and it wasn't so much doubling up like we see—you have three families living in a one bedroom apartment or a two bedroom house. . . . I know a few families right now—it's like six adults, fourteen kids, two bedrooms. (activist, African American, female)

Another spoke up, "And now it's going to be hot outside. School's going to be let out so you have all these kids cramped in this one house" (activist, African American, female).

A low-income woman in her fifties who had worked for several years and recently lost her job due to health problems explained that she was living with her daughter and four children: "It is tense. I think she is going to kick me out. It's just too much you know. Then I have got nowhere to go. The next step is the shelter for me" (low-income resident, African American, female).

In spite of the housing crises in Milwaukee, neoliberal and new urbanist policies seldom addressed this shortage, instead emphasizing downtown, exclusive, market-led developments. In fact, federal and urban housing efforts in the 1990s and onward often focused on converting public housing into new urbanist mixed-income developments. This conversion amplified the housing shortage, rarely produced deep and beneficial interactions and "community" among residents of different incomes, and displaced thousands of families in Milwaukee (many female-headed) and elsewhere (e.g., Chaskin and Joseph 2009; Hanlon 2010). Furthermore, community development block grant dollars for black community organizations involved in housing production went from 21 percent in 1988 to 0 percent in 1997. During the same period, funding for black organizations working on housing rehabilitation also declined (Bonds 2007). Most poor African American women and families lived in insecure situations, spending up to 50 percent of their income on rent and likely to experience a forced eviction (Desmond 2016). In addition, walkable downtown and neighborhood housing developments, which increased rapidly in the 1990s and early 2000s, did not serve low-income families. Costs of condominiums ranged from $150,000 to $900,000 and provided no social infrastructure for children or families, as one interviewee articulated[5]:

> All this woo-ha-ha about these condos and what we're going to do is serving a certain person. Because there aren't any schools on Water, you know. But there's a school on Twentieth right off of North Avenue and my kids go there. And what are the implications for them that that's being forgotten. That side of town is in the worst kind of blight that there can be there's no other way around it. . . . You know, if you look at the Business Journal, and I do, there are like all this worry about what's going into the Grand Avenue and blah, blah, blah. And it's just so frustrating. (activist, African American, female)

In fact, some Milwaukee developments led to gentrification, fueling concern about the displacement of moderate- to low-income families (Kenny and Zimmerman 2004). One interviewee, despite being employed by a nonprofit organization, described her inability to live in the neighborhood where her parents lived that had been recently redeveloped via new urbanism: "For example my mother, she bought her house probably for thirty thousand dollars. It's probably worth probably close to two hundred thousand. . . . It's outrageous. I can't afford to live there" (activist, African American, female).

While emphasizing "urban walkability" and "live, work, and play" through developments such as the Milwaukee Riverwalk and upscale downtown retail, the city government did very little to ensure that housing, employment, and child care services improved or were within walking distance for low-income women and families. The majority of job growth occurred in the suburbs, rather than in working-class neighborhoods, and the number of business establishments declined during the 1990s in Milwaukee's inner city (see Levine 2006). This made juggling jobs and child care extremely difficult. According to the Census Bureau, the majority of African American households were concentrated in just a few neighborhoods where jobs were scarce, and over one-third of African American Milwaukee households had no private vehicle in 2006. This lack of investment in employment led one economic planner to quit in frustration, arguing that the "city believes that investment in buildings and handsome streetscapes makes the city's hard-hit economy more competitive" (Schmid 2006).

Even moderates in Milwaukee conceded, "The new urbanist stuff—let's face it, was more of an elitist agenda. It appeals to people like me, generally middle to upper class. Projects like the Riverwalk, the idea of walkable cities at a human scale, more green space . . . but it is really not a 'human' agenda that concerns the majority of citizens" (historian, white, male). National studies echoed this sentiment, arguing that "new urbanist doctrine emphasizes the importance of diversity in neighborhoods, yet new urbanist practice offers few strategies that directly support diversity" (Day 2003, 84–87) and that new urbanist developments have generally served the elite (Cabrera and Najarian 2013).

In addition and in spite of his new urbanist interest in walkability and accessibility, Norquist rarely advocated for improved bus transportation. He did lobby for light rail transportation in the city, a project that lacked political will and legislative support from the region and state. However, bus service, used primarily by African Americans, had been declining for years. Instead, the city heavily marketed a "live, work, play and learn" program focused on downtown amenities, living opportunities, and careers for young elites and urban retirees. A local architectural firm, hired in 2000 to research and market downtown Milwaukee as a place to live, work, and play, received over three-quarters of a million dollars in funds (Milwaukee Downtown [Business Improvement District 21] 2006). According to the Department of City Development's website, "Whether that investment is in time (attending a concert, earning that MBA) or money (buying a condo, or developing a new building), Milwaukee's downtown offers a solid return" (Milwaukee Department of City Development n.d.). The local business improvement district even hosted a spirit week for downtown employees. This event "boosted morale and built camaraderie through a week of daily office challenges, like dunk the boss, steno chair relay and office airplane, a Bucks Basketball Shootout and the Office Rock Star singing competition" (Milwaukee Downtown [Business Improvement District 21] 2006)—leaving little doubt about what type of walking worker was being celebrated.

Concentrated Power and Profit: Men and Markets in Milwaukee's Neoliberal, New Urbanist Era

While Milwaukee's new urbanist and neoliberal developments failed to benefit many women and racialized, low-income families, it did continue to consolidate power and profit among urban elites. Elite groups including the Greater Milwaukee Committee—mainly led by whites and men—helped frame the discourse and design and execute new urbanist projects. New urbanist practices channeled public financial and human resources toward developers in the form of marketing, infrastructure, subsidies, and other resources. Norquist boasted that the overall number of developers increased in the city in the 1990s and 2000s. However, there remained a small number of local, white, male developers who completed most Milwaukee development projects. For example, one local developer—whose company earned sixty-five million dollars in 2010—was involved in nearly every major downtown project in Milwaukee, including the Hyatt Regency, Schlitz Park, the Riverwalk, and the Midwest Express Center.

In a survey completed by 203 Milwaukee leaders, this developer was voted the most powerful man in Milwaukee (Van de Kamp Nohl 2001). A similar tale applies to two other prominent local developers.

According to interviewees, Milwaukee city development staff and officials catered to these elite developers.

> The unbelievable amount of access and influence that a small handful of developers have. I did an open records request and went down and looked through boxes and boxes of files at DCD [Department of City Development]. They had a box that had stakeholder files in it, and some of them were just a manila folder with one or two pieces of paper in them. The [developer] file is an accordion file it is like two inches thick. They've had dozens and dozens of meetings with him and his staff, their negotiations with him and his site, he wants a new road built off of Water Street. That building was a really old tannery building—it's in a state of disrepair, but he got it waived off of the historic building list. (scholar, female, white)

City officials and the Milwaukee media praised developers and noted their interests aligned with those of the city. In 1999, Milwaukee's head city planner lauded one developer as "the leadership from the private sector you really like to see" (Gould 1999a). Borrowing from a small film title, a sanguine article in the *Milwaukee Journal Sentinel* described one developer as "the guy behind the guy behind the guy" (Gould 1999a).

This pattern of coinciding interests and elite (white, masculine) urban leadership was not unusual or exclusive to Milwaukee's neoliberal, new urbanist phase. Urban developers are nearly all white men, and women held 20 percent or less of city council seats and large-city mayoral offices across Wisconsin and the United States for the first decade of this century (see Center for American Women and Politics 2014; Fainstein 2001; Wisconsin Women's Council and Women's Fund of Greater Milwaukee 2006). There was a short period in the 1980s in Milwaukee when female elected officials composed 30 percent of the City Council, but by 2000 all women were gone (Milwaukee City Council Records). This reflected both a larger trend where the growth in women's representation in elected office plateaued in the United States as well as path-dependent gendered and raced power relations in cities like Milwaukee. As I argued in chapter 3, elite and masculine actors and entities have dominated the city and accumulated wealth since colonialism, and more so with the advent of the Greater Milwaukee Committee in the 1940s.

At the same time, new urbanism and neoliberalism created new discourses and practices that helped legitimate and in some cases strengthen elite, masculine power relations in Milwaukee. For example, the framing of *architectural design and development* as a solution to urban problems (re)positioned local developers as especially redemptive for the city. As I argue in chapter 7, Milwaukee was situated as so desperately in need of development that urban developers who made investment "risks" were revered. Meanwhile, they profited greatly.

In addition, the private sector became increasingly seen as the natural executor of urban projects, and the city granted private-sector entities vast autonomy in shaping developments. Milwaukee's Downtown Plan and the Park East Plan for Redevelopment, for example, were primarily drafted by developers and architects. Because local government had been stripped bare under neoliberal policies and often lacked the staff to carry out projects, and because neoliberal policies implied that the private sector knows best, there were blurred boundaries between developers and the state.

I have already argued that increased flows from the state to the private sector generally reinforce existing patterns of white, male wealth accumulation while redistribution tends to benefit women, minorities, and low-income people (see chapter 2). In addition, many architects, developers, and real estate representatives who promote and execute policies and projects actively benefit from them. As one interviewee noted about Milwaukee's City Hall, "the place is practically run by developers." In this way, Milwaukee politics were both dominated by elite men and also characteristically neoliberal.

What was distinctive about Milwaukee's neoliberalism is that the state played a subdued role, allowing the private sector to orchestrate urban development unfettered by governmental constraints. Accompanied by a discourse that suggested that excessive regulation stifles urban creativity, the local state consequently shifted from a hesitant probusiness stance to offering wholehearted support (and often subsidies) to real estate developers (Hubbard 2004).

The tight and relatively small circuit of policy makers, business leaders, and developers in Milwaukee lacked gender and racial diversity. As suggested above, this was partly a result of a historic legacy of patriarchy and uneven race relations in Milwaukee. But there was also a deeper issue of mutual constitution related to this period of new urbanism and neoliberalism in Milwaukee. These narrow rationalities emphasized a market-led "design and development" strategy for governance, automatically narrowing the field of actors in the urban political arena.

A comprehensive urban agenda, conversely, might have brought a richer array of people into leadership, including neighborhood and nonprofit leaders who tend to be female and/or represent different ethnic, racial, and sexual identities. The opposite is also true: given that a narrow group of masculinist elites were shaping urban policy in Milwaukee, it may not be surprising that the agenda was limited in scope and vision and also benefits these actors. It was a narrowing of both scripts and subjectivities, a theme echoed by Ananya Roy (2003) in her study on masculinist politics in Calcutta, by Leslie Kern and

Gerda Wekerle (Kern 2010a, 2010b; Kern and Wekerle 2008) in their studies on women condominium owners and city building in Toronto, and by Adam Tickell and Jamie Peck (1996) in their study of "remasculinization" of Manchester politics:

> But it is not just in the sexual composition of the new governance institutions that local politics have become (re)masculinized in Manchester; their favoured discourses and their modus operandi also serve effectively to exclude women from the political process. . . . The regendering of local politics should, rather be understood as a consequence of the replacement of electoral-democratic structures with those which confer political power on economic elites. . . . In particular the privileging of economic over social interests, and the ascendancy of decision-making structures based on elite networking rather than consensus building seem to be associated with the masculinization of local governance. (Tickell and Peck 1996, 607)

In the Milwaukee regime, a small circuit of urban elites—both elected and nonelected—proposed, marketed, and executed a narrow policy that aligned with the wishes of this same circuit. Danae Davis Gordon, Mayor Norquist's former personnel director, noted, "We [staff members] were really all soldiers whose job it was to make John look good. . . . A few minorities, including Marilyn, had influence in the mayor's office, but except for Mike Dawson [a woman], all the plum political positions always went to white males" (cited in Van de Kamp Nohl 2001). Developers, real estate moguls, and elected officials were male as well.

The absence and/or exclusion of women *in itself matters*. In various interviews, elected officials and activists in Milwaukee argued that men can represent women's interests as well as women. However, substantial research and a broadly feminist perspective suggest that this exclusion of women in high-level municipal administrative positions and elected offices is consequential. Historically, female reformers have emphasized a "homelike" and "city social" agenda, addressing poverty, neighborhood development, and community and social needs, while male leaders focused on monuments, boulevards, and infrastructure (see Hayden 2002; Parker 2011; Spain 2004; Wirka 1996). This was not so different from the "design and development fix" promoted by new urbanism. In the 1980s and 1990s, feminist geographers pointed to patriarchal patterns in urban governance that excluded women and emphasized economic over social concerns (e.g., Beckis 2001; Brownill 1994; England 1991). In a 2009 study, Alec Brownlow demonstrated how patriarchal leadership misrepresented rape statistics in a New Jersey city, intentionally putting women at risk in order to enhance economic development. In her study of urban politics in Newark, Isoke (2013, 126–27) found that even lengthy leadership by African American males had not disrupted the city's heteropatriarchal governance structure, which was described by activists as "non-democratic," "hostile," "despotic," and, even more shocking, "a contemporary vestige of slavery."

A recent report titled *Men Rule* by Jennifer Lawless and Richard Fox (2012) argues that women's underrepresentation at all levels of governance "raises grave concerns regarding democratic legitimacy and fundamental issues of political representation. Electing more women increases the likelihood that policy debates and deliberations include women's views and experiences." In addition, multiple research studies have shown the positive effects of women's visibility and participation in urban and state governance. Women govern differently, in part because of their gendered social experiences. They prioritize social reproduction issues like child care, domestic violence, and health. They also tend to solicit more opinions from their constituents, be more inclusive in decision making and budgeting, and seek broader participation. Women's visible presence in government positively affects aspirations, political participation, willingness to run for office, and confidence in government by women and girl constituents and populations.[6] A recent study found that females mitigate the most restrictive and punitive aspects of welfare reform and incarceration, as do African American and Latino men. Women of color have the strongest countervailing effect on state welfare reform (Reingold and Smith 2012).

Importantly, these studies and my research do not suggest that all female-identifying persons are progressive or govern differently than all men. Nor do they suggest that any governing differences are rooted in biological differences between "male" or "female" or "black" or "white" or "brown" bodies. It is more likely that socially proscribed gendered and raced roles, ideologies, and marginalizing experiences (e.g., as caregivers or with the racist state) play an important role. As I argued in chapter 1, those with the most social and economic power are often unable to see the effects of their domination and/or not interested in changing it. Conversely, the lives and perspectives of marginalized individuals can shed light on needed changes in cities and governance, and those with "shaky" power may be willing to challenge the status quo (see chapter 1 of this book; see also Bourdieu 1989; Harding 1993; Sánchez de Madariaga 2013; Smith 2005; Young 1995).

Thus, these studies and the case of Milwaukee imply a need for greater balance in values, discourses, bodies, and practices in urban governance. They suggest that a diverse or differently constituted group of urban leaders and power brokers in Milwaukee may have not so readily favored a simple cocktail of competitive new urbanism, neoliberalism, and creative-class politics. The domination of elite, white, heteronormative masculine bodies and discourses (about competition, autonomy, and paid work) was a persistent and sometimes alienating feature of urban governance in Milwaukee and elsewhere (see chapter 2). Recently, a feminist activist pointed out that it was very difficult to elicit compassion or interest from the (still) all-male Milwaukee City Council about the needs of low-income women and families in Milwaukee (activist, African American, female). Debates in Milwaukee around the planned Park East Development focused on economic development and profit rather than social needs of the city (see chapter 7). Another activist interviewee suggested that the current blend of patriarchal and economic influence in Milwaukee was also reminiscent of an earlier era: "The last official event that Mayor Norquist attended was a groundbreaking for a major developer. It was in December and the newspaper showed this picture of all these men in long wool coats, and I was just like 'oh the robber barons'" (feminist, white, female).

While often subtle, these power imbalances were visible at multiple scales of interaction and policy making. For example, in one meeting, an articulate female activist was testifying about the need for affordable housing in a planned development. A prominent developer, whose work she was opposing, leaned toward her and said, "You know—you could come work for me" (activist, white, female). In interviews, the female elected officials expressed pressure to conform to prevailing norms and priorities: "Well, I do think it is harder when you are in the minority, when you are a woman. I mean I speak my mind. But you don't want to be the one who is always raising issues or being different. Then I think they don't listen to you much in the end because they think 'oh she's the problem'" (elected official, white, female).

The interviewee's comments square well with research that argues that a critical mass (of 30 percent or more) is needed for women to challenge deeply rooted cultural, professional, and organizational practices in male-dominated fields (see Sánchez de Madariaga 2013). Additional studies have shown that black women in office advocate more for women's issues when they are not marginalized and outnumbered (Bratton, Haynie, and Reingold 2007). Conversely, tight circuits of often like-minded urban players will continue to reinforce specific logics and rationalities, especially when they derive personal benefits from them. They can more easily subvert potential challenges from diverse viewpoints. Those outside of the dominant gender norm or occupying minority subject positions might easily bend to overarching rationales (which explains why the token presence of a few women or progressives does not often elicit change). To do otherwise involves confronting both gender and political norms and risking the disciplinary effects of further marginalization.

This returns us to some broader raced and gendered governance problems. Limited presence in leadership is a product of the sexist and racist organization of both capitalism and governance—an intersection where new urbanism as a rationality of rule lies. This involves questions not only about "presence" and "absence" and representative democracy, but also about what rules women or racialized individuals have to follow, about who takes them seriously, about access without the capacity to transform the apparatus, and about the reproduction of subjectivities and power differentials in governance and cities (see Brush 2003; Charlton, Everett, and Staudt 1989). Charlton and colleagues (1989) long ago pointed to an important political dilemma: "Why should women clamor for inclusion in institutions that can never really be ours?" Pushing this question and critique further, I argue that diverse feminist voices and visions for urban governance, everyday lives and labors, and urban development and housing in Milwaukee remain excluded.

Conclusion

In concert with the normalization of neoliberal, raced, and masculinist subjectivities and practices, Milwaukee's new urbanist politics centered on a "development and design" strategy. As a discursive and material project, "new urbanism" was purveyed as a salve for a wide range of Milwaukee's urban woes, from unemployment to economic stagnation to a widespread urban ennui over the purported loss of meaning and community. Under Mayor Norquist, a local and national protagonist for new urbanism, Milwaukee aggressively courted private development, pursued a downtown-centric planning agenda, and delineated the city as the natural habitat for the creative class and for elite empty-nesters. Decrying intrusive government, Milwaukee's new urbanism staked its hopes on bootstrap and self-help rhetoric that celebrated autonomy (see Rodriguez 2014). While some design stipulations were placed on developers under the new urbanist rubric, Norquist's neoliberal agenda concentrated on removing barriers that might hinder private development or restrain the city from reclaiming its rightful role as an unfettered "natural" marketplace.

As a rationality of rule, new urbanism helped animate and normalize neoliberal projects in Milwaukee and associated dictations of competition, autonomy, self-help, and market citizenship. Conjuncturally and contradictorily, new urbanism also mobilized raced and gendered discourses and inequalities. New urbanism, as promulgated by Mayor Norquist, romanticized capitalism and a nostalgic, sanitized version of the past. In doing so, it erased uneven gendered and raced relations and the unpaid labors and community-building work often done by women. Milwaukee's new urbanism selectively silenced dark histories of racism and sexism in the city, along with the contemporary racialized effects of new urbanist and exclusivist neoliberal urban economic development practices.

From an antiracist, feminist, materialist perspective, Milwaukee's new urbanism was troubling in that it endorsed and legitimated urban policies that benefitted elites and privileged design over social needs in Milwaukee, as had happened decades before. New urbanist developments were often concentrated downtown and too expensive for low-income women who needed housing most, and did little to create walkability for poor families or connect low-income women to nearby services and jobs. The discourse, advertising, price points, and physical design of new urbanist developments were tailored for affluent singles, couples, and those with full mobility. In some cases, privileged women, constructed as liberated urban dwellers and consumers, were targeted by and benefited from these developments (also see Kern 2010b). However, as others have shown, this emphasis on market subjectivities and market emancipation for women obscured critical inequalities and feminist demands for justice, while women's critical housing and social needs were persistently unmet (Fraser 2013; Kern 2010b; Rankin 2001; Walby 2011; see also chapter 2).

New urbanist and neoliberal approaches to development in Milwaukee in some cases exacerbated racial, income, and gender polarity in the city through gentrification and the diversion of economic development resources away from neighborhoods. Investments in new urbanism were investments in the social reproduction and consumption of the elites. The "live, work, and play" environment eluded all but these elites, and a housing and job crisis among poor women and families went unabated. In addition, neoliberal policies shifted resources toward the private sector, while reducing critical services and supports that would have helped low-income women. In this way, the theoretically progressive and feminist aspects of new urbanism, such as accessible public transportation, affordable housing, shared resources, job development, and neighborhood development, rarely came to fruition.

Finally, new urbanist and other practices described in this chapter shed light on broader issues related to race, gender, and governance. In Milwaukee and elsewhere, urban politics and development remained a masculine and elitist sphere. This is more than a representative democracy problem. The "design and development" focus of new urbanism emphasized economics and the aesthetics of city building rather than human needs, something female urban reformers first challenged a hundred years ago. New urbanism and neoliberalism, in concert with broader backlashes against women and feminism, deepened and perhaps (re)masculinized this arena. They did so by reifying developers as redemptive risk takers; facilitating accumulation for racialized, masculinized elites and developers via subsidies; emphasizing the economic over the social; and giving control of public projects and resources to private developers. Masculinist and neoliberal subjectivities about autonomy and competition were celebrated.

Furthermore, in a circular manner, a small, tight-knit group of male elites and their vision for development were rarely challenged or diversified via different perspectives. Women, who tend to prioritize social reproduction, vote against punitive programs (especially if they are feminist and/or black or Latino), and sometimes govern differently, were underrepresented and often absent as elected officials and developers in Milwaukee. There was also a lack of diversity with regard to nonconforming gender and sexual identities or differing physical abilities. When women were part of this circuit in such small numbers, they held only "shaky" power and were often pressured to conform to extant norms and the masculine culture. In this way, redundant recipes for Milwaukee's success (design and development, new urbanism, creative-class attraction) endured, regardless of their effects. Of course, this was not a simple matter of seemingly female or male bodies acting in predictable ways based on their biology. It was a failure of inclusivity, democracy, and debate that should characterize urban governance in Milwaukee and elsewhere. It was also an absence of feminist visions of urban life.

Rather, there has been a tight range of social and embodied experiences, discourses, and perspectives that has historically comprised urban leadership in Milwaukee. To say that neoliberalism upended democracy or feminist governance would imply that it flourished in Milwaukee previously, which is not true. To say that the prioritization of design over human needs was innovative is also inaccurate. However, new urbanism and neoliberalism tied the urban development script (and associated winners and losers) more tightly to markets, design, and development. They tightened the city's bootstraps as they walked by and over the urban poor. Competition and autonomy continued to outshine feminist and alternative values of justice, care, and collectivity. Rather than moving toward such visions, new urbanism helped recirculate and reconstitute the discursive and material rule of privileged white masculinities and markets in Milwaukee.

CHAPTER FIVE

Could the Violent Femmes
Save Milwaukee?

Richard Florida, the Young Professionals of Milwaukee, and Embodied Creativity

> [The creative class] favor active, participatory recreation over passive,
> institutionalized forms. They prefer indigenous street-level culture—a teeming
> blend of cafes, sidewalk musicians, and small galleries and bistros, where it is hard
> to draw the line between performers and spectators. They crave stimulation, not
> escape. They want to pack their time full of dense, high-quality, multidimensional
> experiences. . . . They do not consciously think of themselves as a class. Yet they
> share a common ethos that values creativity, individuality, difference, and merit.
> **RICHARD FLORIDA, 2002B**

In the early 2000s, Richard Florida, professor of geography, extolled his creative-class message to Milwaukee and other cities that would listen: human creativity is now the "decisive source of competitive advantage," and cities can thrive by tapping and harnessing such creativity (Florida 2002a, 4–5). The primary ingredients in this sweeping recipe for urban success were a group of young, mobile, diverse, "creative" professionals, who constituted a social class of their own, according to Florida's popular book, *The Rise of the Creative Class* (2002a). This creative class—if cities could attract and retain it—operated as its own economic machine, producing jobs, enhancing productivity, and increasing the overall well-being of the city. From an urban economic development perspective, the role of the city was to create the conditions in which this creative class and associated sectors can flourish. By the time Florida published his book, Milwaukee was already on board, having spent a decade pushing for walkable, consumption-oriented new urbanist developments—the ideal habitat for the creative class.

Scholars, in sanguine support or scathing scorn, hurried to engage in a spirited creative city debate that continues today. From different vantage points, academics and urbanists argued that the creative city script offered a fresh set of policy prescriptions for cities, that it traversed well-trodden neoliberal urban terrains, or that it was vapid urban economics. Despite these extensive debates, few scholars or activists paid attention to gendered and raced inequalities and the related material-discursive practices of creative-class politics.[1]

Milwaukee's creative city politics, along with the broader agenda promoted by Florida, provide key insights into raced, gendered, and classed subjectivities and material inequalities in urban politics. In particular, creative-class discourses and urban development policies in Milwaukee seemed to reinforce masculinist and racialized values and hierarchies related to competition, "work," autonomy, consumption, and community. Creative elites were celebrated in the city, while complex lives, labors, and inequalities faced by many Milwaukee residents were obscured. Even as creative-class discourses celebrated "human capital," the city's agenda remained squarely focused on design, real estate development, and narrow visions of economic growth, while social and equity agendas idled. This was made particularly visible through the embodied performances, practices, and promises of Florida, members of an organization called the Young Professionals of Milwaukee (and later FUEL Milwaukee), and Milwaukee city leaders.

Race, Gender, Privilege, and Embodied Creativity

Florida stood in front of six hundred members of Young Professionals of Milwaukee, a professional organization affiliated with the Chamber of Commerce, to "showcase the talents of Greater Milwaukee." The crowd was buzzing—it was the first birthday of the young organization, and its youngish, white, urbanite members laughed, talked, and mingled with policy makers.

Florida was impeccably dressed in black. He had spent the night with local musicians and visited Milwaukee's hippest and hottest spots. "You guys need to better promote the fact that the Violent Femmes, one of the best rock bands ever, are from Milwaukee," he told the eager crowd. He also praised Milwaukee's unique old character, the Riverwalk, condominium developments, and interesting neighborhoods. According to a local news report, "He was amazed that the downtown had an event every night of the week in the summer and he loved the buzz and the scene at Jazz in the Park" (Sherman 2002).

AUTHOR'S FIELD NOTES

Here, as he had done in countless other cities, Florida assured Milwaukeeans that they had all of the important ingredients for urban success (such as music, nightlife, character, and "diversity"). He urged Milwaukee to "think big" and to remember that constructing a vibrant downtown festering with creative people was more important than business recruitment, redistribution, or formal economic development plans. This event in Milwaukee, one of Florida's many speeches to politicians and poets from Austin to Freiburg, was embodied, emotional, and political.[2] It brought together many key actors who ultimately emulated, circulated, and implemented creative-class ideas in Milwaukee and elsewhere—nonprofit organizations, young professionals, urban elites, business leaders, politicians, and, of course, Florida himself.

While many scholars have pointed out that creative-class discourses fit neatly with neoliberal policies and existing political economic conditions, this chapter suggests that the embodied emotional nature of its delivery was also central in generating traction for this urban growth strategy. There are several elements and reasons for this. First, Florida bears many bodily signifiers of privilege and naturalized authority.[3] He is white, male, tall, and middle class, for example, and studies show that such speakers are presumed more credible than others due to historic bias and stereotypes. Second, Florida embodied and performed the creative-class subject: when posed against a range of other urban policy actors, mayors, developers, and academics, he is colorful and engaging. He is a physical exemplar of the idealized "super–creative class member," a thin, fit professor with expensive glasses who loves bicycling, cafes, and hip music. Not only that, but he *physically invites* creative emulation and emotional connection. When he intimately leaned into his audience and conspiratorially and cheerfully informed them that their city had creativity, that there was hope, and that they, the audience of creatives, were poised as important agents of urban salvation, he invoked an emotional response. Teenagers may not exactly have swooned, but policy makers and urban dwellers sighed in audible relief, and maybe even swelled a bit with pride. One audience member explained to me during an interview, "It just made me see, you know, that *I'm* a part of what is happening here in Milwaukee. That is cool, actually."

These audience members, too, then *performed* and *embodied* the creative class, breathing life into ideal types. This occurred not only at this energetic birthday bash, but also through the adoption and circulation of creative-class subjectivities and discourses by organizations like the Young Professionals of Milwaukee. City leaders and business leaders took part too; perhaps too "aged" to claim creative-class status themselves, they nonetheless propagated the policies and discourses of urban creativity.

Of course, it is impossible to discern how well Florida's ideas would have traveled if they had remained in only book form, if different bodies had purveyed them or given less enthusiastic performances, or if urban leaders and organizations like the Young Professionals of Milwaukee had not so readily embraced and embodied them, breathing life into idealized subjectivities. However, according to substantive research on bias and stereotypes, gendered and raced privilege likely helped legitimize Florida's messages, as did their emotional appeal and performance. This would have been insufficient, however, if the creative-class discourses had not fit neatly within the city's historical urban development strategies and priorities, as well as extant gendered, raced, and neoliberal urban discourses related to competition, work, and community.

Embracing Creativity and Competition in Milwaukee

In 2003, Mayor John Norquist wrote,

> The best role of the city was to create pro-urban zoning and otherwise get out
> of the way, letting the markets work to create the setting for an attractive urban
> life style. . . . Milwaukee area had more college-educated people in their late 20s
> and 30s moving in than moving out. . . . Richard Florida has looked closely at this
> generation and says where they live is very important to them. They're attracted
> by diversity. They like tolerance. They like the buzz found in latte shops and hip
> cocktail lounges—and the convenience of living and working close to these places.
> They like cities like Milwaukee. (Norquist 2003)

Like new urbanism, creative-class discourses and politics could be considered
a "rationality of rule" that helped legitimate neoliberalism in Milwaukee. As the
quote suggests, creative-class theses were linked to a set of governing logics and
practices about urban competition and entrepreneurialism. They articulated
what kinds of citizens and subjectivities were more valuable to Milwaukee (i.e.,
autonomous, self-governing, consumption oriented, entrepreneurial, competitive, mobile, and individualist). Such logics were endorsed by organizations
like the Milwaukee Chamber of Commerce and the Young Professionals of
Milwaukee, which embodied creative-class subjectivities and helped carry out
related agendas.

In line with historically masculinist and capitalistic rhetoric, creative-class
discourses scripted certain subjects as desirable and compelled cities to fight for
them: "Those [cities] that have the talent win, those that do not, lose" (Florida
2005, 50). This concept was not lost on planners and policy makers in Milwaukee, who were eager to win and adopt neoliberal policy prescriptions. As
I argued in chapter 4, they had built a new urbanist habitat ideally suited for
consumption-oriented elites, and some stood to profit from downtown development and gentrification. The city's 1999 downtown development plan sought to
attract creative-class types and create a premier "live, work, learn, and play" environment for them, in order to "add value" to the market (Zimmerman 2008).

The Young Professionals of Milwaukee, whose name later changed to FUEL
Milwaukee, was founded with a similar mission: "To position and establish the
Milwaukee region as the destination for world-class talent, in all its diversity"
(MMAC FUEL Milwaukee 2008).

Florida, the Young Professionals of Milwaukee, and the government of Milwaukee devoted a great deal of attention to studying and articulating the pref-
erences of creative-class members. Milwaukee scurried to produce the proper
amenities (like latte shops) and to aggressively market them and proposed a
new urban marketing scheme to replace the old vision of "beer and brats": "This

is the New Milwaukee, a place that welcomes and nurtures the creative class" (Schmid 2007b).

Importantly, city leaders sought to attract "theoretical" creative-class members even though Florida's research suggested they wouldn't want to volunteer, foster inclusive communities, or make long-term investments in Milwaukee. Rather, members of the creative class like to consume coffee and culture, establish their "own identity," and contribute to building places that validate their identity (Florida 2002a, 230).

As an organization, the Young Professionals of Milwaukee similarly emphasized consumption, place promotion, and market subjectivities. The majority of organization events focused on informal socialization and consumption at local bars, restaurants, or similar venues. Occasionally, the group hosted artistic events. However, the Young Professionals justified these events as articulating "the economic impact of visual arts in the community and its importance to retaining 'cool' community status" (Young Professionals of Milwaukee 2004a). The group took pride in these efforts. As one member shared about the organization:

> They are helping to break down that whole perception of the city of Milwaukee of being a cheese and beer town. First of all, the fact that there are a lot of new places opening up; a lot of new retail, a lot of new clubs, bars, restaurants are opening up that we want to highlight. So that exposes our membership to these new places getting a fresh look and makes them feel a little exclusive about these places. Plus, it gives these new owners of these establishments exposure to our membership, which is like their target demographic, so it helps economic development and a little bit of the business for the downtown area. (Young Professionals of Milwaukee member, nonwhite, female)

Aligning with neoliberal market subjectivities and reflecting now-ubiquitous discourses about competition, Young Professionals of Milwaukee members argued that these endeavors constituted important forms of urban citizenship:

> We can do a great job showcasing Milwaukee and telling you that you should be here. Not just because I say so, but here let me show you the Milwaukee Art Museum, let me show you the festivals, let me show you all the attributes that I think make us great, that hopefully will make you stay. That's going to be very beneficial for the city because we're going to keep the increase of young professionals in this city and that's going to help us over time. What we are doing is so critical in that way. (Young Professionals of Milwaukee member, nonwhite, male)

This perception was echoed and endorsed by city officials who viewed the creative class as a panacea for Milwaukee. New Milwaukee Mayor Tom Barrett

(2004) joined the Young Professionals for their "third birthday bash," and his office called the organization "a hotbed of leadership."

The Young Professionals of Milwaukee embraced neoliberal norms of self-governance and individualization. While officially a "collective" organization, they took a hands-off approach to nonmarket activities and social issues. The organization's website encouraged members to think of the organization as "a group that informs and educates its members . . . rather than a group that takes sides, advocates or endorses." When one member was asked if the Young Professionals of Milwaukee was challenging inequalities in Milwaukee, she argued, "We are trying to address it on a more personal level and I think it is more personal responsibility. . . . So I think that that's what YPM is doing. We're not really addressing or going out there and trying to rally around neighborhood segregation and things like that because we don't feel that that's where the change has to happen" (Young Professionals of Milwaukee member, nonwhite, female).

From a more critical perspective, an interviewee described members' approach to school inequalities in Milwaukee: "There is still an individualistic mentality where, 'I just go in and mentor. Everything will be better.' It's like no, no that's nice, and that will be a nice help but that's not the solution" (Young Professionals of Milwaukee member, nonwhite, female).

In this way, the Young Professionals of Milwaukee often articulated and reinforced competition- and consumption-oriented discourses, practices, and subjectivities surrounding work, development, and communities. While engaging in consumptive or instrumental "community-building" practices (which I discuss in more detail below), with some exceptions, they often eschewed feminist and progressive visions of collectivity or collective action.

Constructing Creative Work in Milwaukee

The man sitting before me is relaxed, in boots, jeans, and a long-sleeve T-shirt. We are sitting at a coffee shop, and he has his laptop open while I interview him. We have talked extensively about his work habits and ideals. "I work a lot of hours. Probably about fifty to sixty hours. Well, sometimes up to seventy [laughs]. But I can dress in jeans or whatever, and come and go on my own schedule and the work is really interesting so it doesn't feel like work much of the time. So, I don't know. It's what my friends do too, we all work a lot." (Young Professionals of Milwaukee member, white, male)
AUTHOR'S FIELD NOTES

My interviewee is like the discursive hero of creative-class practices. He is creative and consumption oriented. He is fit, finicky, and flexible. He is talented, transcendent, and time deprived. He can locate himself wherever he pleases, and the city that fortuitously snags him is purportedly guaranteed a prosperous future. According to a prominent Milwaukee architectural firm, the creative class "refers to computer programmers, professors, lawyers, engineers and architects who collectively constitute an economic force that can breathe new life into old urban centers" (Schmid 2007a). This description was derived directly from Florida's characterization of a "supercreative core" of scientists, engineers, professors, writers, artists, entertainers, actors, architects, and other professionals. Florida argued that the creative class was the "norm-setting class of our time . . . reshaping the way we see ourselves as economic and social actors— our very identities" (2002a, 22). According to Florida, creative-class members choose independence and autonomy over security, choose impermanent relationships and affiliations, and flourish in no-collar workplaces marked by the "soft control" of peer pressure and intrinsic motivation (Florida 2002a, 12–15).

In fact, Florida's reification of such creative-class workers might be seen as one such form of "soft control." Along with other material-discursive practices, the creative-class discourses helped normalize a type of hypercapitalist overwork and the bodies that conducted it in Milwaukee. Michel Foucault, drawing on Marx, has explained how, throughout history, laborers had to be "constituted" before they could be exploited: "Life time must be synthesized into labor time; individuals must be subjugated to production cycles, habits must be formed etc. Economic exploitation first required a prior 'political investment of the body'" (Foucault 1977, 25).

Theorists have argued that contemporary neoliberal capitalism is marked by similar adducements and social norms. Without an onerous factory environment, dispersed, flexible, and technological-savvy employees perhaps need to (re)commit to work and overwork in novel ways. The construction of certain work as "creative" and essential to urban economies helps interpellate elite workers and enroll the specific labor investments of their bodies and more. As Italian philosopher Franco Berardi (2009) argues, "the immaterial factory asks instead to place our very souls at its disposal: intelligence, sensibility, creativity, and language." These investments are shaped by broader neoliberal norms that enjoin workers to engage in competitive economic struggle against one another and to engage in self-making practices like entrepreneurialism and self-branding, among others (see Dardot and Laval 2013; Mirowski 2013).

Yet, some of the losses and inequalities associated with such investments and self-making are buried deep in neoliberal and creative-class scripts. So too are the deeply uneven gendered, raced, and classed terrains of labor. For example, according to Florida, the idealized creative is a "workhorse." Construing long work weeks as normal and creative and inevitable—even if they benefit companies more than workers—minimizes opposition among employees. Furthermore, researchers have drawn connections between cultures of overwork, competition, and masculinity, particularly in the creative fields. Masculine norms produce "macho" motives to put in long hours and assert the "demanding" nature of creative jobs, perhaps to ensure that creative jobs—lacking traditionally masculine tasks—are not perceived as "soft" or "feminine" (see Nixon and Crewe 2004). Refusing to adhere to masculine cultures of overwork not only produces a loss in status, income, and interesting job assignments, but also threatens one's gender identity (Cooper 2000; Jarvis 2002; Massey 1995; McDowell 1997; Nixon and Crewe 2004). In Milwaukee, these pressures were particularly pernicious for gay, nonwhite, and female workers, who are expected to conform to dominant norms. One female interviewee from an architectural firm in Milwaukee commented that she would not think to leave the office before six or six thirty in the evening because her colleagues might think she is not sufficiently dedicated.

Furthermore, Florida's idealized creative worker is purportedly mobile and unencumbered, with few ties to family, community, or place. This valorization fits neatly with neoliberal and capitalist rhetoric that celebrates the endlessly available, flexible, adaptable worker who has only himself to blame for success or failure (see Brown 2015; Mirowski 2013; Sparke 2013). The valorization of such subjectivities reinforces individualistic capitalism and simplistic notions of autonomy, but it also undermines other values, such as a feminist "ethic of care" based on connection, collaboration, and community (see McDowell 2004). It "disappears" social reproduction work like child care, cleaning, and community building (often done by women in households or by low-wage service workers) that bolsters the paid economy and is rendered uncreative.

Furthermore, and directly related, it scripts a narrow field of actors. Single parents who rely on communal networks are often constrained in their mobility. Women in heterosexual partnerships commonly limit geographic mobility in deference to their husband or partner's career. If they are mothers, they often restrict work hours, limit work moves and commuting distances, and adjust their schedules to combine caregiving with paid work (see Cooper 2000; Crittenden 2001; Jarvis 2009; Williams 2000). As a group, women—still dominant caregivers for elder and sick relatives—are more likely to "stay put" to provide emotional or physical care for their kin. For African Americans in the United States, slavery, racism, and related segregation have dramatically shaped their spatial practices and choices in cities like Milwaukee. Thus, one's mobility and autonomy—when conceived in liberal or neoliberal capitalist ways—along with associated networks and exposure are deeply framed by gender, race and ethnicity, education, and economic status (see chapter 2).

While mobility, job status, autonomy, income, and access to opportunities and jobs are affected by race, class, and gender, Florida contended that "creativity is the great leveler" (2004, 18). He argues that talent and creativity overcome such structures. In doing so, he obscures fundamental inequalities in labor markets, which are salient in the top creative fields (see Negrey and Rausch 2009;

Parker 2008). These career sectors, including advertising and architecture, are often marked by exclusive cultures of masculinity, racism, heteronormativity, and circumscribed gender codes (e.g., Gill 2002; Hall 2013; Handelsman et al. 2005; Nixon and Crewe 2004; Rosser 2004).

Furthermore, several studies have shown that creativity and talent are filtered through raced and gendered lenses. Women with skills or achievements equal to those of men have their successes in the workplace attributed to luck rather than competence. Women and minorities are perceived as less competent than white men; and mothers rate more poorly than nonmothers with precisely the same experience, skills, and education. In cases where unyielding evidence proves a woman to be a top performer, she is often deemed as less likable than a comparable man. In the arts sector, one study found that a woman's chances of being selected for an orchestra increased 30 percent when she was placed behind a screen so that evaluators could not see her apparent gender (Goldin 2002). These and other issues contribute to a wage gap between men and women, especially between white men and minority women and between mothers and nonmothers.[4] Furthermore, studies show that gender gaps in earnings far surpass any regional wage gaps between the "most" and "least" creative regions (Negrey and Rausch 2009).

Uneven gendered and raced labor markets were particularly tenacious in the Milwaukee region as Florida's creative class ideas ascended. In 2007, full-time female workers earned 76 percent of the wages of full-time male workers; and black women in the same category earned 55 percent (Levine 2013a). This wage gap for white women has been improving in the city, especially as it caters to single women and men, but wages remain substantively uneven by race and gender. The lack of attention to such structural gaps contributed to a misrepresentation of opportunity and merit within and outside of the supposed creative sector and discursively placed blame on individual subjects in the Milwaukee area. As Peck (2005, 759) argues, "their only salvation [is] to get more creative."

Again, this is a larger problem whereby neoliberal capitalism and discourses like the creative class incite a series of behaviors and beliefs in individuals, including *personalization*—individuals are encouraged to see their histories as of their own making (Mirowski 2013). Notions of market freedom obscure gendered and raced inequalities and social reproductive labor even as capital markets benefit from these labors and disparities (e.g., Collins and Meyer 2010; Roberts 2013, 2015; see also chapter 2). As feminists and antiracist scholars point out, obfuscation and undue optimism about inequalities and the perception that one's success is one's own making have long been in circulation among those with privilege and power. For example, in one study of the high-technology industry, only 38 percent of men thought women faced a glass ceiling, while 62 percent of women believed so (Molina 2001). Furthermore, whites often do not easily see racist discrimination in housing, labor markets, and other areas and are slow to acknowledge white privilege (Knowles and Lowery 2012; Pager 2007).

In this way, a normative, elite, white male subject (even as a regulatory fiction) seemed to most unambiguously thrive in the "idealized" creative class and supercreative core in Milwaukee. This was evident not only in the composition and earnings of the creative workforce in Milwaukee and nationally (see Negrey and Rausch 2009; Parker 2008) but also in organizations like the Young Professionals of Milwaukee, the vast majority single and white, who worked in paid jobs forty-five or more hours per week (Young Professionals of Milwaukee 2004b).

With that said, both male- and female-identifying interviewees who were members of the Young Professionals of Milwaukee often commented favorably about their flexible working arrangements and opportunities for independence and self-expression in their work. As one interviewee explained, "I am really in charge of my work; I get to design products the way that I want using my own ideas . . . and really, I seldom get negative criticism from my superiors." Some middle-class nonwhite members had jobs that they found productive and rewarding, such as expanding diversity in their organizations or providing recruitment and training.

Thus, while critiquing the valorization of neoliberal and creative-class subjectivities and the silencing of its unequal and coercive dimensions, it is worth considering both the forces that have helped transform the nature and structure of work and the potential benefits of this transformation. As Janet Newman (2013) argues, feminism, not only neoliberalism, has privileged reflexive, flexible forms of subjectivity and empowered information-rich actors. Feminism raised stark criticisms of patriarchal and hierarchical forms of governance and organizational structures that characterized Fordism and politics prior to the 1980s. These critiques, whether co-opted by neoliberalism or not, helped create an emphasis on "soft" management skills and person-centered leadership that characterized "creative" and other workplaces in Milwaukee and elsewhere. They also created new opportunities for both men and women as consultants, trainers, and partners, for example. While these opportunities have been subject to uneven raced and gendered relations in sometimes unpredicted ways, they have also extended middle-class women's opportunities, wages, and career experiences.

Dabbling with Diversity

The Young Professionals of Milwaukee, an organization founded in 2001 and four thousand strong in 2006, are hosting one of their popular "mosaic" events, which bring together people to discuss contemporary topics related to culture and diversity. The topic is race and diversity, and the room is packed densely with circular tables and predominantly white people mingling about. Some brief chitchat reveals that some of the audience is here by choice, some by compulsion (several employers, who have a corporate membership in the Young Professionals of Milwaukee, have mandated attendance). The facilitators, Young Professionals of Milwaukee leaders, soon ask the group, numbered at perhaps two hundred, to take a seat at a round table. Our activity for the evening, we are told, follows the popular "speed dating" model. At each table, a group of six people will introduce themselves, talk for approximately ten minutes about their feelings and experiences about race, ethnicity, and difference, and then move to a new table with different people.

After some silence, an awkward conversation unfolds at my table with the earnest suggestions that more religious holidays be observed at the workplace and that everyone should "have lunch with one person that is different than them." When some deeper issues are raised, such as the helpless feelings of an African American teacher in stemming the violence in her school, the conversations stop abruptly as we are moved to a new table. After several rounds of these conversations, the facilitators signal an end to the activity. They pass around microphones and invite individuals to share their experiences. Some people volunteer their thoughts—how the event made them realize some issues about race, or how they planned to reach out to "different" people in their workplace. One lone body stands up to suggest that these conversations are insufficient, that there actually needs to be concerted action that challenges poverty and segregation in Milwaukee. Some murmurs occur.

The event comes to a close, and the audience is reminded that the Young Professionals of Milwaukee is not an activist organization. Rather, participants are encouraged to take knowledge from the conversations and build on them in their own personal lives. For example, one should expand one's friendship groups and watch films that reflect other cultures. Like other attendees, I left the event somewhat dazed.

AUTHOR'S FIELD NOTES

"Diversity matters to young professionals," leaders of Young Professionals of Milwaukee told me repeatedly, and that is why they hosted events like the mosaic. Milwaukee's Mayor Norquist frequently claimed that younger generations value diversity and tolerance, citing Florida's research (Norquist 2003). Accordingly, as one interviewee told me, "the whole drive of Young Professionals of Milwaukee is attracting and retaining diverse people in Milwaukee" (Young Professionals of Milwaukee member, white, female).

In this way, diversity was construed as central to young professionals and to the success of Milwaukee. On one hand, this could be a progressive position. However, the mosaic event, interviews, and surrounding discourses presented a more paradoxical picture, which both called attention to and muted inequalities in some ways. Before hosting the mosaic event described above, the Young Professionals of Milwaukee did some homework, posting on their website that "research shows that cities with diverse talent are economically more successful." They drew on popular studies by Florida that suggested that "cities without rock bands and gays are losing the economic development race" (Florida 2002b). Hoping to attract diversity and "put the Milwaukee region on the world map in a whole new way," the group launched a study of its own. This 2004 report, referencing legacies of segregation and racial inequality, found that "our city's most significant barrier to attracting diverse talent is our image." In like manner, a report by the Department of City Development argued, "We have an image that is Laverne and Shirley, beer and brats. We need to change that image so we can get young people to come here." Such discourses and rationales had several consequences. First, they reinforced and extended neoliberal logics of urban capitalism and competition. In this case, diversity became important, not in its own right but for its instrumental links to economic development and accumulation in cities. Similarly, several companies attached to the Young Professionals of Milwaukee sought to improve their reputation and links to consumers by "diversifying" their staff. In the process, substantive racial inequalities in Milwaukee became diffuse and deflated. Race became "an image problem" that kept diverse young people from coming to Milwaukee and thus hindered economic growth.

The mosaic event occurred amid this central problematic: Diversity had already been labeled by the Young Professionals of Milwaukee as an "image problem." The organization's events were supposed to attract a large audience and to boost Milwaukee's image (FUEL Milwaukee 2007). The event itself—attended by mainly white elites—was then scripted in a way that propagated superficial conversations about diversity. Ten-minute "chats" ended before becoming too contentious or challenging. This enactment of "diversity" discursively displaced other, more urgent discussions. In addition, as participants in a sanctioned event on diversity, attendees were interpellated as tolerant urban citizens in ways that did not disrupt neoliberal subjectivities. In the creative-class script, they were agents of positive urban transformation via their supposed interest in diversity (e.g., Florida 2002a). More circumspectly, they could be seen as unintentional perpetrators of the unequal status quo.

While the city of Milwaukee had a population that is approximately 50 percent nonwhite, "attracting diversity and really showcasing Milwaukee" was a serious endeavor of city leaders (Young Professionals of Milwaukee member, African American, male, April 2004). In an article about his world travels to attract talent, the director of the Metropolitan Milwaukee Chamber of Commerce dichotomized the attraction of talent and jobs *out there* in juxtaposition to Milwaukee's current population:

> There are two paths the city can take. One puts Milwaukee in a place where it can compete on a worldwide basis to attract talent, investment and jobs and the other puts us in a place where we're struggling to keep the community above water because we've got such a large portion of the population without high school degrees,

too many teenage pregnancies, too much of the inmate population being returned here, too much being directed to the police because crime is too high. The choices we make today determine which path we go down. (Ahlers 2007)

In other words, Milwaukee's economic development agenda suggested not so much a path of inclusion or transformation for the city's current population, but one of replacement by other, more "economically contributive" citizens. The instrumental and selective nature of calls for diversity in Milwaukee was thus surprisingly blatant. Florida's research had long suggested that "tolerance and diversity" (construed as high populations of immigrants and gay and lesbians) would drive economic growth or serve as "canaries" signaling eventual growth. However, broader analyses of "diversity" were less frequently explored or celebrated. Many of Florida's (rotating) top ten creative cities had small African American populations. Furthermore, racial and economic inequality have been consistently high in these creative cities (Donegan and Lowe 2008; Leslie and Catungal 2012; Parker 2008).

Thus, the celebrated cities of "openness and tolerance" were not necessarily canaries of hope for black families or poor women in Milwaukee. Importantly, according to feminists and social justice advocates, equity and inclusion ought to be imperative for all citizens, regardless of whether they contribute to economic growth or not, principles that were undermined by instrumental approaches to diversity.

The message that certain types of embodied, elite diversity were "preferred" in Milwaukee and by the Young Professionals of Milwaukee was reflected in the organization's primarily elite and white membership, and its community reputation (Young Professionals of Milwaukee 2004b). An article in the *Milwaukee Journal Sentinel* asserted that "many young professionals who work in non-profits or belong to a minority group (ethnic groups, lesbian, gay, transgendered and bisexual, etc.) see the Young Professionals of Milwaukee as more as a stomping ground for traditional white-collar professionals, not necessarily the 'diversity' minorities were looking for" (Evans 2006). Some of my interviewees echoed this sentiment, describing organization events as experiences of exclusion and alienation. For example, several teachers (some of whom were African American) suggested that they didn't fit in with the "culture" of the Young Professionals of Milwaukee. Other interviewees felt the conception of "professional" was limited: "I just don't care to hobnob with like the up-and-coming business class. . . . Plus we [activists] are never a part of those conversations, you know. They talk about 'professionals' and we are sort of left out" (Young Professionals of Milwaukee member, nonwhite, female).

Thus, the selective discourses and practices surrounding diversity and inclusion in Milwaukee were of concern. A simple rendering of the discourse might read like this: if one's "diversity" adds value to the market economy, improves the image of the city, and raises real estate prices, it is acceptable and advantageous. From a feminist and social justice perspective, this approach is deeply problematic, as it, among other things, situates the market and public spheres—already described as raced and gendered—as the place in which one's value is evaluated and constructed.

Notably, Milwaukee's pursuit of diversity was framed within neoliberal, autonomous, and voluntaristic frameworks. Florida argued that "the creative people I study use the word a lot, but not to press any political hot buttons. Diversity is simply something they value in all its manifestations. . . . Talented people defy classification based on race, ethnicity, gender, sexual preference, or appearance" (Florida 2002a, 79). Like much neoliberal discourse, this argument simultaneously delegitimized structural and hardened disadvantages that many female, nonwhite, non-gender-conforming, differently abled, immigrant, LGBT, and other residents faced. Framed as a negative "political hot button," critique and collective action were devalued. Instead, creative-class recipes recommended an "appreciate diversity" fix instigated by a fickle creative class and framed in and through the market. This type of diversity cocktail—like those served at the mosaic—had no progressive punch. According to feminist Judy Wajcman (2013, 22–23), "Ideas like recognizing diversity can actually undermine the proposition that women as a group are targets of discriminatory practices. There appears to be a shift in the discourse on managing diversity away from any sense that specific groups experience 'disadvantage.'"

Even more critically, Dana Davis (2007, 351) and others argue that a pseudo "racial emancipation" and multicultural diversity agenda prevents more direct engagement with racism (Bonds and Inwood 2015). However unintentional, this seemed to be the case with the Young Professionals of Milwaukee and city leaders. They hosted events like the mosaics, they provided training to members and employers about expanding diversity in the workplace, they created a "diversity council" composed of individuals and nonprofit organizations that largely held progressive perspectives. But ultimately, more radical voices in the organization were silenced, and "doing diversity" via the mosaics remained light and uncontroversial, undercutting political resistance. This approach to diversity was constrained by design and echoed a neoliberal perspective of individualism in which issues such as racism, white privilege, and patriarchy were muted (see Davis 2007). As one self-described progressive who was a member of the Young Professionals of Milwaukee stated, "People don't want to go to these stupid mosaics anymore. They're done with the mosaics; they don't want to sit around and chitchat about, you know, racism and stuff. They want to be able to say okay, what are we going to do?" (Young Professionals of Milwaukee member, nonwhite, female).

This does not mean that greater tolerance, diversity, and justice could not have been a side effect of the creative city prescription, especially if executed differently. Nor does it mean that authentic feminist and progressive "creative" arts initiatives, differently defined and carried out, could not radically challenge spatial inequalities and neoliberalism. Current research has explored these possibilities, with mixed findings. For example, Heather McLean has shown how artists can leverage heterogeneous arts-led regeneration strategies to make space for "radical social praxis" and challenge hegemonic regimes (e.g., McLean 2014a, 2014b; Weiss 2005). Even within the Young Professionals of Milwaukee, I observed conversations among members and within the organization's diversity council that demonstrated interest in equity and social activism. In the end, the group's efforts may help produce a middle-class Milwaukee workforce with more women and underrepresented minorities. As I suggested in the previous chapters, this kind of improvement does matter. However, the overarching practices and discourses of the Young Professionals of Milwaukee and the city subverted more radical actions. Instead, these soft diversity initiatives created and affirmed illusions of action, valorized the "creative class" for their supposed tolerance, muted other kinds of collective mobilizations and conversations about care, and reproduced a narrative of impending progress via the creative class that belied stark inequalities.

Salient Silences and Discursive Dismissal in Creative City Discourses

The woman sits across from me in her household. She stretches out in her chair and breathes a sigh of relief, as her young toddler climbs on her lap and starts to run his handheld train up and down her arm, murmuring "vroom, vroom." Her older daughters are watching television and she calls for it to be turned off for now and they ought to start their homework. Then, this mother is quiet for a moment. She has just returned home from her work at a local fast-food restaurant, and she also cleans houses on weekends. She tells me that we can't talk long, she needs to fix something for dinner and she doesn't have a plan.

AUTHOR'S FIELD NOTES

Is this mother creative? Certainly she is "diverse," if one considers her skin color. I've watched her as she manages multiple jobs, works more than seventy hours a week at home and at paid work, somehow makes time to laugh with her children, and magically puts food on the table when her jobs pay only nine dollars per hour. She is trying to take night classes so she might earn a job in the higher paying health sector. Yet this mother and all the activities surrounding her were seemingly uncreative and invisible in Milwaukee's creative-class urban development agenda. The efforts of feminists and activists to make households visible, to make the "personal" political, and to assert the value of all urban residents and types of labor fell relatively silent in the creative-class cacophony. Instead, the creative-city thesis was structured around a hierarchical creative hero who is primarily located in the "masculinized" urban public sphere. He was in his office, being creative. If he was at home, he was laboring at the computer or putting together music. He may be designing art for public consumption. He and other creative-class members were the "natural—indeed the only possible—leaders of twenty-first-century society" (Florida 2002a, 315). In Florida's texts, implicitly and passively arrayed beneath these heroes were the gendered and raced service workers. In Milwaukee, around 80 percent of these cashiers, food service workers, personal and health care aides, and child care workers are female. Most earn less than ten dollars per hour, and many are African American (Levine 2013a). Deeming it elitist, Florida bemoaned a dualistic social order in "which some people are considered natural creators while others exist to serve them, carry out their ideas and tend to their personal needs" (Florida 2002a, 323). Yet Florida, the Young Professionals of Milwaukee, and Milwaukee city leaders—not an unknowable unnamed society—(re)defined certain people (the creative class) as natural creators, instantiating difference and inequality.

Young Professionals of Milwaukee members were valorized by themselves, by city officials, and in the media, and they also gained access to the mayor, city leadership, and other elites through their participation in the group, thus building and sustaining the social reproduction of elite networks. According to geographer Jamie Peck (2007), members of the creative class "are held to have *earned* their superior position in the creative city, by virtue of raw talent and creative capital, validated through the market, and it is *they* who must be catered to in what amounts to a post-progressive urban policy." Meanwhile, city resources and policy prescriptions were formed and allocated in Milwaukee based on these creativity labels. At the same time, as I argue elsewhere and throughout this book, the complex lives, paid labors, and needs of many Milwaukee residents and households were obscured and ignored in the creative-city discourse (see Parker 2008). Florida made happy proclamations about outsourcing his cooking and cleaning, universally claimed that young people were deferring childbearing, and noted that only workplace perks that enhanced creativity would stick around. However, caregiving and social reproduction duties still confound many households. This is especially true for women, who, for various reasons, still conduct the majority of caregiving labors and whose triple burdens of production, reproduction, and community work have intensified under neoliberalism (Bianchi et al. 2012; Nagar et al. 2002).

It is reasonable to suggest that workers perhaps do not wish to be relentless twenty-four-hour workers in the paid economy and that this might not be good for cities. Studies have shown high-technology workers who are fathers "sneaking away" from work and mothers and fathers conducting work from home during paid maternity and paternity leaves (see Cooper 2000; Williams, Blair-Loy, and Berdahl 2013). Meanwhile, cultures of "intensive mothering" and "new momism" have emerged that raise expectations of maternal perfection and time and resources parents are expected to devote to their children (e.g., Douglas 2010; Douglas and Michaels 2005; Hays 1996). As I reported in chapter 2, increasingly people of differing genders, races, and ethnicities and those in varied situations report stress in balancing work and family life, especially low-income women. Even as Florida celebrates happy young childless workers supposedly without caregiving duties, the data present a more complex picture. Over 50 percent of first childbirths still occur to women in their twenties, and the median age of mothers at first birth is deeply varied by race and geography (as low as twenty-two for African American and Puerto Rican women in the United States, for example; Centers for Disease Control and Prevention 2012).

Thus, the creative-class discourse scripts a racially and gendered narrow "creative," childless, mobile population of bodies and activities. It also devalues or discursively erases the social reproduction labor that in practice confronted even "creative" workers in Milwaukee and elsewhere and arguably helps sustain communities. In doing so, Florida's claims legitimate neoliberal market subjectivities and persistent U.S. state and employer practices that individualize social reproduction at the household level. As feminist scholars have long pointed out, because women still do most caring labor, women's equality in part hinges on the redistribution of and/or increased state support for such labor.

In addition, since women and femininity are often associated with caregiving of all types, greater esteem and visibility accorded to this work would likely increase women's status and equity and improve the social fabric of cities via investments in care and collectivity (e.g., Sánchez de Madariaga and Roberts 2013). The lack of affordable child care, support for youth, paid maternity leave, high-quality schools and parks, and other social supports disproportionately affects the financial and emotional well-being of women and low-income families (Crittenden 2001; Fraser 2013; Klodawsky, Aubry, and Farrell 2006; Orloff 1996; Shriver and Center for American Progress 2014; Williams 2000). The trend of privileged households paying for social reproduction assistance via the private market has contributed to a low-wage, transnational, racialized, and gendered domestic and caregiving workforce. This both instantiates racial, gendered, and ethnic hierarchies and creates even more intensified and precarious work-life situations for such workers and their households (e.g., Burnham and Theodore 2012; McDowell 2007; Parreñas 2001; Pratt and Johnston 2013). Thus, grappling with social reproduction and its gendered dimensions (including work-life tensions, child care, and community building) is necessary in order to create more equitable cities, as I argue in chapter 6 (also see Parker 2008). However, creative-class discourses devalorized these labors and associated concerns. Often, too, did the Young Professionals of Milwaukee.

The Milwaukee government, for its part, did little to engage with social reproduction for the nonelite, as is argued throughout this book. Rather than a clamoring for investment in public schools and poor children, there was a silent concession that the desirable "creative" families with children would move to the suburbs or remain in elite pockets of the city, for example. The economic and social situations of other residents were of less concern. In addition, by legitimating and valorizing the dedication of scarce urban resources toward elite real estate development and the attraction of the favored creative-class elite, the creative script indirectly targeted women, families, and minorities in cities. As argued above, these groups are direct beneficiaries of urban and social services and desperately needed affordable housing and jobs (see Nagar et al. 2002; Wekerle 2005a; see also chapters 2 and 4). They also directly suffer the effects of creative-class-stimulated gentrification. In 2006, the local parks district announced that it would close 90 percent of its swimming pools due to budget shortfalls. However, the same agency earmarked a generous $200,000 for additional public art in the upscale corridors of the city's downtown (see Zimmerman 2008). The city also lost 11 percent of its jobs between 1990 and 2005 (Schmid 2006). As is articulated throughout this book, poverty, unemployment, poor educational access, and the lack of affordable housing and child care have been a racialized and gendered phenomenon in Milwaukee.

However, even amid this crisis, the city remained a "real estate development" machine, spending a whopping 70 percent of its $413 million economic development budget on real estate projects (Schmid 2006). The city developed urban land and directed scarce resources to shopping centers, street beautification, and new urbanist housing in the hope of attracting the creative class. This urban development strategy, defended by the mayor's office and the city's cadre of white masculinist elites who profited from it (see chapter 4), perhaps intentionally missed the targets that could have benefitted from holistic economic and social investments in Milwaukee.

Conclusion

In Milwaukee and beyond, creative-class members were seen as idealized urban subjects, occupying new urbanist dwellings, purportedly driving economic growth, and propagating and embodying neoliberal autonomy and self-management practices like self-commodification, competition, and entrepreneurialism. This process was hierarchical and uneven, in that some bodies and practices were reified and others were devalued, demeaned, or made invisible, generally building on and exacerbating extant gendered, raced, and classed inequalities. The manifestations and performances of "desirable" creativity (however contradictory) through primarily elite, white, and often masculine subjects like Florida and members of the Young Professionals of Milwaukee gave fuel to these narratives.

The creative-class script and associated actors and practices aligned with and bolstered neoliberalism in Milwaukee. The creative-class discourses combined market and masculinist concepts of "creativity" in a way that endorsed hyper-capitalism, individualism, and narrow conceptions of valuable work. Creative-class economic development policies and discourses made invisible an important range of creative practices and people, such as mothers juggling unpaid and paid labor, radical artists challenging gentrifying space, and poor people negotiating access to service in austere neoliberal cities (e.g., McLean 2014a; Parker 2008; Wilson and Keil 2008). Instead, a mobile, unfettered, highly paid worker in the "public sphere" and some of the most masculinist fields like technology, architecture, and law were idealized. These subjectivities were marked by raced and gendered inequalities that took new and novel forms and were most easily occupied by white, male, elite heterosexual subjects and those who benefited from associations with white hegemonic masculinity. Yet this fact was obscured in claims about creative "meritocracy."

While the Young Professionals of Milwaukee and city leaders made claims about tolerance and the importance of diversity, these assertions were often instrumental and superficial in practice. Diversity was partly seen as a strategic tool for economic growth. The Young Professionals focused on soft diversity efforts by hosting events like the cultural mosaics that fostered thin conversations and framed deep inequalities as image problems in Milwaukee. Such actions muted the brutal and banal forms of racism in Milwaukee and the need for redistribution or collective action to address them. Meanwhile, city leaders focused on recruiting "diverse" workers from other places, in spite of a large population of minorities in the city in need of work and inclusion into the broader social and economic fabric of the city.

In addition, the Young Professionals of Milwaukee and the creative-class discourse writ large valorized liberal/neoliberal conceptions of competition, consumptive-oriented communities, individualism, and autonomy. Creative-class members were validated for improving the city via their presence, consuming around the city, and engaging in broader place-marketing activities that would add value to the city. The group shied away from an advocacy agenda. While there were some exceptionally progressive members and earnest interest in social issues, these were generally muted in the broader organization. Amid the clanking of "young professional" talk over martinis at hipster urban joints, there was limited clamoring for social change.

Rather, the Young Professionals of Milwaukee seemed to help reproduce extant class, raced, and gendered elite urban networks. The study of such networks is an important agenda for urban researchers (see Kern 2007). In these networks, white, single, middle-class women who did not have significant caregiving responsibilities often did "fine." Although not completely, and amid gendered exclusions and hierarchies, they were able to embody and profit from historical white privilege and many facets of supposedly nongendered, idealized neoliberal subjectivities and practices.

Meanwhile, creative-class discourses and policies helped continually point urban policy and development dials *away* from social reproduction concerns (especially among the nonelite) and human needs. Florida's voluminous writings and speeches deprioritized and caricatured many of the "messy, fleshy" social reproduction activities that sustain human life and cities more generally—including caregiving, cleaning, and community building. In a U.S. and urban climate that has continually devalued and disinvested in such activities and surrounding institutions like public education, the creative-class discourse fits quite well.

The discursive and material inattention to social reproduction has had nefarious and uneven effects in Milwaukee. Women, still socially responsible for most caring labors, bore the brunt of social and economic disinvestment. This was especially true for low-income, African American women and families who experienced years of dispossession and racism in labor markets and housing and would benefit most from social and urban services and investments in social reproduction.

The Milwaukee government invested in these creative-class elites via special attention that was given to the Young Professionals of Milwaukee and by structuring an urban development plan tied to their presumed consumption habits. Such a plan involved investments of millions of dollars in downtown real estate development, elite housing markets, and attempts to strengthen the creative industries. In this and other ways, inequality was further exacerbated through policies surrounding and attached to the creative-class vision in Milwaukee. Drawing on David Harvey's (1989) concept of urban entrepreneurialism, creative-class attraction policies may be a pinnacle form of speculation premised on elusive bodies, and inscripted in space via city-building and consumption strategies. Amid unequal gendered labors, crises in education and housing, and racialized and gendered poverty and other inequalities in Milwaukee, the creative city urban development strategy involved spectacularly uncertain rewards and certain targets.

CHAPTER SIX

Getting By in Milwaukee

Amplified Lives and Labors for Low-Income African American Women

> My barriers have been abuse, housing, employment, and education. I think just
> basic life is a barrier.
>
> **KAREN, AFRICAN AMERICAN, LOW-INCOME MOTHER**

Karen heaved these words from her lips, took another sip of coffee, sank into her chair, and looked silently at me. Her experiences were very different from those of most of the elite creative class and new urbanist dwellers in Milwaukee, even though they lived in the same city. Like those of many poor African American women whom I interviewed, her life and labors were often intense and heavy.

Karen's story and others shed light on important dimensions of urban politics and life in Milwaukee according to feminists: everyday life and labors, households, and social reproduction. *Social reproduction* refers to the labors, practices, and social relations that surround and sustain households, cities, and, more generally, human life, including caring for and clothing children, providing education and health care, and creating community networks. Appropriately, Cindi Katz (2001) has described social reproduction as "the messy, fleshy indeterminate material components of human life."[1]

In Milwaukee and elsewhere, the complex daily lives and labors of women were often ignored or caricatured by government, the media, and even academics. Historically, the labors of black women have been devalued or co-opted, in part through racist, heteropatriarchal systems. Under Norquist's neoliberalism, investments in most forms of social reproduction declined precipitously, especially for poor women and families. The narratives of low-income black women whom I interviewed in Milwaukee challenge this silence and disregard, contextualized by social reproduction theories and black feminist thought.

I came to know most interviewees through their participation in a poverty support network for low-income women; others were their friends, family members, or activists contesting urban development projects. Like 45 percent of African American women in Milwaukee, my research subjects were poor and had been their entire lives. Many had connections to paid work, Milwaukee's welfare-to-work (w-2) program, and various support networks, which were contingent or temporary. I talked with these women in their homes, in coffee shops, and at meetings, protests, or other organized events. Their stories highlight their survival and resistance strategies, the complicated power relations and spaces they negotiated, and the intersectional processes of marginalization in Milwaukee.

In the pages to follow, I zero in on the theme of *amplification*. Amplify means to make louder, so I present the sometimes invisible narratives and quotes of my interviews, as they described daily life and social reproduction in Milwaukee. Amplification also refers to intensity—the intensity of African American women's work, life, and resistance, of laborious days when the tasks of work and love were never done and rarely rewarded. It also refers to the emotional and bodily intensity of living lives of precarity, and of responding with creativity and alternative subjectivities. Critically there was also an amplification of the gulf between white women's experiences and black women's experiences vis-à-vis the neoliberal state and related institutions.

African American Women: Unequal Labors and Experiences with the State

bell hooks (1981) has written, "No other group in America has so had their identity socialized out of existence as have black women. . . . When black people are talked about the focus tends to be on black men; and when women are talked about the focus tends to be on white women." As the women whom I interviewed in Milwaukee helped convey, black women in the United States have always had deeply unequal experiences with paid and unpaid labor. After years of forced slavery, African American women, compared to white women, participated in the paid labor force at much higher rates, but always in lower wage and lower status jobs. Even among similarly educated and full-time female workers, far more African American women that whites are in poverty. Recessions and labor market changes are harshest for African American men and low-skilled African American women—the latter having never experienced the high-wage, low-skill jobs that some men found (e.g., Gilmore 2007; Jones 2009; Trotter 1985). Furthermore, employment-related racism and disparities persist, with black female workers in the Milwaukee area earning only 56 to 70 percent of the wages white males earned in 2010, depending on their specific geography.

For black women in the United States, caring labors have usually been balanced with forced or paid labor and often controlled and/or characterized by whites. This has produced stereotypes such as the black "mammy" or "welfare queen" (see Hill Collins 2000a; McKittrick 2011; see also chapter 2).

The labor of black mothers and their children has rarely received the generous support of the state. Instead, welfare payments, urban renewal, child protective services, domestic violence services, and various forms of state "aid" have been profoundly shaped by sexist and racist assumptions.[2] Also, mothering for African American women takes place in a broader context of racism. Nurturing children involves shielding them and preparing them for unequal treatment at school, at work, and with the criminal justice system (e.g., Alexander 2012; Gilmore 2007; Hill Collins 2000a; Jones 2009; Sue 2010). Other unique features of black motherhood include the tendencies of African American women to be "other mothers" to nonbiological children, to engage in community care, and to assume the role of motherhood as a symbol of power and a basis for political activism. Beth Richie (2012) notes that black mothers shoulder uneven demands for community care and social life maintenance. In part, this emerges from a faulty analysis that claims that black women have it "easier" than black men and are therefore blamed for failings in black neighborhoods.

Always Amplified: Life's Work for African American Women in Milwaukee

These intersecting oppressions and the complexities surrounding social reproduction for low-income black women in neoliberal times were imminently clear in the voices of my interviewees. As one woman stated, "I have a teenager, my oldest turned fourteen today. I have a daughter that is twelve and I have a three-year-old little boy. Working, I can say that I work eighteen hours a day, being at work and then at home (Audra, African American, female).[3]

Interviewees cared for up to six children of varying ages and labored up to twenty hours a day. Commonly, their children had special needs, ranging from attention-deficit/hyperactivity disorder to diabetes and asthma. Their labor was often intensified by changes in labor markets and austere social policies that characterized neoliberalism. Most interviewees cared for other family members or children and earned wages through temporary agencies, restaurants, and/or informal work, such as sex work and plasma donations. There was periodic volunteer work and the navigating of state and "shadow state" provisioning options, such as traveling to food pantries and churches; meeting with social workers, teachers, and food stamp offices; and the endless waiting at agencies and health clinics: "Yesterday, I got up at five. I left Jerome at my sister's place to get the bus [laughs]. I mean the buses. If it all works out, I get to work at nine. . . . I don't eat lunch. I can't afford it. . . . It's dark when I pick up the baby, seven usually" (Cheryl, African American, female). In a few cases, paid labor appeared to provide independence and welcome relief for women, a finding that echoes some research and aligns with neoliberal rhetoric about autonomy and work. Since many feminists have long argued that economic independence is essential for women's equality, workforce involvement is a space where feminist aims at justice and neoliberal policies have perhaps treacherously coincided (e.g., Fraser 2009, 2013; Lister 1990; Orloff 1996). A few of my interviewees found personal value and respite in paid labor: "Work is a, like I said, it's a place of refuge for me. . . . I can focus on what I need to do at work and get it done, and then, you know, look forward to that afternoon or that evening with my kids. . . . I love them true enough but, you know, I don't want to feel like I'm stressed [at home] to have to deal with them. . . . So, I'm that type of parent where if you have homework, let's talk about what you did at school today" (Tamara, African American, female).

However, most interviewees described a different reality, one that was para-doxically insecure and controlled. This reflects a critical problem with gendered and raced neoliberal capitalism, described in previous chapters. Women (and all subjects) are supposed to be full-time, autonomous, rational, economic sub-jects and laborers in the paid economy. Yet the capitalist paid economy is often discriminatory, humiliating, and precarious and pays low wages. And, under a protracted neoliberal state, women have had minimal to nonexistent support for their caring labors, so they must do both.[4] In this "amplified" workday, for my interviewees, there was little energy for children's activities and a loom-ing gulf between their desires surrounding motherhood and their capacities: "Because you're spending fourteen hours a day on an eight-hour a day job. So when you get home you're too tired to help them with their homework" (Audra, African American, female).

These women's labors were filtered through both the low-wage neoliberal economy and the state, which played a critical role in differentially mediating, supporting, and unhinging social reproduction, particularly through Wiscon-sin's welfare-to-work program, Wisconsin Works (w-2). Among the most work focused in the nation, the program provided some health and child care, but required women to engage in over thirty hours of work per week in order to receive assistance.

As described earlier, the w-2 program was crafted and pursued avidly by conservative think tanks, politicians, and even Mayor Norquist, who argued in 1996 that "abolishing welfare is key to the health of cities." To discourage "dependency," participants were offered only services that they specifically re-quested, and there were terms and lifetime limits. This meant that many women were living on food stamps as a sole source of income by the early 2000s. In leg-islative debates that I witnessed, a twelve-week exception from work for moth-ers of newborns was described as an excessively generous feature that would "condone the very problem of irresponsibility we are trying to resolve" (author's field notes).

Women in the w-2 program, including my interviewees, were sanctioned if they were late or missed work:

They've got a very short window for excuses. If they would say, okay, I've got your doctor's statement. You'll get your hour paid for the time you were here, which I think is five fifteen an hour, but they won't include time on the bus or whatever. And they don't accept my excuse, then I don't get paid. Or let's say I have a sick child. And maybe I can't take him to the doctor, but I can stay home with the child. And I don't come back with an excuse, that's a whole day of pay I lose. That means food for my kids. (Kimberly, African American, female)

Such sanctions were doled out more frequently for women of color than white women (Courtney and Dworsky 2006; Mulligan-Hansel and Fendt 2003; Wisconsin Legislative Audit Bureau 2005). The threat of sanctions forced my interviewees to make difficult decisions, such as forgoing a job to take a child to the doctor or leaving a child in the car while they worked.

Furthermore, the specter of sanctions or referrals to Child Protective Services had a disciplinary and isolating effect on mothers. In one study, 25 percent of w-2 participants had children removed from their homes over a four-year period. As Dorothy Roberts (2000, 2008) points out, black children are more likely to be placed in foster care, in part because of cultural standards and because the state is more willing to intrude on the autonomy of black mothers (see also Collins and Mayer 2010; Courtney and Dworsky 2006). For these reasons, fear loomed large among my interviewees and hindered activism. According to one community organizer,

Women were very upfront. They were there, the energy, the anger, the speech, the—everything. They had their voice. . . . However once Pay for Performance came into play, women backed off because it was an extraordinarily punitive thing and they were very afraid because they were being sanctioned like crazy. And also they were concerned that the little they had, and the most precious thing they had, namely their children, could be forfeited if they became too public and too adversarial. So they backed off and they backed off so badly that we can barely get them into the public arena. (Mary, activist, white, female)

My interviewees who participated in w-2 indicated that they had little input in their work sites and tasks, a finding echoed by academics and advocates (Collins and Mayer 2010). Women complained of picking up garbage and repetitively folding the same clothes. According to a Milwaukee policy activist whom I interviewed, "Participants in the Milwaukee area were commonly being assigned menial and repetitive tasks such as counting hangers in thrift stores or packing and unpacking the same box of books over and over. These activities did little to boost the skills of w-2 participants. Nor did they offer any sense of the real experience of holding a job. Instead, they leave participants feeling less gratified by work then they had before" (Margaret, testimony to the Senate Committee on Health, Children, and Families).

Low-wage temporary employment—which constituted 42 percent of w-2 placements and was a main source of work for my interviewees—was particularly precarious. First, workers had no control over the tasks or work environment. Second, mistreatment and ambiguous dismissal were common, and discrimination and stereotyping were persistent in many industries (see Peck and Theodore 2001). Finally, like a double-edged sword, transportation was often provided by the agency. This made temporary work an attractive option for the w-2 program and for women who had limited transportation. However, it was often a form of wage dispossession and impinged on mothering labor, as described by one interviewee:

> Whenever you work temp agencies this is how you do it. If the job pays eight dollars an hour, they charge you eight dollars a day in transportation. . . . But if they have to pick you up, say your kid gets sick, from the working scene, they're going to charge you thirty dollars for that one pick up. It isn't because it cost them thirty dollars to come get you. It's because they're mad that they're losing money because you're not on the clock now. . . . So if somebody calls you to say your kid is sick, you want to know exactly how sick that child is before you leave. They've got to be damn near dying for me to leave. And that's not right. (Lori, African American, female)

To these women, combining paid work and motherhood was a Faustian bargain that usually ended badly. Women could rarely meet their children's needs given their unstable, low-wage working arrangements. Yet the financial support of the state or employer was one of the few ways to provide for their children. While w-2 policy language reified "working" poor mothers, employers were suspicious of my interviewees' moral and maternal commitments. One woman commented, "But, he wasn't you know, it's like he didn't understand even with my doctor's excuse. You know . . . I mean some employers—he acted like I was just, you know, purposely not coming to work, and that's hard. That's very, very hard" (Jara, African American, female).

Nine women whom I interviewed lost jobs because their employer did not believe them or they needed to take off work to care for sick children. In other words, these women were caught in traps of racial and gendered differentiation. The state portrayed them as "responsible, good, hardworking" mothers if they worked at inflexible, low-wage jobs. Yet, most media and policy discourses still valorized stay-at-home white mothers, and mothers in the larger paid work faced discrimination in pay and promotion when compared to nonmothers (e.g., Correll, Benard, and Paik 2007; Douglas and Michaels 2005; Williams

2000; Williams and Boushey 2010). Overtly raced and gendered discrimination, microaggressions in the workplace, and media stereotypes of poor racialized mothers deepen the problem (e.g., Clawson and Trice 2000; Fraser and Gordon 1994; Jones 2009; Sue 2010).

Ultimately, my interviewees maintained a precarious toehold on their provisioning and caring capacities, one constantly unhinged by practices of employers and the state. Regarding w-2, one study reported that "more than four years after they sought help, most of these applicants were no better off, and, in many cases, they were worse off than when they sought assistance" (Courtney and Dworsky 2006).

Black women's paid and unpaid labors were negatively enmeshed with the state in other ways, particularly with regard to criminal justice and incarceration. One interviewee asserted, "We got to be supporting each other 'cause there is some women out here right now that I do know that are struggling with the fact of loneliness and not having a daddy for their child or their daddy may be locked up. Their daddy might be dead" (Audra, African American, female).

As the quote suggests, prisons featured prominently in the life's work of my interviewees. Only one interviewee had been incarcerated, but many interviewees' friends, brothers, sisters, and children and the fathers of their children had been. In Milwaukee, 50 percent of African American men aged thirty to forty-four have been incarcerated, compared to approximately 5 percent of white men and 5 percent of Hispanic men (University of Wisconsin–Milwaukee Center for Employment and Training 2011). Wisconsin incarcerated a higher percentage of its black population than any other state in 2010. Women expressed anger and grief about this and the problems it created. They were often temporarily "housing" prison returnees, providing bail or financial support, or otherwise negotiating the criminal justice system. They were accurately fearful for their children and relatives, as black men are arrested and sentenced for drug-related crimes such as marijuana possession at six times the rate of whites in Wisconsin, despite similar patterns of use and distribution (Alexander 2012; American Civil Liberties Union 2013). In addition, certain government benefits like low-income housing were restricted if felons lived in households, so my interviewees were wary and watchful. They could not tell employers they needed leave from work to go to court with their sons or daughters, and could rarely advocate for them within the penal system.

Women spoke in sometimes coded ways about cultures of violence and masculinity that were produced and deepened in prisons, as well as neighborhoods. Interviewees reported that they sometimes preferred to tolerate abuse, rather than turn to the police: "Things have to be really, really bad for you to go and call the police. You don't want the police at your house. You don't want them there because next thing you know somebody is in jail or they're after you"

(Brenda, African American, female).[5] Black feminist Beth Richie (2012, 14–15) describes this as a "trap of loyalty," in which black women often have their needs denied and victimization ignored because of the false notion that black women have more advantages then black men. "At a very concrete level, if a woman involves the criminal legal system following an abusive episode or assault, it can be viewed as turning a Black man over to the police." Richie also documents how poor black women who turn to police for assistance may be manipulated or assaulted.

Incarceration affects not just black men in Milwaukee. Female incarceration rates increased by nearly 400 percent during the 1990s, and women were often subject to violence in prison or jail (Richie 2012). Approximately two-thirds of incarcerated women are mothers, and one in every thirty women admitted into correctional facilities is pregnant (Glaze and Maruschak 2008; Maruschak 2008). The incarceration of fathers and mothers has profound consequences for social reproduction and bodies that are not fully understood. For example, in most states, women can be shackled during labor and childbirth, and the kinds of separations, violences, and penal experiences surrounding incarceration permeate and stunt the physical and emotional well-being and social reproduction of entire families (Women's Prison Association 2011). Upon leaving prison, the paid and unpaid labors of women and men are deeply affected through, for example, diminished employment opportunities, increased poverty, stigma, and a lack of access to state resources and citizenship rights (Alexander 2012).

Overall, for the poor African American women whom I interviewed, their paid and unpaid labors and engagement with the state were occasionally liberating, but mostly amplified, grueling, and insecure. However, it seems worthwhile to point out that many of these experiences were not *new*. My interviewees expressed a history and expectation of engagement with marginalized paid work balanced with caregiving. Here, neoliberal studies that focus on "new" subjectivities and precarities surrounding labor and the stingy neoliberal state fall short in explaining my subjects' experiences. My interviewees largely rejected neoliberal discourses about work and motherhood. They viewed themselves as *always, already* workers, as *always, already* unsupported, differentiated, and/or penalized by employers and the state, primarily because of their status as racialized, low-income women. With various words, they described their complex maternal labors as "work." This work, they argued, had only ever had fleeting or fickle support from the state. While interviewees did talk about poverty, rarely did unprompted reflections on capitalism and labor markets enter into our discussions. Rather, in a spectrum of material-discursive power relations, they pointed mostly to racism and its evolving and insidious forms, including mass incarceration.

Poverty, Provisioning, and Politics

Amid these amplified unpaid and paid labors and encounters with the racialized state, how did my interviews get by? And what kinds of politics of resistance did they employ? They often meshed their lives and labors together. My interviewees took their babies with them while they drove the bus for work; they made calls and appointments if they had access to phones. Some women worked for wages in their own home as child care providers, while caring for their own elderly mothers or children. Some mothers worked in community service jobs, such as at thrift stores, and their children joined them there to do their homework.

Women and families in Milwaukee also lived together as a means of survival, forming alternative political homescapes, and as a way of bundling labor and resources. Not uncommonly, two or three families lived together in a one- or two-bedroom apartment. There, women watched each other's children while one person "provisioned" the household through paid labor; informal activities, such as prostitution, blood or plasma donation, or drug sales; or visits to social service agencies or churches. Women described this kind of bundled living and labor as difficult: "It just creates—not only do you have more people going to into mental institutions (after living in shared households), because just imagine—just me dealing with my dad and he's over there, imagine if I had him in my house all day. I already live with my sister and take care of my niece who also has a handicap and then let's say I've got to take Cindy and her kid" (Tamara, African American, female).

While these kinds of relational arrangements were all too familiar for interviewees, their comments show both the ways that reproductive work is deeply bound up with other labors and how individual, household, and community labors are integrated. This may be especially true for African American women, who conduct much "community mothering" and are often seen as responsible for the well-being of communities (see Hill Collins 2000a; Richie 2012). The above quotes also hint at the stress produced by these kinds of arrangements, stress that sometimes resulted in homelessness for families.

Importantly, these home spaces, whether occupied by one or more families, were sites of political resistance and autonomy. They were both a rejection of the incarceral state and the way that plantation histories still shape African American communities via state intrusion and control (hooks 2000; Isoke 2013; McKittrick 2011). In some ways, they were a repudiation of middle-class, white, nuclear households. Bringing family and friends home was a way to ensure they did not end up homeless and/or arrested and that children did not end up in foster care. Even though they risked losing public assistance, interviewees let formerly incarcerated relatives, partners, and friends live with them, sheltering them from further state encroachment.

The women I interviewed also survived daily life by consuming cheaply and managing materially, with implications for broader social relations and theoretical understanding. First and somewhat obviously, my interviewees tried to spend as little money as possible, and to purchase goods as cheaply as they could. Often, they forwent material needs, like shoes and coats, for themselves as mothers. They also relied heavily on the shadow state (nonprofit and community-based organizations) for food, personal supplies, clothing, and housing assistance whenever possible. They were clearly not alone—even in the period of economic expansion before these interviews were conducted, emergency service needs in the city of Milwaukee had increased by up to 94 percent (Fendt, Mulligan-Hansel, and White 2001).

However, relying on the shadow state was often very time-intensive and infringed on possibilities for other labors. Mothers and families might spend an entire day waiting in the emergency room, at health clinics, or even at social service agencies and churches. The huge demand and unpredictability of social services often led to wasted trips, expenses, and time delays. In addition, women experienced humiliation and gender and racial mistreatment in these encounters. Their ailments were questioned, their reproduction practices were derided, and their children were snubbed. "It's like you're not even a person, not even a human being," said one exasperated interviewee.

For provisioning, my interviewees turned frequently to discount stores like Walmart as a source of cheap food and, on rare occasions, for new clothes for their children. In this way, as is true for households of all incomes now, poor racialized women in U.S. cities have been able to buttress their household provisioning and reproductive capacities in part through the expansion of globalized corporations, supply chains, and poor, racialized labor in all parts of the world. In fact, from my interviewees' perspective, one of the most important and beneficial shifts in their capacity to "get by" and "provide" for their children was the continual cheapening of goods and new possibilities for consumption.

Women in my study relied on not just cheap goods, but a broad range of provisioning spaces and materialities beyond the household. Automobiles and buses were of particular importance, not just as sources of frustration and lack, but also as a place where care work took place and was enabled. More than one interviewee reported having lived in a car for a short period of time, and one reported leaving her children in the car while she went to work, a choice that troubled her immensely and that she hoped she would not have to do again. Another woman was thrilled to have found paid work as a bus driver. She would bring her infant son to work with her, and he would ride the bus all day long with her. Also, mothers carried out other care tasks on public transportation, where they sometimes spent over two hours per day. On buses, they slept, held children, and supervised homework.

Cell phones, too, helped in the labor of these women. When available and affordable, they provided a rare form of security and "crisis management" amid the fragmentation and chaos of life's work: "And I got to call the teacher, and then my sister because she's got to watch the kids because my babysitter isn't showing up. You know, it's always something. This phone saves me. It saves me" (Brenda, African American, female).

Religion, churches, and spirituality were prominent in Milwaukee women's lives, as spaces of community, resistance, subject formation, and material provision, and mechanisms of daily survival (see also Isoke 2013). While I did not set out to inquire specifically about religion, church, or faith, subjects frequently spoke about church and God during interviews. The vast majority of my subjects attended a church. For them, church was a place to connect with people, resist power impositions, seek advice, and practice their spirituality. In many cases, churches also provided material support to women. "In bad times, I get meals from church. . . . I even got help for my baby—a crib and clothes," described one interviewee.

Churches were entities of political and community resistance and connection. They were often "homeplaces," or autonomous spaces for relationship building between black people that foster hope, leadership capacity, and a strong, stable, and positive sense of self-identity (see hooks 1990; Isoke 2013). The women I interviewed connected with friends and neighbors and received support. Sermons often critiqued broader power relations surrounding African American communities, and many churches engaged in direct policy advocacy and activism in Milwaukee. As discussed in chapter 7, I observed church pastors sitting on the floor in crowded meetings in City Hall demanding that officials commit to building community and creating good jobs and affordable housing on city-owned land. Declaring "this land is our land," church leaders and the women I interviewed articulated alternative subjectivities and discourses different from dominant neoliberal ideologies. They challenged "market" discourse with "morality" discourse. If neoliberal rationalities configure human beings exhaustively as market actors, as scholar Wendy Brown argues (2015, 31), then many of the spiritual spaces and practices in black churches challenge or operate outside this dominance.

In other cases, for my interviewees spirituality and prayer were forms of getting by and explaining fractured worlds to themselves and their children. "It must be God's will," my interviewees might say if they lost a job or lost housing, and their church leaders at times echoed similar sentiments. This points to complex issues related to institutional spaces of interpellation and resistance, and neoliberal practices and subjectivities. As discussed elsewhere in this book, some churches materially benefitted from the rescaling and privatization of social services. Such churches were eager to deliver services but also to secure funds by, for example, managing welfare reform programs. Some articulated or enforced "neoliberal" tendencies toward self-management and depoliticization, occasionally framing political marginalization or misfortune as "God's will." I interviewed several activists who argued that this approach kept interviewees and institutions from challenging the actions and choices of humanity. Masculine power structures were also evident in many religious spaces, as touched on in chapter 7.

Regardless, I observed prayer, religion, and spiritual subjectivities as tangible and forceful, if immaterial and "otherworldly" (see Isoke 2013). These topics would transform the faces of interviewees as they spoke, and they considered them as essential as the roof that sometimes was over their heads. My interviewees sometimes indicated that God and prayer seemed to be the only reliable constants in their lives: "I just pray to God that I can get up in the morning. . . . I pray for my babies and that I can take care of them and that I can keep going. . . . I pray for everything" (Tanya, African American, female). As I suggested above, it was also a motivating force for structured political activism and everyday resistance.

Embodied Social Reproduction

Another way to understand the materiality of women's lives and labors is through the concept of embodiment. In recent years, feminist and antiracist feminist scholarship has explored bodies and embodiment as a critical component of life and political experience, but this scholarship has limited interface with social reproduction studies (see Meehan and Strauss 2015). Yet, social reproduction is an embodied and multiscalar experience, as my interactions with interviewees made clear.

For women, social reproduction might involve an expanded abdomen and the extreme exhaustion of pregnancy; the flares of anger and irritation at children that reach deep into one's chest and then gradually settle into a pounding headache; the palpitations in one's heart when receiving the first hug of the day; the submission of one's body to menial labor or sex in order to pay for heat to stop the shivering of oneself and family members in a cold apartment; the heaving of one's elderly mother off of the bed to help her to the bathroom; the gripping of a sign that says "our lives matter."

Nearly all of my interviewees had experienced bodily abuse, assault, and trauma, carried out by family members, boyfriends, police officers, pimps, or strangers. This does not include the trauma of ongoing state violence and witnessing violence in their neighborhood. Recent research shows that gendered violence is very common, affecting up to one in three women, regardless of race or income. In recent years, black women have been killed by intimate partners at four times the rate of white women. Moreover, black women who are young, do not live with their intimate partner, reside in low-income urban areas, and rely on government assistance are particularly vulnerable to physical and emotional abuse (see Richie 2012). This kind of trauma affects the body in immediate and direct ways (e.g., broken bones). Crucially, it also produces systemically poor physical and emotional health and coping behaviors (e.g., panic attacks, autoimmune disease, and substance abuse) that seeps into paid and unpaid labor (Reading 2006). In fact, women who have been raped by a household member are ten times more likely than others to abuse illegal substances or alcohol (Richie 2012).

In addition, studies have shown how poor, racialized bodies experience injustice, discrimination, and related poor health. For example, perceptions of racial discrimination have been correlated with higher blood pressure, anxiety, and depression and lower birth rates for pregnant mothers (Collins et al. 2004; Williams, Neighbors, and Jackson 2008). Health problems such as diabetes and obesity are common among inner-city African American populations, as is mortality more generally. Furthermore, poor and racialized communities are unevenly subject to environmental toxins at work and at home, such as pollutants from coal plants or lead in old buildings—the latter true for many of my interviewees. The dynamics and complexities of such bodily experiences and inequalities are not well understood, although discrimination and unequal access to resources are an important part of the story.

An emphasis on the body reminds us how sometimes only a theoretical veil separates production and reproduction: the same person toils on the fast-food line and helps her children with homework, the same splitting headache joining the two moments. And of course, ill and abused bodies do not easily carry out labor. This also reminds us that bodies are sites of resistance. This resistance might not be only collective action, but also bodily sacrifices that are made in order to protect oneself, and create, nurture, and reproduce political space (see Klodawsky 2009). As Isoke (2013) and others have argued, black women's resistance is often articulated affectively through discourses of care, belonging, emotion, and relationality rather than through logic, objectivity, and rationality (also see Hill Collins 2000a; hooks 2000).

My research subjects' labors, lives, and bodies were shaped by illness. Many of the women whom I interviewed lived with significant pain and disease. Arthritis, diabetes, breast cancer, and a host of other health problems plagued them. One woman moved only with a walker, slowly and methodically. She could not navigate stairs nor pick up her crying three-year-old. Another woman had posttraumatic stress disorder from childhood abuse and suffered severe panic attacks: "I take medicine but when it happens there is nothing I can do. I can't even leave the house sometimes. My kids have seen it. I can't keep a job, either" (Mary, African American, female). Studies suggest that the poor health of my interviewees is reflected in the overall population of w-2 participants, 40 percent of whom report mental health problems and 20 percent of whom have a disability (Courtney and Dworsky 2006).

Many of my interviewees were also caregivers to ill children. In Milwaukee and elsewhere, poor children have significantly more health problems than nonpoor children. They have higher rates of asthma, developmental delays, and lead poisoning, for example. They also have higher rates of hospital admissions, disability days, and death (Milwaukee Center for Urban Health 2010; Wood 2003). One woman whom I interviewed spoke of her child's inhaler (he had severe asthma) as an object without which she would never leave her home—it was her lifeline in the most literal sense. "Watching him work so hard to breathe and not knowing if something is going to happen to him . . . it kills me, it kills me every single day." Another mother talked about her son's struggle with juvenile diabetes, and many talked of learning disabilities and struggles at school. In my observations, the illnesses of the children seemed to affect the physicality of the mothers. They exhaled in shallow breaths and hunched over as if a weight hung around their neck when they spoke about their children and their associated worries.

Interviewees also talked of the physical and emotional labor involved in caring for sick children—physically subduing tantrums in emotionally impaired children, living with fear of forgetting an important medical device, visiting hospitals and health clinics and schools whenever possible. Hours and days spent waiting at clinics. Ultimately, women often forwent important medications and treatment for themselves and their children. They did this because they were overwhelmed with responsibilities, there were limited health care facilities, and they lacked the time and financial resources. They were also always afraid of the possibility of losing jobs or being sanctioned when their child's illness interrupted work. This fear was present even when women lost someone they loved to death, an experience far too common for my interviewees: "I mean out of that question alone I got one lady that I asked what's the worst thing that's ever happened to you? And she said that her daughter got shot in the head. And that cut her off from the system because she didn't feel well enough that after her three days of bereavement they wanted her to come back to her csj job. And she was like—you can't. You just can't do that" (Annette, African American, female). In fact, morbidity and violence loomed large. The trauma and depression that accompanied the loss of children and family members shortened and impaired my interviewees' lives. Morbidity was linked in some cases to the illnesses described earlier, but also to direct violence in cities that pursued racist, sexist, neoliberal politics. Interviewees had witnessed violence as children and had been abused as children and women. They knew young infants who had died and had relatives and children who had been subject to gang and other neighborhood violence.

Underpinning these experiences was the sense among my interviewees that the state and other people cared little about the African American population in Milwaukee. As one interviewee told me, "They left the city because of our children. And now they want to come back. And they don't care if our children are sick or dying. It seems they just want us out of the way" (Audra, African American, female).

These direct and discursive experiences of neoliberalism, racism, violence, sexism, poverty, abandonment, and death were burdens literally "carried" and "resisted" in the bodies of my research subjects. In some cases, this happened through brutal violence and indifference. In other cases, the chronic stress of trauma, racism, and poverty, coupled with insufficient supports, state violence, and austerity, produced subtle and cumulative bodily burdens. Babies were born with low birth weights and related health problems; children and mothers were depressed and untreated; poor ventilation led to asthma; and immune systems that are depressed led to stroke, diabetes, cancer, and other chronic diseases (see Conroy, Sandel, and Zuckerman 2010).

In spite of such experiences, the women whom I interviewed practiced embodied resistance and rejected dominant values and neoliberal subjectivities, confounding state officials and disrupting some of the scholarship on neoliberalism. They confronted police officers who harassed their children. They gave hard-earned money to neighbors or homeless people and shared food stamps. My interviewees expressed apathy and resistance to neoliberal narratives about self-reliance, work, choice, market behaviors, and "good" motherhood (see Brown 2015; Sparke 2013). Their perspectives are better understood through black feminism, which pays attention to the historical contradictions, dilemmas, and subjectivities of black women and black motherhood. They relied on each other for community care and support and nurtured one another's children as needed. They creatively depended on material and immaterial resources to survive and push back against various power relations. They articulated values of connection, belonging, human life, care, and autonomy—not neoliberal versions, but visions of self-sufficient and caring black neighborhoods and communities (see hooks 2000; Isoke 2013; McKittrick 2011).

As I discuss in chapter 7, some of these women were active in a campaign for a community benefits agreement, larger feminist and antiracist campaigns, and a support network for low-income women. In some cases, they testified at local or state hearings, helped organize neighborhoods, or worked on political and labor campaigns. Similar to the respondents in Isoke's (2013, 4) book on urban black women and activism in Newark, the women in my study created political subjectivities that "re-imagine(d) the role of the citizen subject in relation to the political system" and made "space for caring, impassioned, affective, volatile, and socially unfettered subjects whose motivations are often otherworldly."

Conclusion

The narratives of low-income African American women provided insights into everyday life and social reproduction in Milwaukee, which are connected to urban governance and broader intersecting power relations. This chapter began with the theme of amplification. My interviewees experienced "intensified" lives and labor, stalked by racism, sexism, violence, poverty, and neoliberalism. These amplifications were embedded in racialized difference, where poor black women are more likely than white women to experience poverty, die from intimate violence, lose children to death or illness, and suffer severe health problems. While some scholars would pin such poverty and precarity solely to neoliberalism, the daily lives of my interviewees painted a more complicated picture. Their lives were shaped by sustained and intersecting exclusions and dominations, and their own decisions, practices, and strategies of resistance. In a racist culture, African American women continue to be represented as the "other," marginalized in social and economic spaces. As women, they are sometimes subject to misogyny, male power, and secondary status in social and economic arenas. Amid these relations, the African American women whom I interviewed present sustained critiques and alternative subjectivities.

But amplification also means to make louder or more salient. This chapter makes more audible the voices and subjectivities of my interviewees and the social reproduction of communities and cities. Social reproduction as a concept gives us a language by which we can connect the common tasks and the associated emotions that make one human and vulnerable: the feeding of newborn babies, the gathering of neighbors for a common purpose, the grieving over a loved one who has been lost.

While, of course, this awareness of shared vulnerability and labor is not sufficient grounds for ethical action, as Judith Butler (2006) argues, it is, nonetheless, a contrasting language amid the anomie of supposedly disembodied, rational capitalism and governance. It is tangibly unjust that one mother might send her child (a recreational drug user) off to college while another visits her son (also a recreational drug user) in prison. As a theme, social reproduction attunes us to such injustices and might unite disparate activist and policy efforts. For this to be true, however, we need to keep returning to, understanding, and challenging the multiple forms of differentiation and violence that shape social reproduction.

With this in mind, I turn to a third meaning of amplification—to expand or intensify understanding through deeper analysis. Here, I suggest that social reproduction theories should be unhinged from narrow Marxist frames and would benefit from further conversation with black and antiracist feminism and other approaches. Social reproduction and its relationship to neoliberalism and other power relations needs further theoretical and empirical probing. Scholars, including myself, have critiqued the state's abdication of social reproduction as a key dynamic of neoliberalization in Milwaukee and beyond. Yet, we have not fully nuanced this argument to account for historical continuities and racialized differentiation. As chapter 5 showed, the city invested in the reproduction of elites through new urbanist developments and creative-class endeavors. However, government support for social reproduction in Milwaukee and elsewhere was rarely generous to African Americans prior to this period of neoliberalization, and it recently abandoned my interviewees even as it saturated their spaces of social reproduction. Such differences and intensifications were and are produced through intersecting inequalities that are not temporally disconnected, but cumulative. In other words, the same communities and individuals have been affected not just by the recent round of policies described as neoliberal, but also by slavery, Jim Crow, white flight, housing, segregation, disinvestment, and more recent rounds of school restructuring. Gendered inequalities have also stalked these women, who spoke to me about traumas of intimate and state violence and disregard, perpetrated by men, police, and institutions. My interviewees made connections among these different forms of historic and contemporary violence as a politics of memory and resistance and refused to render them normal or invisible.[6]

Power relations and resistance come in labyrinthine and subtle shades, some colored neoliberal, some less so. Research demonstrates how racism, family abuse, and trauma, for example, tenaciously take hold of children's bodies. This means that political-economic "path dependencies" do not operate in isolation and are not the only ones of concern. We need carefully traced explorations of the multiple and compounding material-discursive power relations that situate everyday life and labor in cities like Milwaukee. We need these narratives to be articulated in conversation with those that encounter and resist them with their bodies, through memory and the creation of alternative spaces and subjectivities, and through shared nurturing and collective action.

CHAPTER SEVEN

"This Land Is Our Land"

Race, Gender, Neoliberalism, and Contested Urban Politics

> We believe the beauty of a [development] project is measured not only by the
> structures and streets it builds but also by the lives it enhances. . . . The quality of
> jobs, environment, and neighborhood services ought to drive the development at
> least as much as the character of buildings, landscapes and trendy businesses.
>
> **GOOD JOBS AND LIVABLE NEIGHBORHOODS COALITION BROCHURE, 2004A**

In early 2000, the Milwaukee government announced plans to remove an underused freeway spur in downtown. A visual eyesore, it was starkly reminiscent of decades of freeway development decried by Mayor Norquist and other proponents of new urbanism. The removal of the freeway made available a sixty-four-acre parcel of land in downtown Milwaukee, known as the Park East Corridor. The Park East Redevelopment Plan was drafted, and in 2005 the city announced plans to invest nearly twenty million dollars into the dismantling of the freeway, infrastructure improvements, and subsidies (City of Milwaukee Resolution introduced February 2005).[1] Milwaukee's leading developers also had ambitions; one would invest seventy-five to ninety million dollars in apartments, condos, and neighborhood retail space (Daykin 2002).

The scope, location, investment resources, and anticipated revenue of the Park East Corridor generated excitement in Milwaukee. City leaders described the area as a "catalyst" for downtown development that would inspire confidence in the market and bolster "unprecedented growth and revitalization of downtown."[2] Such hyperbolic claims are typical in contemporary neoliberal development projects in U.S. cities. A group of community-based organizations in Milwaukee, however, mobilized to present a different imaginary for the Park East Corridor. Eventually called the Good Jobs and Livable Neighborhoods Coalition, they saw a unique opportunity in Park East to create economic opportunities for city residents, to reassert the value of the public good, and to foster a diverse downtown community that affirmed the progressive values of Milwaukee while challenging its unequal present.[3]

The announcement of the Park East Redevelopment Plan and the contestations that ensued both reflected and refuted Milwaukee's uneven neoliberal trajectory. Elite and exclusive politics run deep in Milwaukee, as do feminist, antiracist, and social justice impulses. Raced, gendered, neoliberal, and resistance efforts were bound up with one another as activists and politicians envisioned different futures for the city, deferred to markets and often masculinities, and wrestled with inequalities that persisted in both mainstream and progressive politics.

To understand the context of community organizing and the emergence of the progressive coalition that challenged the Park East Development, it is useful to look back to the time of Norquist's election. As suggested earlier, the late 1980s represented a leadership change in Milwaukee and the deepening of neoliberal politics locally and nationally. Milwaukee activists worked in creative collaborations to challenge these politics but with serious frustration. Several inner-city churches formed a coalition focused on racial and social justice. Feminist organizations joined with unions and other organizations to contest welfare reform, lobby for family leave and sick pay, support progressive economic development, and challenge racial and gender injustices. Milwaukee's labor unions continued to be forces for change and became increasingly oriented to the community. Progressive collaborations influenced individual urban development projects through lobbying and protests, forcing hotel developers to sign agreements with employee unions, for example. In addition, over seven thousand Milwaukee residents marched to secure prevailing wages and jobs for minorities in the construction of the Milwaukee Convention Center.

In the 1990s, the broadly scoped Campaign for Sustainable Milwaukee, composed of community organizations, universities, research organizations, labor associations, and businesses, was active. This campaign articulated an inclusive vision of social justice, helped sponsor a movement for living wages and other activist efforts, and created several business-community partnerships oriented toward improving jobs and economic opportunities for inner-city residents. It did not produce a sustained, transformational grassroots movement, and one interviewee argued that the Greater Milwaukee Committee "co-opted what was a progressive effort and it became sort of a training initiative as opposed to an activist movement" (academic, white, male). Meanwhile, raced and gendered poverty and elite development continued unabated.

Thus, in spite of several victories and unique collaborations, progressive, feminist, and antiracist influence on urban development and equity was neither systemic nor sustained in Milwaukee's recent past. Even before Mayor Norquist was elected in 1988, the progressive movement was "quiescent, dispirited and kind of demobilized" after dealing with many of the social service cuts in the 1980s, according to one community leader. When Mayor Norquist presented himself as a liberal, even "socialist," mayor,[4] the progressive community was slow to react to a different reality, according to one Milwaukee scholar:

> Norquist made some rhetorical flourishes that would sound vaguely leftish and anticorporate. So I think some of the disconnect between the reality of his ata-vistic market oriented policies and his obvious neoliberalism and the perception was sort of a historical lag in those social relationships. My sense is that eroded as his tenure as mayor went on. His first term there was a lot of "whoa—what is he doing?" And a lot of the community organizations that we spoke to were like "oh, he needs to establish with the business community, but he's really our guy." (academic, white, male)

A historian of Milwaukee also described this conversion by John Norquist: "There was a moment when John Norquist all of a sudden was no longer a progressive. I mean if you read his book, it's all about the market, about cities as natural marketplaces. But I'm not sure when that conversion happened" (historian, white, male).

By the time Norquist's positions became transparent, there were additional political and funding barriers to activism. For example, Mayor Norquist used his leadership to immure opponents. As a *Milwaukee Magazine* editorial explained, "most politicians reward their friends and punish their enemies. But [Norquist] seemed to be pushing this maxim to extremes" (*Milwaukee Magazine* 2008). In particular, the mayor used federal funds distributed to cities for community and social investments (community development block grant [CDBG] funds) "as a political hammer" to demobilize activists and discipline community organizations or to build a base of local influence (Bonds 2007; also see Rich 1993; Weir 1999). In an unconfirmed sexual harassment case against Mayor Norquist that the city settled for $375,000, the Hispanic victim argued that, among other threats, Norquist threatened to withhold block grant funds from community organizations that she supported or that might employ her (*Milwaukee Magazine* 2008). Organizations that hired community organizers with CDBG funds, pushed progressive agendas, or spoke out against the mayor risked losing the capital. For example, Michael Bonds (2007) showed a dramatic decline from 1988 to 1997 in CDBG funding for black community organizations for housing, community organizing, economic development, and other activities. For example, nearly 50 percent of economic development funds went to black organizations in 1988; in 1997, this had declined to 22 percent. Many of the organizations that saw this decline had been adversarial to the mayor. Bonds also found that black community organizations were more severely penalized and lost funding more routinely that did white community organizations that struggled with similar or more substantial performance or financial issues.[5]

Foundations, governments, and agencies were generally unwilling to fund activism and had strict accountability requirements. According to one feminist activist, "All they care about are outcomes. Funders want to know that you served this many people. . . . But we are trying to build a movement. You don't build a movement overnight" (activist, white, female). Community organizers pointed out that funds came with "placating" ties and technocratic measurement and service delivery requirements: "The truth is there's a lot of money that goes to big groups that have no [member] base. It's much harder for groups that do grassroots organizing to get that kind of support. . . . Our work is more radical. . . . It's about empowering people at the bottom" (activist, white, female).

Privatization and devolution of social programs were also critical parts of the Pavlovian (stimulus-response) funding landscape. The welfare-to-work program in Wisconsin (w-2), for example, allowed community organizations to compete for lucrative contracts to locally administer welfare benefits, monitor participants, and provide job training and placement. The same was true of other kinds of services and programs, such as educational privatization. Both education privatization and welfare reform efforts were partially funded and promoted by powerful conservative foundations that spent considerable money to shift public opinion and perhaps divide communities. In fact, ideological, practical, and economic conflicts surrounding privatized and semiprivatized schools divided the African American community. Many African American leaders viewed the historically racist and ineffective Milwaukee Public School system as flawed beyond repair and thus supported vouchers (see Pedroni 2005).[6] However, the Bradley Foundation, which lacked interest in broader concerns about race, equality, and education, elevated their school voucher campaign and intensified conflicts in the African American community. Churches, leaders, and organizations that worked on education and social justice were pitted against one another. As one Milwaukee pastor described, "It is so evident that [Republicans] are keeping the leaders divided so they don't come together to look at what is really happening." Because of school vouchers, "We have pastors and churches that don't even speak together, don't have fellowship together, or even now, talk against each other" (quoted in Miner 2002a). For example, the Bradley Foundation funded churches to run "charter" schools (independent and often privately run schools) and welfare reform programs. One church received over one million dollars from the foundation, increased its membership from forty to four thousand, and was praised as an exemplar by President George W. Bush (Bradley Foundation 2006).

The capacity for churches, black communities, and sometimes feminists to deliver education and social services was a mixed blessing. These organizations finally had some resources and autonomy. As one community leader suggested, "We've been fighting racism for so long in Milwaukee, and so if the chance comes up to get some resources for our community, then how do we turn that down? How can we think about turning that down?" (activist, African American, male). Organizations could now provide tailored, compassionate, and culturally appropriate programs, after years of critiquing the state's cold racist and patriarchal systems. Feminist-inspired programming often dramatically changed the life experiences for women oppressed by poverty and domestic violence. Feminist advocates shifted languages, policies, and programs within and outside of the state to reflect specific needs of different women, including gay women, minority women, and those balancing work with child care or experiencing sexual harassment at work. Safety and transportation needs of women in cities began to receive attention. Local politicians were able to create some jobs for their constituents.

Yet, nonprofit organizations and activists had substantially fewer resources than needed to deliver services in a climate of welfare state retreats and austerity (see Brodie 2007; University of Wisconsin–Milwaukee Center for Economic Development 2001; Walby 2011). They couldn't help the women pouring into health clinics and domestic violence shelters. They couldn't purchase or renovate enough housing to meet the needs of low-income families waiting for a place to live, and hospitals could not meet health needs.

In addition, many activist and protest endeavors were eventually co-opted or converted into training or social service initiatives. Organizational time was bound up in meeting the basic needs of individuals and communities, and it was much harder for groups to collaborate, to launch broader activist and informational campaigns, and to protest specific policies.[7] Rather than building a coherent political movement, community organizations "tended to their own projects in their own neighborhoods," according to one Milwaukee scholar. Organizational survival was often tied to funds and restrictions against community organizing, sometimes provided by conservative foundations. As one Milwaukee community activist described:

> We had been under this onslaught of organizing by the Bradley Foundation and the Heritage Foundation—sort of testing ground for both school vouchers and welfare. Systematically, we've seen that the huge amounts of foundation money that went in support of those two programs undermined the social justice traditions of both community organizations and churches. And to see that when a church got a charter school or a community organization became a w-2 (welfare reform) center—then their level of political activity dropped dramatically—or at least their engagement around a social justice agenda dropped dramatically. (activist, white, male)

Some evidence suggests that foundation efforts to undermine activism might have been intentional. For example, in 1997, the Bradley Foundation funded a ninety-four-thousand-dollar research project focused on the progressive movement in Milwaukee (Bradley Foundation 1997). In the late 1990s, when the progressive Campaign for Sustainable Milwaukee was collaborating with the Greater Milwaukee Committee to encourage better jobs and wages, the Bradley Foundation released articles stating that the "GMC has been duped" by a group of activists with "communist" and "Socialist leanings" (see Reynolds 2002).

Amid this climate, one elected leader decried the decline of vibrant feminist activism in Milwaukee by the late 1990s. She said, "what we have are a lot of social service agencies that are run by feminists and have some sort of feminist outlook" (cited in Boles 2001, 80). On one hand, it is important not to dismiss direct and tailored service provision and the integration of a "feminist outlook," or what some feminists have labeled an ethos of "working in and against the state" (Newman 2013). As career paths opened up within the state, feminists often transformed these agencies to be more gender sensitive, client centered, and attuned to critical feminist issues like gendered violence. I observed female heads of state and Milwaukee-based agencies host meetings with welfare-to-work participants, soliciting opinions about how to improve services. At other times, "feminist-sensitive" leaders and female and minority elected officials were able to stave off some of the harshest policies and reforms, ensuring, for example, that poor women receive child care vouchers (however insufficient) as part of welfare-to-work reforms. In a recent study, Reingold and Smith (2012) found females, Latino and black males, and especially Latino and black females mitigated the harshest welfare reforms during the time period while Norquist was in elected office. Furthermore, many grassroots and feminist endeavors persevered in Milwaukee, forging new alliances and using new strategies, and influencing the state's agenda via partnership and pressure (see Larner and Butler 2007).

Nonetheless, it is clear that feminist, black and antiracist, and social-justice-oriented movements suffered in Milwaukee during Norquist's reign and under neoliberalism. In addition to the reasons above, there was also a national reinvigoration of white masculinities and markets (with contradictions and disruptions). This invigoration took the form of discourses, policies, and practices and can be seen as reactive to female and minority power and rights acquired during the 1960s and 1970s.[8] Neoliberalism is only part of the story.[9] Susan Faludi (2006), Sylvia Bashevkin (1998), and others have described the cultural assault on feminism and associated rollback in women's rights in the 1980s: "Women were expert policy insiders who successfully lobbied, testified before congressional committees, wrote legislations, and influenced the wider public. It was just when they reached this point that the Reagan revolution came to town" (Bashevkin 1998, 35).

Strategically, political discourses and media caricatures framed, and continue to frame, feminists as radicals, declaring that equality had been achieved. Then politicians and the media (dominated by white men) cleverly blamed feminists for the effects of racist, patriarchal, and neoliberal policies. For example, they blamed "the women's movement for feminization of poverty, when legislature blocked one bill after another to improve child care, slashed billions of dollars in federal aid for children and related licensing standards for day care centers" (Faludi 2006, 14).

A similar, intertwined backlash occurred against civil rights movements. The popularity of "rights" discourses faded among the white population. Policies and discourse instead focused on a generic or "banal" multiculturalism and soft diversity policies.[10] Neoconservative, racist, and neoliberal agendas emphasized (differentiated forms of) personal and heteronormative family responsibility and success through the market.[11] They demonized an overbearing "nanny" state and caricatured feminist politics so much that the possibility of making claims based on gender or race vis-à-vis the state declined, making feminist organizing more difficult.[12] As I mentioned in chapter 2, a study found that the primary reason that Americans opposed welfare was racist sentiment (Gilens 1995). Similarly, one poll in the 1980s showed the vast majority of men did not support women's rights or a women's movement, as they thought women had already gained enough (Faludi 2006, 76). Importantly, these processes do not simply reflect an economic colonization of the social realm.

Intersectional and nefarious policy formations and ideologies, related reluctance among women to be seen as complainers or radicals, and false but ubiquitous beliefs that equality has been achieved have contributed to what Roth (2004) called a "structural fading" and "marginalization" of feminist politics in the United States. Similarly, Carolyn Whitzman (2007) described engaging in long-term feminist urban politics in North America as "the loneliness of a long distance runner."[13]

The work of Sara Ahmed (2010), a race and cultural studies scholar, offers further insights into such hostilities. In a blistering critique of happiness as a cultural pursuit, she argues that happiness and consent have historically relied on and silenced marginalized bodies, including women. For example, middle-class women's entry into the workforce and related feelings of pleasure or independence often rely on the underpaid labor of women of color. A feminist killjoy, then, is one who exposes sexism, heterosexism, racism, and other power practices only to be criticized for stealing happiness. Paradoxically, as Faludi (2006) and Braithwaite (2004) suggest, feminists' unhappiness is also construed as a result of achieving the equality they wanted (e.g., having it all). A backlash blames feminism for producing women's misery. All of these factors helped displace genuine feminist critique and marginalized but not erased feminism, antiracist activism, and other kinds of social justice endeavors.

In fact, diminished support and hostility toward civil rights and antiracist efforts were evident in the 1980s (e.g., Gilens 1995; Mink 1990; Williams 1995) and have continued nearly unabated into the 2000s, deepened by the events of September 11, 2001, and the rise of drug wars and the racialized prison-industrial complex.[14] Neoliberal policies that reduced state investments in equity efforts like welfare, school integration, or affirmative action helped ensure nonwhite populations and women (as a group) did not gain substantive economic or political power. Neoliberal intensifying shifts of resources toward markets also promote white men, whose dominance in local and global capitalism is relatively secure (Campbell 2014; Connell 2013; Runyan and Peterson 2013; Walby 2011). In 2011, while over 50 percent of African American female workers in Milwaukee earned less than twenty-five thousand dollars per year, the CEOs of Milwaukee's four largest companies (all male) received over thirty million in compensation. In 1990, a parallel group of CEOs (also male) received nearly five million (Levine 2013a). These numbers do not include stock options. Specific discourses around autonomy, freedom through markets, and self-sufficiency further ensconce this dominance and give those associated with privileged masculinity credit for "earning" it (see chapters 2 and 3).

Other dimensions of raced, gendered, and neoliberal politics dampened activism in Milwaukee, especially among vulnerable populations. As shown in chapter 6, women in the welfare-to-work program could lose benefits for missed work or other infractions, and the threat of losing their children to foster care loomed large. The sanctioning environment combined with broader local and national disciplining discourses and the penal state to divide communities and sometimes squelch activism among African Americans, including women.[15] On some occasions, discourses of "individual success and responsibility" were taken up by some community members with divisive effects, according to my observations. One interviewee's comments embodied this approach: "I do talk to the ladies in my community and I tell them, I say if you're truly seeking to better yourself in life or do something for yourself, you know. . . . You, yourself as an individual have to be willing. A lot of us are not willing to get up out the bed at seven in the morning" (low-income resident, African American, female). This quote articulates neoliberal conceptions of individual responsibility that, when combined with neoliberal and welfare reform materialities, at times interfered with notions of collectivity and solidarity important to feminist, antiracist, and antineoliberal organizations in Milwaukee. Such proclamations shifted politics and responsibility for inequalities toward households (Isoke 2011). Reflecting these discourses, conservative foundation campaigns, and perhaps a real desire for change, a black opinion survey in Milwaukee in 1995 found that most respondents supported "individual responsibility" or quid pro quo within the welfare program in 1995. They also supported taking money out of paychecks for fathers who refused to make child care payments (White 1995), a project that has had some support among feminists. However, these respondents were either opposed to or ambivalent about other "punitive" parts of the welfare project, such as denying benefits based on out-of-wedlock birth or removing children from homes of "unfit parents."

By 2004, when I was conducting my research, the harsh realities of welfare reform were clear to many African Americans in Milwaukee. They were strongly opposed to the punitive nature of the program, its failure to improve living conditions or address poverty, and the lack and quality of jobs in the city. They were angry about historical injustices from slavery to segregation to incarceration.

However, collective action against these inequities was limited. Ongoing marginalization and punitive policies as described in chapter 6 affected the emotional, social, and physical well-being of many individuals, households, and communities. Survival under austerity was the ultimate task. Finding food and a roof to sleep under or cycling in and out of prison consumed the time of many poor African American women and men in Milwaukee and elsewhere. Others consciously chose a politics of the home rather than collective mobilization (see Isoke 2011; Morgan and Maskovsky 2003; Wilson 2009). In fact several studies have shown that raced and gendered neoliberal policies have impeded the organizing capacity of feminist and community organizations and often allies like labor unions, and have discouraged civic participation in many low-income Latino and black neighborhoods.[16]

In addition, some Milwaukee community organizations and individuals strategically embraced and/or benefitted from neoliberal policies. Kantola and Squires (2012) argue that many women's organizations have shifted from "state feminism" to "market feminism" to pursue their objectives, reflecting the reality of downsizing, offloading, and restructuring of the state. At the individual level, this might be seen as the exertion of subaltern agency in which marginalized individuals calculate and "make do" with opportunities available to them. For example, some African American women in Milwaukee supported school vouchers as a way to best serve their families' interests, even if they opposed marketization of schools and knew that neighborhoods suffered as local schools declined (see Pedroni 2005, 96). Several researchers have explored how community organizations adopted neoliberal terminologies and practices, with paradoxical or even perilous outcomes,[17] an issue I explore later in regard to the Park East case.

In summary, feminism, antiracism, and other forms of activism in Milwaukee were constrained by a punitive mayor who presented himself as a progressive, changing funding structures and powerful foundations, often divisive neoliberal policies and discourses, feminist and antiracist backlashes and politics, and amplified burdens and punitive policies especially for the poor, women, families, and communities of color. These uneven power relations worked in both contradictory and collusive ways. They also spawned resistance and a sense of urgency among marginalized populations. As one feminist activist argued, "Poor women of color have the most potential power. . . . They have the least to lose and therefore have the most at stake in the change that is to happen. They can't afford to stop fighting because there isn't anywhere else to go" (activist, white, female). However, raced, gendered, and neoliberal power relations made the collective terrain for such resistance much more difficult. There was not overwhelming political change in Milwaukee at this time.

However, activist and progressive projects persisted in Milwaukee, presenting alternative imaginaries related to everyday life and justice, achieving success on individual projects, transforming the state through direct participation, and sometimes adopting neoliberal practices and frames in order to pursue agendas.[18] Activists, including feminists, increasingly turned to collaborations to try to make an impact. Into this climate entered the Park East Development Plan and its contestation by a community coalition of feminists, labor unions, progressive African American churches, and others.

Community Contestation and the Park East Development: Different Imaginaries

The Park East Development Plan, as introduced by the Milwaukee government in 2000, reflected the imaginaries of primarily white male elites intent on market-centric development and a downtown-based creative class. The project fit evenly with neoliberal policies and Milwaukee's history of unequal and segregated spatial development. In spite of the constrained terrain for community organizing described above, a coalition of Milwaukee activists and organizations responded, eventually naming themselves the Good Jobs and Livable Neighborhoods Coalition. They viewed the Park East Development Plan as an affront to equity and a neoliberal inscription of space. In a prolonged battle between activists and urban elites (that extended beyond what is captured here), alternative but intertwined imaginaries were presented, and efforts for justice were troubled by neoliberal, racist, and sexist impulses on both sides.

The city's vision for Park East came through in interviews, public testimonies, and the Park East Development Plan document.[19] With some nuance, the plan emphasized new urbanist design principles and private development to increase the tax base and visually enhance downtown Milwaukee. The invoked subjects of the new spaces were the creative class, retired empty-nesters, and other elites. These emphases largely accorded with neoliberal practices in other cities and Milwaukee's historical patterns of elite-led development.[20] Absent in the plan was commentary about inclusion, social reproduction, ethics of care, connection, or justice, although some of these issues received attention when the community coalition raised them at public meetings. The Park East Development Plan was prepared in large part by private developers, with input and guidance from the Department of City Development. Coinciding with the composition of urban elites and developers, fewer than one-third were minorities or women. The plan included typical neoliberal and new urbanist language about efficient, economical, and productive use/reuse of land. It prescribed precise window placement and aesthetics like "defined street edges and corners." The plan restricted what types of activities were allowed to occur at the street level in structures built in the Park East area. Reception areas, lobbies, and cafeterias were allowed, but individual offices, which might need closed blinds, were not (HNTB Corporation and Planning & Design Institute 2003).

This Park East Development Plan and the entailed regulations reflected a common paradox in purportedly neoliberal practice. That is, in a supposedly "free market" and "reduced government" regime, the state actually regulates and intervenes, for example, with subsidies and design and code requirements.[21] The plan did not mention human and economic development or social reproduction issues. While this omission can be partly attributed to the nature of development plans, the silence was also reflected in practice, as a Milwaukee activist argued:

> I noticed an article in the newspaper in December 2002 that in City Hall rotunda there was going to be a model of Park East Development Plan and there were going to be people from DCD [Department of City Development] there to talk about it . . . so I asked him "what kinds of jobs are going to be involved?" He looked at me like I was from Mars and said "that is really not what we do." Well, I just couldn't believe that was what the DCD's position on that question was. They hadn't contemplated it. That they didn't think that the fact that the city was investing all of this money in infrastructure at least and likely some other money and subsidies for individual development as well that there wouldn't be some strategic view about what sorts of jobs should be created down there. (activist, white, male)

When the Good Jobs and Livable Neighborhoods Coalition raised these concerns and stalled the redevelopment plan, the city resisted adding to the plan regulations related to housing, social reproduction, and jobs. The city attorney, at the request of the Department of City Development, issued a written opinion that "these community benefits could not legally be included in a formal redevelopment plan," a position that was contested by the coalition and eventually retracted by the city attorney's office (Memorandum from the Office of City Attorney to Julie Penman; Memorandum from Alyssa Talanker).

The Park East Development Plan and city leaders emphasized unencumbered, market-led development. One elected official suggested that the city should "just let the market force just kind of takeover, let the market dictate what should be done on this property."[22] City leaders conveyed a sense of powerlessness in the face of competition and seemingly inevitable capitalist forces: "We are not Los Angeles; we are not a high-growth city. We've lost population and tax base and we need to provide incentives for development, and some-times that means subsidies when we're competing with other cities to lure busi-ness, encourage parking, and developers like [name], quite honestly. . . . If we place these restrictions and mandates on this development opportunity, there is a significant risk that developers will not be able to make deals work—as [developer] testified, the land will lie fallow for many years."[23]

This quote aptly illustrates the development mentality that marked Milwau-kee. Job creation and racial and other inequities might be dealt with, but only after development occurred. This approach and surrounding rhetoric about competition were laden with fear and insecurity. As urban geographer David Wilson (2009) has argued, many cities deploy the discourses of fear of global-ization and competition to "assist their restructuring ambitions" and serve cap-italist needs. In Milwaukee, local and regional threats loomed larger than global competition, but served the same market-justification function: "[Y]ou know you're competing as regions and in many respects it's not just Milwaukee ver-sus Chicago versus Indianapolis/Minneapolis . . . but a greater Milwaukee area too. . . . I'm in favor of higher wages as much as possible for these jobs, but to the point where we may provide a hindrance and encourage a developer to look at an alternative location because we drive up the cost here, I don't think that that's in the best interest of the city of Milwaukee" (elected official, white, male).

Developers amplified the discourse of competition, arguing that wage and housing restrictions would "render the developments not feasible." One devel-oper stated, "the returns in Milwaukee are substantially less than you would receive in other marketplaces. Milwaukee is rated the thirty-eighth best apart-ment market in the United States." Importantly, this developer did not have development projects in other cities, but was using the comparison in a disci-plinary way. Presenting himself as a risk taker and a benevolent, place-based de-veloper with little profit margin, he continued, "We don't have investors flocking into Milwaukee and we don't have outside developers coming into Milwaukee on a regular basis, because the returns are not enough to justify investment."[24] Such testimonies moved the City's Comptroller Office to write a letter in oppo-sition to the community benefits agreement. Citing cost estimates provided by developers, he wrote, "my primary concern is the ordinance's adverse impact on development. . . . Projects will certainly be lost to other communities."[25]

In fact, there was insufficient evidence to suggest this loss would occur. Many developers continued with construction and marketing plans during the Park East debate, apparently anticipating positive returns. More than one developer testified that they *would* continue to work on their developments, but that re-strictions would make it cumbersome: "I think any mandate on a piece of dirt makes it more difficult by definition. Is it unobtainable? Of course not. Are there market deals going to be done in this market, in this area? *Of course . . . that's the way I look at it. I'm going to do everything I can no matter whatever happens. I'm*

*not going to walk away and not try to do deals here. I'm going to try to get deals
done. No doubt about it. And [prominent developer] is not going to walk away."*[26]

Similar statements were made privately to elected officials, my interviews
revealed. The fact that city leaders fought the community benefits agreement
even when developers indicated they would develop in spite of restrictions
demonstrates in part how disciplinary neoliberal imaginaries function and are
reproduced (see, for example, Fairclough 2002; Gill 1995). There was a preemp-
tive subjugation to the "market," or at least to developers, even when actions and
words indicated it was perhaps unwarranted. Social theorist Stephen Gill (1995,
420) describes disciplinary neoliberalism as the ability of capital to promote
fear, uniformity, and obedience, and to deny alternatives. In Milwaukee, city
leadership was seemingly being disciplined by market rationalities and capital
and/or exerting neoliberal disciplinary techniques on community members
who expressed their aspirations for participation and justice. Developers and
media articles preyed on fears, arguing that Park East would become a "wasteland" and that Milwaukee needed the risk, competition, and masculinity that
developers could offer.

The Community Benefits Agreement: An Alternative Sociospatial Imaginary

The Good Jobs and Livable Neighborhoods Coalition opposed the city's vision
for Park East and its apparent indifference to social needs and everyday life
(e.g., Leitner, Peck, and Sheppard 2007).[27] In December 2002, a group of organizations prevented the city's Park East Development Plan from being passed
through the Common Council. After this success, the Good Jobs and Livable
Neighborhoods Coalition of twenty-five nonprofit organizations formed. Attuned to progressive movements in cities like Los Angeles, the coalition pursued
a popular community benefits agreement strategy. Unlike previous community
benefits agreement that had been between developers and the community, this
was the first in the country attached to redevelopment legislation.

The symbolic and physical space of the Park East project amid persistent
social inequality mobilized community members. One activist described a
monthly meeting of African American leaders where the Park East progressive
coalition "created a huge amount of energy because people had been frustrated
by these issues for so long and there had not been a good way to package this
before." Another activist said, "It really was the power of how simple this is. . . .
Every place we went people were saying 'where have you been all of our lives'
because they are always talking about subsidies for this and how terrible they
are and this was reframing the discussion about subsidies and saying, 'why
should we be subsidizing these developers? If we are going to invest our tax

dollars we should see a better investment for our community." That was liberat- ing to people" (activist, African American, male).

Amid multiple power relations and compounding disparities, the concreti- zation of the city's neoliberal vision via the Park East Development Plan com- pelled citizens to act. Some scholars have argued that when neoliberalism is spatialized (rather than theoretical), it may be most vulnerable to resistance. In fact, the city's plan for Park East galled coalition members: "Why would you deliberately make a plan that would create a bifurcated section of the city when you have a chance to start from scratch and build something in a deliberate way? This a huge swath of downtown that can be developed and you're really saying that all you want to do is make a gold coast of condos and you're all right with that? . . . It is going to be racially skewed. . . . Why do you think that is okay?" (activist, white, female).

The Good Jobs and Livable Neighborhoods Coalition's vision for Park East was not simply an antineoliberal one. Like many resistance projects, it drew on a number of alternative imaginaries and challenged a range of historical and contemporary exclusions and power relations in Milwaukee (see Larner and Butler 2007; Leitner, Peck, and Sheppard 2007). Broadly, it articulated feminist values such as collectivity, care, and equity, but it did not use words like "femi- nism" or specifically pay attention to "gender." The proposed community ben- efits agreement included six areas: good jobs, affordable housing, local hiring and training, environmental issues, community involvement/accountability, and community services including child care. It argued for extensive commu- nity involvement in economic development, a regulatory role for the state, and opportunities that would especially benefit low-income racialized residents. According to the agreement, 25 percent of jobs in Park East would be reserved for disadvantaged or minority businesses, and 5 percent for women during con- struction. Furthermore, at least half of postconstruction jobs would have to go to low-income, local residents; these jobs would also pay a living wage and offer health benefits. Affordable housing requirements and linkage fees to subsidize child care for working parents in the development area were also outlined in the plan.[28]

Coalition members argued that development and tax-funded subsidies for private development should benefit the "public," including poor and disenfran- chised residents. They argued that infrastructure and design should not take precedence over people. They decried the legacy of spatial and social racial in- equality in Milwaukee and its seeming reproduction in the Park East Plan. As stated in the epigraph to this chapter, the coalition argued that a project should be assessed by not just its physical beauty (as implied by new urbanist prin- ciples) but how it would improve the daily lives of residents.

Many coalition members conceded that there were some attractive aspects of

popular new urbanist planning practices for the Park East area. This was particularly true among white, middle-class coalition members. Still, they were cautious about new urbanism, envisioning compromise and diversity in Park East:

> We do think that there is an opportunity here to create something for everyone. . . .
> It does feel like downtown is becoming an island for very wealthy people and that
> Park East could become that. . . . And you know on one hand we appreciate the
> need to increase the tax base in the city and that's important and we hope that
> comes from this. Um, on the other hand I think that the first dollar of increased
> property tax revenue is better than what it was when it was a highway so . . . yeah
> I think that we'd be excited about mixed use and that it's very inclusive. . . . Um,
> income-wise, racially, and different families. Um, so to us inclusivity is probably
> the key word. (activist, white, male)

Other coalition members suggested more radically that neoliberal and new urbanist strategies intensified racial segregation: "I think it's just another way to
segregate people, a group of people. I mean whether you know I've heard in
the past you know when the expressway went up or the freeway, that was also
a way of you know isolating people. And I just know that the whole downtown situation is another way . . . to draw a boundary" (activist, African American, female).

The Good Jobs and Livable Neighborhoods Coalition produced a series of
maps of the areas surrounding Park East showing the area as a demarcation
zone for race and income. To the west of the proposed development area, the
neighborhoods were dramatically African American and low-income in composition, with an average median income below twenty-five thousand dollars.
As such, Park East could become economically and racially diverse if affordable
housing were mandated in this area. But an unregulated Park East Development
Plan would amplify existing inequalities. They called on the city to "build a
bridge between the two Milwaukees, here and now."[29]

In fact, a working-class African American community had been destroyed
when the Park East freeway spur was originally built in the late 1960s. Yet there
was no effort to remedy it in the reimagining of Park East. "A community gets
moved out to build a highway and when that highway is gone, that same community is then told you're not welcome back here" (activist, white, male). The
coalition pointed out racial disparities in Park East and in the city of Milwaukee,
noting that "pastors and leaders would be driving around the city watching city
construction projects and not seeing people of color on those projects." These
disparities fueled the anger and passion of many activists, especially African
American church leaders (activist, African American, male).

Finally, the coalition's vision coalesced broadly around space, the public
good, and public resources, as illustrated in a protestor's sign: "This land is our

land." They also drew on messages of morality, persuading the city to "do what is just." They held prayer vigils in City Hall as a form of protest.

Tactics, Concessions, and Discourse: Gender and Race in the Battle for a Community Benefits Agreement

The clash over the community benefits agreement at the city level lasted for two years, as city officials attempted to pass an unrestricted plan and the coalition sought to stall and restructure the plan to include a community benefits agreement.[30] An early task force composed of developers and activists (appointed by the mayor) was unable to negotiate an agreement. The coalition then pressured elected officials through protests, prayer vigils, and public testimonies. Amid election season, several pieces of legislation related to a community benefits agreement failed to pass. In response, the coalition eventually scaled back its proposed agreement to make it more palatable and less potent.

Throughout the debates, discourses and practices highlighted the ascendant— or at least persistent—role of markets and privileged white masculinities in both mainstream and "resistance" urban politics. These were often complex and contradictory and included dominant market imaginaries and often the exclusion of feminism, gender, and social reproduction; deference to developers and masculinist subjectivities surrounding them; tight-knit relationships between city officials and urban elites; and internal raced and gendered exclusions within the coalition and broader urban governance.

DEFERENCE TO DEVELOPERS AND ELITE RELATIONSHIPS

In task force activities, meetings, and public events, the elite relationships among city officials, developers (all mostly male), and other elites were apparent, as was a general deference to developers. Even the small number of city officials who supported some regulations on developers insisted the regulations apply only once developers received five hundred thousand dollars in subsidies *above and beyond* "normal" subsidies. A city official clarified, "We can still do infrastructure improvement, roadways, streetscaping, sidewalks, street lighting, harp lights—all the amenities that we've provided for many projects in this city. We can still do river walks with public funds and not cross the five-hundred-thousand-dollar threshold."[31]

These comments revealed the eagerness of the city to subsidize development, and to avoid regulating developers. In this way, the city's development imperative seemed to override any free market imperative, as did perhaps their interest in maintaining good relationships with developers, many of whom were local. As I argued in chapter 5, the (masculinist) framing of design and development as the solution to Milwaukee's problems positioned developers as redemptive to the city. In testimonies, citizens, elected officials, and elites heaped lavish praise on developers, arguing that they "risked" much to help a city desperate for development. In one meeting, at least five testimonies commended one developer. He was described as "the leader in the rebirth in downtown development" and "a very, very good man."[32] In this way, the developers were depicted as an idealized, masculine neoliberal subject—risk taking, competitive, autonomous, capitalistic, and deserving of reward. A *Milwaukee Magazine* (2012) profile of a prominent Milwaukee developer exemplifies this well. Titled "He Built This City," the story mentions that when the developer was hesitant about taking on a new project, his wife asked, "Are you going to be my man?" Even more, the story leads with a tale of competition between the developer and a president of the local construction company. In a dispute over twenty-five thousand dollars in construction costs, one man challenged the other to a swim race. The developer, who had trained hard, was the victor, just as he was in securing millions in subsidies from the Milwaukee government and others, the article boasts.

The neoliberal paradox—that the developer's risks were subsidized by government and his rewards were privately reaped—is often invisible. Even more surprising, his demands for subsidies are seen as "manly," as earned through tenacious deal making. One of many, a citizen testified that the developer "took on Park East when nobody wanted it."[33] Another local business owner testified that developers willing to "take a risk" for Milwaukee should not have hiring regulations placed on them: "These guys have got to start somewhere, and why in the world can the developers that are taking this risk not have the opportunity to choose who they're going to hire?"[34] The developer had received over eight million dollars in direct remediation and aid for his Park East apartment development. Years later, he would secure another two million in aid and thirty-six million in low-interest loans and tax-exempt bonds (some supposed to help with unrelated floods). The media, city officials, and others continued to heap accolades on the developer and his creative efforts to access funds and get things done. The city, meanwhile, was still waiting in 2012. It was reportedly "hopeful" that property tax revenue would help pay back the thirty-seven-million-dollar debt the city accrued preparing the sixty-four-acre Park East area for development (*Milwaukee Magazine* 2012).

It is worthwhile to point out the contradictions and the relationships among constructions of risk, markets, and masculinities. Urban developers (nearly all male) in Milwaukee and elsewhere were commended for being aggressive, tenacious, independent, persistent risk takers. Conceptions of successful neoliberal development are based on this same rhetoric: cities that develop downtowns can compete; cities that compete win; cities have to be aggressive to win. Substantive research has shown that such characteristics are bound up with notions of masculinity and male power. The absence of women among developers and in city governance is perhaps telling, as studies show that women in corporations and government that exhibit aggressive qualities are often denigrated and disliked.[35] Thus, it seems the perceived masculinity of these developers compensated for the fact that they were asking the city for handouts. In gendered neoliberal discourses, a poor woman who accepted nine thousand dollars a year to pay for rent and food was deemed a "dependent welfare queen." A rich man who asked the city for ten million in subsidies and had the city "hoping" for tax revenue years later was an "independent hero" who was saving the city. Masculinity and money may work magic.

There are other occasions when the interplay among developer deference, elite relationships, and masculinist privilege was salient. For example, one newly elected female official described a meeting with a developer: "It was clear that he had expected me to go along with him. That he was used to getting his way. Like he thought just because I was a young woman that he was going to be able to bully me. And, then I had done my homework and I knew some stuff and he was, I don't know, surprised" (elected official, female).

The deference to developers affected policy making. For example, Department of City Development staff and city officials described their commitment to "educate" rather than "mandate" developers. The rhetoric and positions of the DCD aligned with developers more often than not; staff used developers' data to make arguments, and the city attorney argued against mandates on developers. Even the few city officials who favored a community benefits agreement were careful to venerate developers. Coalition members described feeling like "outsiders" amid this climate. One coalition member described a meeting in which the DCD director and a prominent developer walked into the meeting "arm in arm," a closeness I also observed among urban elites. In interviews, coalition members described DCD staff as adversarial and even hostile to them. This construction of community members as interlocutors in urban development was not incidental, accidental, or unique to Milwaukee but a product of the city's practices and broader neoliberal ideologies and masculinist practices that framed the private sector as the natural executor of development and exclude a range of citizens from decision making.[36]

MARKET TRICKS

Newspaper editorials and City Council debates suggested that "good citizenship" in Milwaukee was contingent on participation and allegiance to the market. In meetings and during testimonies, people constantly referred to and deferred to the market (i.e., its importance, its viability, or its potential failure in certain instances).[37] It was hard for the coalition to challenge these dominant subjectivities, so they attempted to expose contradictions. That is, once the coalition realized there was limited support for the community benefits agreement, they worked with elected officials to pass an agreement that applied only in the case of "market failure," defined as subsidies over half a million dollars. One elected official described his position: "I expect the market to work. And when the market works, it means that the government's not involved and we don't subsidize. And if we don't subsidize, none of these restrictions apply."[38]

The coalition, then, could make only partial critiques of the market. For example, coalition members and some supportive elected officials argued that the market did not "naturally" create jobs for minority (nonwhite) workers. One activist testified, "The private market is just not doing it. . . . If it's left to the marketplace, as we're urged to do, the status quo will essentially be business as usual; predominantly majority workers working for the same old contractors and the same old developers and no real change in social and economic conditions in many neighborhoods of our city."[39] The coalition also noted that subsidies reflect a market failure: "The problem is that the free market has not been working for people in our community. As has been pointed out, one, we've had hundreds of millions of dollars of subsidies for downtown projects, so we already have the free market being impacted by those subsidies. And in spite of those subsidies . . . there have been very few good jobs created, and for the good jobs that have been created, they've gone to people that don't live in the city of Milwaukee."[40]

In arguing that the market was not benefiting citizens of Milwaukee, progressives asserted a role for regulatory intervention, and presented ways of *evaluating* the market. They asked, "Is the market in its current form good for the people of Milwaukee?" By arguing that the market does not fairly distribute jobs, they challenged the fundamental neoliberal contentions that markets reward merit and hard work, are just, and are race- and gender-neutral. They also raised issues about the autonomy of workers within markets, hinting at problems such as historical racism and geographic inequality. By focusing on subsidies, they exposed the fallacies of "free" markets embedded in neoliberal urban discourse.

However, market dominance was sometimes normalized in this progressive discourse. For example, the community benefits agreement kicked in only when subsidies exceeded half a million dollars. This "accepted" the fact that nearly every development project in Milwaukee received extensive subsidies including tax abatements and infrastructure improvements. In several cases, developers had to pay only one dollar for buildings owned by the city. Thus, when markets were defined as failing *only* when subsidies included extensive infrastructure and more than half a million dollars, the discourse of *failure as exception* was subtly reinforced. In reality, if subsidies are a useful measure, than market failure is the norm in Milwaukee and many other cities.

Furthermore, the market was still the central subject around which the debate was managed (e.g., Is it failing? Is it authentic?), and so the discussion remained largely on and within neoliberal terms. As one coalition member argued during a debate, "We are not against the market. We are all for the market if the market works."[41] This was a (real or strategic) gesture toward prevailing notions of "good citizenship" in Milwaukee, as represented through editorials, debates within the City Council and city departments, and arguments by urban boosters. As researchers have noted, neoliberalism helps constitute citizen-subjects as those who act in socially approved ways, not because of force or coercion but because their choices align with presumed community interests (see Ilcan, Oliver, and O'Connor 2007; Rose 1999). In interviews, coalition members expressed a desire to at least perform, if not completely conform to, this role of citizen-subject. They commented that they were viewed as "unpatriotic" and "communist," without concern for the greater good of Milwaukee by city officials and editorials. Positioning themselves in a more "liberal" discourse was politically opportunistic and also helped allay fears within and outside of the coalition about their appropriate citizenship status. As one member said, "We don't want to be remembered for ruining development in Milwaukee. We want to show that community benefits and successful development can go hand in hand" (activist, white, female).

Gender and Race Inequalities and Discourses: Salient and Silent

Compared to dominant discussions about markets, raced and gendered practices and discourses in the Park East debates were more complex and—paradoxically—opaque *and* salient. There was one explicitly feminist organization involved in the Good Jobs and Livable Neighborhoods Coalition, which influenced its initial commitment to issues affecting low-income women, such as jobs and child care. The coalition was broad based in representation, was democratic in practice, and proposed an agreement that addressed the needs of a diverse group of citizens. However, the coalition did not define itself as feminist, use gender or women's inequality as a mobilizing frame or central interest, or often emphasize "everyday life" or social reproduction activities in cities. The aspects of the community benefits agreement that would have directly benefitted women were eventually eliminated or became "recommendations."

The reasons for this are not clear. Some factors include the broader urban political climate that devalued "feminist" activism described earlier, silences around gender inequality in Milwaukee and beyond, self-censoring and issue trade-offs by feminists, the limits of coalition-based politics, and masculinist practices and legacies among mainstream society and governance, elites, and within activist organizations. Furthermore, the coalition was confronting a particularly masculinized arena of urban politics: a City Council with zero feminists and zero females, both of whom are more likely to support "social reproduction" and to be less punitive around issues like welfare reform and incarceration (see chapter 5 for a full discussion of this issue).

Antiracist politics and practices played out differently in the Park East debate, even amid the broader backlash against civil rights endemic to neoliberalism and neoconservatism. The coalition effectively mobilized frames of racial inequality in Milwaukee. In some cases, the group successfully showed how unmitigated market forces had worsened racial disparities in jobs, housing, and other arenas in Milwaukee. Coalition members, City Council members, and other actors expressed concerns (real or strategic) about racial exclusions and how to address them in the Park East Development. There were a number of African American male elected officials who expressed concerns about racialized unemployment and inequality. Not surprisingly, there was little agreement on the ameliorative policies. Nonetheless, the coalition effectively politicized relationships between race and urban development and presented an alternative sociospatial imaginary related to employment and integration. Claims for racial equality in employment were raised and often legitimated by city leaders, developers, and activists. In this way, resistance projects successfully influenced the terms of the debate and city politics, as other scholars have found (e.g., Larner and Butler 2007; Leitner, Peck, and Sheppard 2007). However, as was the case with gender, the discussions and attainment of progressive outcomes in Park East were troubled by the racist legacies within urban government and other organizations. Furthermore, the intertwining of gender, race, and poverty (and associated subjectivities) in the discourses and practices surrounding the Park East debate added further complexity.

The initial community benefits agreement, broad in scope and services like child care provisions and low-income housing, eventually devolved into a more limited agreement that was voted on by City Council members. This agreement stated that (1) developers would pay prevailing wages and hire apprentices on construction projects that received over half a million dollars in subsidies and that (2) developers would adhere to the city's preference for hiring local residents and following emerging business contracting requirements and *be encouraged* to employ 25 percent of workers from targeted populations (e.g., minorities and women). If the agreement passed, white men—the majority of members in construction unions—would benefit the most from the prevailing wage requirements. The second requirement would expand racial hiring on construction projects. However, these rules required only 25 percent of workers to be racial minorities. Similarly, developers were required to hire apprentices on the project, but only *strongly encouraged* to ensure that 50 percent of the total number of apprentices hired are "targeted persons who reside in the community block development grant area."[42] The lack of regulatory teeth meant that developers could simply report that they had tried but had been unable to find apprentices from this area and had therefore hired white male apprentices from the surrounding suburbs. Furthermore, the female and community block grant resident/minority requirements could be substituted for one another. In this way, it was theoretically possible for a developer to meet all of the requirements without hiring a single female on a project. As one feminist organization representative pointed out, "local hiring is not really going to affect women in poverty at all."

The proposed final agreement also encouraged the construction of affordable housing and the payment of a living wage for Park East jobs, but this language was vague and unregulated. Furthermore, the affordable housing threshold was so high that truly poor families, especially female-headed households, would be excluded. Thus, the aspects of the original community benefits agreement that would have primarily benefitted African American low-income women were whittled out of the final version. This fact was not lost on some coalition members. Two interviewees from a feminist organization pointed out that "a lot of our issues [such as housing] keep getting taken off of the table": "Well, you know the living wage part of the coalition was cut out pretty early on in the coalition's negotiations so there is not a lot in there right now for low-income women, really. . . . So I don't really know—the affordable housing provisions are really not at a level to help low-income families but it is trying to set a precedent that we are going to think a little more comprehensive about out citizenry" (activist, white, female).

Women and non-gender-conforming individuals were also often absent as subjects in many of the discussions and debates. While the specific challenges that low-income women and families face were occasionally raised, this was more the exception than the norm. There was a mutually reinforcing effect, in which the services that would benefit women were eliminated, and so women were not the subjects of the debates and women and feminist organizations were not the center of the debate, and their needs were not well reflected in the final community benefits agreement. In addition, my interviews suggested that many actors (e.g., elected officials, coalition members) in the Park East case did not consciously consider gender equality to be of concern.

My observations further suggested that gender as an equity issue in urban development has been normalized out of the urban political discourse in Milwaukee and elsewhere. Amid the general backlash against feminism, there is a documented hostility and ennui around gender issues in urban planning and policy in North America and Europe, where ideas like diversity are better tolerated. This notion is reflected in a comment made by a feminist planner: "the concept of gender has not been a best seller. . . . We found that it helped to leave 'gender' out of the title of the session" (Wankiewicz 2013, 143).[43]

Directly related, the scope of urban planning and governance and associated imaginations in the United States has continually narrowed. Social concerns remain unpopular, unless they refer to live, work, and play strategies for the elite.

Equality, poverty, compassion, care, and everyday urban life are often "out" too. Development, markets, the built environment, and the creative class are "in." This is in part about neoliberalism, but it also reflects a historical bias described by Daphne Spain (2004), where women built and advocated for "the city social," while men built the grand boulevards of the "city beautiful." As I explained in chapters 2 and 4, masculine and patriarchal tendencies persist in urban governance. Studies of U.S. and Canadian cities have shown women's safety, poverty, youth needs, and "ethics of care" are often ignored in favor of development agendas (see, for example, Brownlow 2009; Isoke 2013; Kern 2010b; Klodawsky, Aubry, and Farrell 2006). Even in Milwaukee, with a history of socialism, the emphasis on design over human needs persisted. For these and other reasons, gender, feminist values, and the needs of low-income women were rarely salient in the Park East debate.

Among feminists and low-income women involved in the community benefits campaign, the decision not to emphasize unpopular words or concepts like gender, women, sexuality, and feminism was partly strategic. They didn't wish to be feminist killjoys, ruining happiness or dampening supposed solidarity (see Ahmed 2010; Parker 2016b). They recognized that certain issues were more politically palatable (such as prevailing wage and minority hiring—perhaps because they most directly benefited men) and that concessions were needed. Optimistic about the future, one activist for low-income women reflected on both the absence of women's issues and absence of women in power: "Men make laws. Women can't. It is the beginning. You have to start somewhere right? Because in the long run we're going to keep the fight." She argued that feminists could later turn to other organizations in the coalition and say, "We helped you. Now you help us get what we need" (activist, African American, female).

In addition, feminists in the coalition were committed to challenging multiple inequalities and recognized that low-income women's experiences in Milwaukee were deeply racialized. The politicization of race was a feminist cause in Milwaukee, a position shared by many academics and activists: "But if we don't understand that race is an enormous issue for women—that there are women whose brothers, sons, fathers, and husbands are important parts of their lives. And if they can't get out of the poverty and oppression that they're in, we will never win. We have to understand this or we will never win" (activist, white, female).

Also, coalition members felt that once a community benefits agreement was passed, they could continue to promote more inclusive policies. "I think setting a precedent that low-income people as a whole are worthy of attention in public policy would be a good thing," argued one low-income female activist. Another activist argued that something was better than nothing: "Right now I know that we're not going to get affordable housing for our people. But at least even if it's affordable housing for a worker, a real worker. And tomorrow it will be for a person that's on w-2. But at least for right now we need to do something. If not, we'll never get it done" (activist, African American, female).

Not only were benefits for women rather absent in the debates and final agreement, so too were feminist emphases on everyday life, work-life balance, ethics of care, and embodied material struggles. One rarely heard discussions about children or caregiving or embodied everyday experiences of exclusion, violence, and poverty, except as related to housing. Instead most rhetoric focused on paid jobs and wages, reflecting biases among urban planners and politicians, but also among the coalition, which was dominated by labor and supportive but nonfeminist organizations. When asked, one interviewee hinted at part of the problem: "Sometimes I feel like a broken record. . . . Sometimes I feel like this is one more occasion where poor women of color get ignored and we just have to continue to say that is not right" (activist, white, female). Later, the same person said that she doesn't explicitly use the word "feminism" and rarely talked about women or gender in advocating for the community benefits agreement. Reflecting backlashes and an aversion toward feminism in the United States and in urban politics, as well as a desire to not be seen as a feminist killjoy (Ahmed 2010) described above, she argued that people perceive feminism as "too adversarial." In this constrained environment, feminists and advocates for low-income women may have been inadvertently or strategically complicit in making gender inequality less visible. They noted that concepts like family and race were more popular than women. They used strategic language while hoping for an eventual quid pro quo that may or may not happen. Many inequities were at stake in the Park East Development Plan. Community groups and feminists attempted to challenge them collectively, realizing that certain actors or causes might not immediately benefit.

Contrasting their silences around gender, commentators from both sides of the Park East debates spoke directly and frequently about the challenges for African American men in Milwaukee, particularly in relation to employment. These discussions centered on striking and substantial inequities in Milwaukee. Joblessness rates among African American men neared 50 percent in 2005 (see Levine 2006), reflecting that the number of men who were ineligible had simply stopped looking for work. Officially, the median wage for African American men was over five thousand dollars higher than that of African American women, and *official* unemployment rates for African American women were not dissimilar (Levine 2013a). The coalition prioritized male unemployment, as did City Council members. Joblessness, job insecurity, and low wages among poor women and/or their inability to feed and care for their children were less frequently mentioned. African American male unemployment and incarceration were injustices not only against the target population but also for women and entire communities, as feminist activists argued.

In addition, the framing of this crisis in male employment seemed partly rooted in traditional notions of male breadwinners and in construction and contracting work (the jobs prioritized in this debate) as "masculine" work. Testimonies where work issues were debated centered around a male subject. Speakers made statements about "underpaying a *man* what he is worth,"[44] or taking "an *average guy* off the street. . . . You've got to train him. You can't take him off the street and pay him $31.80 an hour."[45] In another comment, a union representative was apologetic for including women in an accounting of "diversity" within apprenticeships, noting that "with our last apprenticeship class, 51 percent are either minorities or women. And we do lump women in there because it's nontraditional."[46]

In otherwise supportive institutions within the Good Jobs and Livable Neighborhoods Coalition, masculinities and racist tendencies were evident. Inner-city churches and unions worked collectively for progressive causes, challenged racist and neoliberal politics, and were partners in feminist-friendly agendas. However, these institutions also had exclusionary histories that were not entirely eclipsed in Milwaukee's fight for good jobs and livable communities. Importantly, this experience was not unique to Milwaukee and its progressive endeavors. Research has shown how racism, misogyny, lingering masculinist cultures, and the marginalization of feminist agendas quietly persist in labor movements, community organizing, political and humanitarian relief work, and antineoliberal mobilizations like the Occupy movement and the World Social Forum.[47]

In the debate over Park East, African American religious leaders were powerful actors, challenging "markets" with "morality" (see also Wolf-Powers 2010). Staff and leaders from churches and religious alliances were pivotal in planning and carrying out tasks related to the coalition's work. They often mobilized congregation members to attend protests and City Council meetings in support of progressive political causes. At one point, the inner-city coalition filled a church with five hundred community members to pressure elected officials and candidates to state their support of a community benefits agreement.

To muster both attendance at such events and testimony at city meetings, church leaders performed personal and pulpit recruitment. On several occasions, attendees at protests told me that their pastor's request was the main reason they were at the meeting.[48] According to one interviewee, "The pastor has a lot of power. And the pastor says we're going to be here, this night on this day, we're going. The bus is going to be here and we're going to load up and people go. We've got a lot of churches where what the pastor says goes." Coalition leaders recognized and deferred to this patriarchal, if benevolent, power. At one protest vigil, one pastor asked the other to lead the prayer because "his flock followed him here."[49] When a local pastor, nearly always male, gave testimony at City Council meetings, the moral authority that he invoked and the effect it had on city leaders were evident. Although feminist or feminine ethics of care were not often evoked as a challenge to markets, the morality of the church was. One meeting was so crowded with community members in attendance that several pastors in attendance had to sit on the floor in front of elected officials. One labor activist explained, "Now if I had sat down in the front of the room then it wouldn't have mattered, but Pastor Markus sits down in the front of the room that's a big deal. The church brings moral authority. The labor movement doesn't make moral authority—we may bring some input in terms of economic justice, but we don't have access to the higher power" (activist, white, male).

Historically in the United States and elsewhere, men have been the "makers" of moral authority via political and religious institutions. This patriarchal pattern was reinforced in City Council meetings, and perhaps also persisted in many African American churches.[50] For example, feminist scholars have argued that even social-justice-oriented denominations give inadequate attention to gender inequality and women's leadership (e.g., Barnes 2006; Cummings 2008). Barnes (2006) found a tendency for African American churches to focus on one specific cause (racial injustice) over others (gender injustice and others). This occurs not only because of limited funds and volunteers and difficulties in addressing multiple problems, but also because of priorities made by those in power. While females constitute 70 percent of black church attendees, they represent only 3 percent of formal ordained leaders. Feminist black scholars such as Beth Richie (2012) and Patricia Hill Collins (2004) have noted that because of historical oppression, African American women are often expected to "stand by their man." This allegiance is often shown in religious circles by supporting men in one of the few arenas where African American men, regardless of their place in society, can hold positions of power (Barnes 2006; Ngunjiri, Gramby-Sobukwe, and William-Gegner 2012, 102). As a result, women and women's issues often confront a "stained glass ceiling": "The great paradox of the U.S. Black church in relation to Black women is that although Black church theology consistently emphasizes Christ's message of deliverance, equality and justice for the oppressed, much of this same Black theology reflects a characteristic Christian male dominance and patriarchy that continues to limit Black women's leadership within Black churches" (Ngunjiri, Gramby-Sobukwe, and William-Gegner 2012, 102).

I did not have adequate opportunity to observe the inner dynamics of African American or other churches to understand the debates and prioritization of issues. My interviews with male religious leaders directly involved in the coalition suggested that they were attuned to justice issues and to some feminist principles. However, my interviews also revealed some conservative attitudes about gender and sexuality. In addition, testimonies and prayers offered by church leaders often focused on race, incarceration, and male unemployment. While racism is a feminist issue, it was rarely framed in this way, and there was much less mention of the constraints faced by women of color. Such silences by church leaders contributed to the overall marginalization of the diverse needs of women and non-gender-conforming individuals in the community benefits effort. Furthermore, the seemingly patriarchal nature of the leadership of these churches and the infrequent presence of women in leadership roles contributed to the overall masculinist tone of the debate over community benefits agreements, alongside other patriarchal political leadership.

Like inner-city churches, unions in Milwaukee have long worked for economic and social justice, participating in many collaborations and coalitions, including the Good Jobs and Livable Neighborhoods Coalition. In the 1990s, unions extended job and apprenticeship access for women and minority residents, and demanded that publicly funded projects in Milwaukee provide jobs for a percentage of minority, female, and inner-city residents (see Reynolds 2002). One feminist interviewee argued, "One of the strengths of Milwaukee is for a long time has been ties between the labor movement and community organizations in a way that isn't true in lots of places. . . . We were able to get the labor movement to speak out about w-2 in ways which—you know if on a massive scale this had happened in 1996—we might be in a very different place right now" (activist, white, female). In fact, several Milwaukee unions had a geographically unique history of supporting feminist endeavors and paying attention to gender equity issues. They also had a powerful member base, political connections, and resources to help form and sustain the coalition and the campaign for a community benefits agreement. They articulated a strong message about economic justice and decent wages.

On the other hand, Milwaukee's labor unions were connected to legacies of gender and racial exclusion. This was sometimes subtle and sometimes salient within the Park East debate. There were few women in leadership within the labor movement in Milwaukee, and workers were generally constructed as male in the discourse. The invisibility of women as subjects within the Park East debate, the erasure of substantive benefits for low-income women, and traditional notions of gendered labor were in part reproduced by the presence and influence of unions. In spite of some progressive unionists, ambivalent support for the community benefits agreement existed among other union members and leaders. One elected official described, "I talked with some of the [union] members. . . . They came forward and ultimately said 'you know what, privately we want prevailing wages, we could give a darn about the affordable housing, but we're being asked to do that because—you know because the head of one union supports the progressive legislation there and he wants that. Frankly we want the prevailing wages, we could give a darn about the affordable housing'" (elected official, white, male).

Furthermore, due to historical and contemporary practices, racial tensions persisted within unions and the Good Jobs and Livable Neighborhoods Coalition. An interviewee reported that one pastor told his congregation that unions had never done anything for the African American community. He also noted that unions and race was something that coalition members "have not really wanted to talk about" (activist, African American, male). Another interviewee was even more candid: "There is a racial component. And part of the racial component is a great deal of tension with the African American community and unions. It's actually shown up with some of the legislators at Common Council who are African American and feeling like unions, you know, the access of opportunities throughout the unions is not for African Americans" (religious leader, African American, male).

In some discussions and debates, African American leaders voiced verbal suspicion about whether unions could be allies or expand job opportunities for people of color. They argued that prevailing wages would be discriminatory and work against nonunion African American and Latino contracting firms who could not afford to pay prevailing wages, although they never mentioned women. Several African American elected officials indicated that they might support a community benefits agreement if a prevailing wage requirement was not included. In these ways, the racist tendencies and histories within unions, in part perceived and reflected through heavy suburban membership, were a barrier in securing a community benefits agreement.

Race and gender may have also produced divisions and silences within the coalition, whose members had agreed to work together and support each other's causes, but recognized varied forms of internal and external power relations. As Sara Ahmed's (2010) work has shown, feminists who speak out against racism, misogyny, or other violences are seen as killjoys and difficult to get along with. Within social movements, these same people potentially become "double killjoys" (Parker 2016b), suppressing joy as well as solidarity and hope in progressive movements. Often, the most marginalized groups are asked to set aside differences for the common cause, to "wait for their turn," or to ignore certain power relations (Barnes 2006; Bhattacharjya et al. 2013; Isoke 2007; Luft 2008; Stevens 2011).[51] These power relations, for example, enabled prevailing wages to remain a prominent element of the community benefits agreement that never left the table. Yet this dimension of the agreement was not going to do much to help poor, African American women or even men and was opposed by several African American elected officials.

Conclusion

Raced, gendered, and neoliberal power relations were evident in the construction and contestation of the Park East Development Plan in Milwaukee. Contradictory at times and collusive at others, these relations were also embedded in broader community organizing and urban governance processes.

Milwaukee's rich tradition of feminist, antiracist, and progressive organizing, with roots dating to the early 1900s, was stymied but not stopped prior to and during Milwaukee's phase of urban neoliberalism. Some of the reasons for this were specific to Milwaukee, others were based in the broader reinvigoration of privileged white masculinities and markets, along with other power relations. Neoliberalism is only partly and contingently to blame.

National and local backlashes and hostility against feminism and women, which have been occurring for at least the past hundred years in the United States, were a critical part of the story. Similar backlashes and racist sentiments have simmered and sizzled in Milwaukee since at least the era of Socialist control.

These hostilities squared well with a general climate of masculinity and limited female and minority presence in local governance and a retaliatory mayor who did not have a feminist track record, to put it mildly. This mayor used "community development block grants as a political hammer" (Bonds 2007, 190), which resulted in activist groups (and black organizations in particular) losing funds for housing and development, and the related ability to organize and challenge policies. Those who challenged the mayor lost money to build houses or provide health services to poor residents in their neighborhood.

The mayor's punitive policies were enabled by a shifting neoliberal political climate of declining resources and devolution, where federal resources to cities to meet human needs were declining and local governments had more control over how to allocate them. Neoliberal discourses, fueled by and in relation to antifeminist and racist sentiment, increasingly devalued community organizing, care, and collective action. Foundations and federal, regional, and local agencies made grants available specifically for social service delivery and not for organizing and activism. On one hand, this allowed feminist, African American, and other organizations to deliver services in culturally appropriate, locally responsive, tailored ways. On the other hand, these organizations and other progressive endeavors (like the labor movement) *needed* to continually organize in order to mobilize and confront systemic injustice and change public opinions. Unfortunately, they had fewer resources to do so at the same time that mutually reinforcing racist, heteronormative, sexist, and neoliberal policy and discursive changes were further restricting the rights of women, laborers, and minorities, as well as the capacity to make claims against the state. Meanwhile, conservative foundations, many based in Milwaukee and dominated by wealthy white men, launched media campaigns that attacked community organizing, reinforced stereotypical images of women and people of color, and bolstered neoliberal reforms like education privatization and welfare reform.

Finally, specific neoliberal and racist policies like cuts in social services, welfare reform, and mass incarceration limited the ability of the most marginalized people in Milwaukee to engage in collective activism and confront injustice. If you were in prison, you couldn't protest. If you spent most of your time finding food for your children or getting your medication in the absence of food stamps and welfare support, it was hard for you to organize your neighbors. And sometimes release from prison and access to the limited welfare dollars that you could get were so fragile and contingent that you dared not speak out against the government or the police. So racist state practices (like police violence) continued and were remade. Meanwhile, popular neoliberal narratives, images in the media, and policy incentives and realities dictated that each individual and/or household should be responsible and autonomous and that equality was possible through the market (even as real wages declined and racial and gendered hiring and pay persisted). Many individuals and/or households often spent more time trying to survive or get ahead in their own ways than banding together. All of these factors, along with identity politics and internal factions spurred in part by the neoliberal funding and discursive environment, profoundly shaped the overall character and capacity of community resistance.

In spite of this constrained terrain, feminist and progressive activism in urban politics persisted in Milwaukee, often in creative and collaborative forms, in some cases adopting neoliberal frames and languages. The contestation over the Park East Development Plan in Milwaukee revealed the intersectional power relations (including contradictions and fissures) related to neoliberal capitalism, masculinities, and racism that were faced by local activists. It showed how resistance and dominant relations are bound up with each other and have complex and intertwined histories. It also hinted at some of the internal manifestations among activist groups of those same power relations.

The city's vision for Park East reflected the continuation and consolidation of capitalist/neoliberal, masculinist, and racialized strategies and projects supported by the city's male elites. It emphasized physical development, competition, the recruitment of the elusive creative class to Milwaukee, and the supposedly free market. According to many developers, city leaders, urban elites, and foundations, this was the commonsense cocktail for urban success. It was certainly in line with Milwaukee's historical patterns of urban politics. The relative absence of attention to everyday life, social issues, and social reproduction, while not new, was significant. So too was a lack of women in city leadership, especially feminists, who may have governed differently and tended to prioritize female and social reproduction issues (see Lawless and Fox 2012; see also chapter 4).

When challenged by a coalition of activists, eventually named the Good Jobs and Livable Neighborhoods Coalition, the city hardened its agenda with some minor accommodations to address racial injustices. There were developers and urban leaders who had become politically and financially invested by that time, and there was now a specter of risk and loss if the Park East Development Plan was not enacted. This played into broader anxieties and prevailing notions of citizenship that are endemic to neoliberalism. "Milwaukee must compete or lose; the incorrigible market must rule," argued citizens and city leaders. Even activists found themselves rhetorically ceding to the market, lest they be labeled socialists or bad citizens. Milwaukee's status as a supposedly second-tier city with economic development woes did not help the situation. City leaders argued that the market could not be weighed down with regulations like affordable housing, or else development would stall or shift to cities like Chicago. Developers claimed that regulations would limit profits. This popular and steely focus on the "free" market (so normalized in public discourse) was difficult for activists to combat. Editorials and media commentators constructed activists as socialists who would create a "wasteland" in downtown Milwaukee.

Paradoxically, this "free" market included substantive subsidies from the Milwaukee government to developers. And even as developers conceded that they *would* still develop if regulations were imposed, city leaders fought against these restrictions. Meanwhile, urban developers were extolled for being aggressive risk takers who were doing good for the city. They were lauded as tenacious deal makers for securing millions of taxpayer dollars for private development. These ironies show contradictions in the pervasive practices and discourses surrounding raced, gendered, and neoliberal urban politics.

They also show how development imperatives and white masculinist values and relationships (among developers, city officials, and other urban elites) can supersede neoliberal commitments. City leaders appeared to want developers to obtain a good deal. In fact, these elite relationships and deference to developers seemed to permeate relations in and around City Hall. The city often used developers' data and arguments; developers were given access to city staff, leaders, and files; and female elected officials and activists described patronizing and patriarchal attitudes by some of these actors.

At the same time, the cacophonous discourses around markets, development, and competition (however contradictory in practice) left little space for alternative imaginaries of the city's urban governance. Gender equality, collectivity, ethics of care, and everyday life were simply not part of the dialogue. Scholars have pointed out that neoliberal ideologies and policies exclude and delegitimize such values. So too do masculinist and patriarchal practice and historical legacies. Cities in the United States have often been spaces where white heteronormative masculinities and markets rule. As far back as the late 1800s, women reformers critiqued male leaders' emphases on functional, profitable, and beautiful cities. They argued instead for the "city social," which would integrate social services into physical design, serve those most excluded, prioritize neighborhood community organization leadership, and improve everyday life in cities for women, among other things (see Hayden 2002; Parker 2011; Spain 2002; Wirka 1996). This vision, moved forward by feminists and others over the years, remains relevant today.

However, feminist, antiracist, and other visions of justice remain vastly un-derrealized in Milwaukee, as suggested in the Park East debate. Instead, nar-row frames and discourses were continually repeated, reproducing sensibilities about competition, supposedly free markets, jobs, autonomy, and development. The Good Jobs and Livable Neighborhoods Coalition's demands that would have directly benefitted low-income women (like child care and living wages) were eliminated from the city's community benefits agreement as they faced strong opposition. Through complex processes and debates, the most feminist and transformative sociospatial imaginaries within the coalition became the least visible. So too were the most marginalized voices, organizations, and is-sues (like feminists and racialized low-income women), in part through self-censorship and eternal patience for a turn that might never come.

In addition, the progressive coalition was not immune to broader power structures and practices related to gender, race, heteronormativity, and neolib-eral capitalism. Racist and masculinist histories and processes within the co-alition created internal divides and exclusions, subverted a truly feminist and racially just agenda from being passed, and were occasionally capitalized on by opponents. These processes were not contained within the debate over Park East or progressive movements or neoliberal politics and discourses. Rather, they were related to intersectional and pervasive power relations, backlashes, and unbalanced political values in Milwaukee and elsewhere. They were part of historical trajectories and broader processes where white men and mascu-linities tend to dominate as real actors and "regulatory fictions" in the urban development arena. Within this context, the coalition worked to expand the debates over Park East to include issues of justice, democracy, morality, and the failure of the market to serve all of Milwaukee. However, the coalition also reflected and reproduced power relations internally and discursively, and re-lented on some feminist demands in hopes of making a small dent in the city's neoliberal armor.

CONCLUSION

Feminist Urban Narratives,
Politics, and Imaginaries

When the steely glare on urban neoliberalism is shifted even slightly, fuzzy processes and images begin to take clearer shape. In this book, I have focused on the continuous and often affinitive raced, gendered, capitalist, state and other power relations that shape urban politics in the United States. Using a feminist intersectional approach—which is not new but still needed—I suggest that these uneven relations are path-dependent and persistent, but not stagnant, invariant, or uncontested. Capitalist, raced, gendered, and other power relations arrange themselves in intertwined and unique ways at different moments in time, manifesting both materially and discursively. They affect not only urban development, policies, and housing, but also the everyday lives and labors of poor women. Understanding these urban power relations and their affinities and contradictions with one another remains an urgent but underrealized task for scholars.

In Milwaukee, the rule of hegemonic white masculinities and markets has generally persevered, but with complexities and incongruities. It has prevailed within a context of dominant values, discourses, and practices that reinforce competition, narrow concepts of work, and individualist autonomy while marginalizing feminist visions and alternatives like cooperation, care, compassion, and connection. Similarly, design, development, and the economy are privileged over human needs, everyday life, and the "social." These uneven priorities and power relations were recently visible in the clinking cocktail glasses of elite creative-class members, the new urbanist development discourses that celebrated consumption-oriented communities while ignoring racism and sexism, the complex traumas and daily resistance of low-income African American women's lives and labors, and the developers who pocketed millions in subsidies yet were commended by the media for "saving the city."

The tale I tell in this book begins with a history more than a hundred years old and centers on urban governance, development and housing, everyday lives and labors, and resistance in Milwaukee. It focuses most specifically on gender, race, capitalist, and state inequalities. Drawing from specific feminist theories and approaches, it considers how bodies, households, everyday life, social reproduction, economic systems, and the state are all interrelated dimensions of urban politics. It argues that Milwaukee both shaped and was shaped by local, national, and international processes and dynamics. There are countless other power relations that might be explored and city stories to be told.

Constructed through colonizing and capitalist processes that decimated the original Native American population, Milwaukee was governed by Socialists not long after its inception as a city. Milwaukee's Sewer Socialists, who challenged cold capitalism and lobbied for improved urban services, greater equality, and social reproduction concerns, did not embrace gendered or raced equality. For example, there was little concern for Native American, African American, and many immigrant populations. Socialists were not in full support of women's suffrage and generally excluded women and nonwhites from leadership. While white women in Milwaukee and nationally secured some influence through women's clubs, partnerships, and eventually voting rights, their leadership and "city social" agenda was curtailed by a masculine agenda emphasizing beauty and boulevards, and a general backlash against women.

Even as women of all races secured jobs (with different pay and conditions) and helped transform the city during World War II, gendered, raced, and sexual anxieties ensured that their roles became more confined soon after. Feminist energies and political organizing were soon squashed amid one of the many feminist backlashes that shaped the city. After the war, Milwaukee envisioned a modern, marketized, masculine city steeped in white privilege and power. White flight ensued, many women assumed a domestic life, and African Americans lost capital, jobs, and entire neighborhoods.

In Milwaukee's recent phase of raced and gendered neoliberalism (dating to the 1980s), new urbanism justified downtown development for elites and sometimes romanticized Milwaukee's racist and gendered past and present. Promoting narratives about consumption and market-centric communities, the city's development discourses obscured and disinvested in social reproduction and the people who often conduct this work. Meanwhile, progressive dimensions of new urbanism, like walkability and affordability, were rarely accessible to Milwaukee's poorest female-headed households and nonwhite communities.

Milwaukee's creative-class politics were also neoliberal, raced, gendered, and elitist. Creative-class discourses bolstered neoliberal rationalities and were embodied and embraced by the elite, in part because they aligned with and affirmed extant raced, gendered, and classed power relations. They venerated marketized and masculinist concepts of "creativity" and obfuscated other values and narratives like collectivity and care. They celebrated a supposed creative meritocracy in labor markets, which are in fact shaped by many gendered and raced inequalities. Creative-class discourses in Milwaukee and elsewhere idealized a mobile, autonomous, flexible, hypercapitalist worker. While my in-terviews suggested that some women had made wage gains and enjoyed flexi-bility and choice in "creative" careers, they often had to conform to dominant neoliberal norms and faced new forms of insecurity. The highest paying indus-tries remained most easily occupied by white, male, elite heterosexual subjects with limited social reproduction responsibilities.

The Young Professionals of Milwaukee, a local organization, was founded to attract the creative class to Milwaukee. Members of the organization embodied the creative class and its emphasis on consumption, autonomy, and competi-tion. They made instrumental claims about tolerance and diversity in Milwau-kee. However, the surrounding practices often lacked substance and diverted attention away from deep and violent racism in Milwaukee. Instead, the city and the organization promoted soft diversity efforts that focused on improving Milwaukee's image problem and therefore improving the city's economy. The most progressive and equity-oriented impulses of the organization went under-realized. Meanwhile, city leaders affirmed and animated existing elite networks and focused on recruiting "diverse" workers from elsewhere, in spite of a large nonwhite population in need of opportunity and inclusion into the social and economic fabric of the city.

While elite social networks, high-end developments, and capitalist profits were reinvigorated by new urbanist and creative-class politics in Milwaukee, social reproduction and everyday life for low-income residents were generally devalued. Social reproduction, defined as the labors that sustain households, communities, and human life and underpin capitalism, has never been highly valued or visible in the United States and its cities. Government supports for household labors like raising children have always been thin, especially for women of color, even as gender and racial equality hinges in part on such sup-port. Creative-class discourses oriented attention further away from such labors and the bodies that conducted them, deeming them "uncreative," neglecting or silencing the need for policy supports (like maternity leave or low-income housing) by employers and government. These discourses helped fuel Milwau-kee's uneven economic development investments and priorities. Rather than attend to an affordable housing crisis or focus on jobs, social services, schools, or even swimming pools, Milwaukee spent nearly 70 percent of its economic development budget on real estate development and amenities for the elite.

Gentrification and local and national reductions in social supports (fueled by racism, sexism, and neoliberalism) took a further toll on poor and moderate-income families in Milwaukee and their social reproduction activities. Nonprofit organizations and churches struggled to meet the needs for housing, food, and health, even during the booming 1990s. This situation fits what Brodie (2003) has titled the "paradox of necessity," in which neoliberalism has stripped away institutional supports while simultaneously maximizing the need for social interventions because of the socially destabilizing effects of unfettered markets. This disproportionately affects women, who benefit the most from state redistribution and social services. The situation became grimmer in Milwaukee as welfare reforms solidified and a recession unfolded. Community organizations, racialized households, and the bodies of African American women, in particular, have absorbed costs of such disinvestments in reproduction.

Without access to affordable housing, poor Milwaukee families lived doubled and tripled up in households. Poor African American women in Milwaukee managed low-paid, precarious waged labor along with community and child care responsibilities, rigid regulations and degrading experiences under Wisconsin's welfare reform policies, and incarceration of family members, partners, and even entire neighborhoods.[1] Nearly all the low-income women whom I interviewed and their children experienced significant health problems, deepened and produced through gendered and community violence, racism, and poverty. Black feminists remind us that their position is not new, as historically the lives of African American women have been marked by racialized, capitalist, and gendered inequalities and loss. However, my interviewees' lives and labors seem to be *amplified* by recent power configurations and through cumulative experiences of dispossession and marginalization in Milwaukee. In spite of this, these women asserted resistance and power through spatialized practices, meaning making, and community organizing, rejecting dominant neoliberal subjectivities and creating material and spiritual home spaces of connection and care.

As I have revealed throughout this book, the deprioritization of social reproduction and human needs and the related emphasis on competition, autonomy, and narrow constructions of work were tied to the composition and priorities of the local government, both recently and historically. These were shaped by heteronormative elite racist and gendered practices and discourses that reinforced "masculine" ideal subjects as regulatory fiction, as well as a narrow range of bodies and perspectives in government.

There is a useful range of feminist scholarship to help us interpret these issues, including but not limited to a "women in governance" and "gender and governance" perspective provided by sociologist Lisa Brush (2003). Women's participation in elected and business leadership increased minimally or in some cases declined; and in the case of the Milwaukee City Council, women were nonexistent by 2004. When reflecting on the past decade, one statewide official noted in 1999, "even rural Wisconsin elects far more women than urban Milwaukee" (cited in Van de Kamp Nohl 2001). My interviews and other data suggested a number of reasons for this, including fewer women actually running for office due to intensified reproductive and productive burdens that were endemic under neoliberalism, a decline in public sector jobs that can be a career stepping stone for elected office, a decline in feminist networks and activist organizations, intensified paid and unpaid labors for women and households, and a masculinist climate that was not often welcoming to women. While specific to Milwaukee, this situation reflects a broader U.S. trend in which women's participation in government is either stagnating or only marginally increasing, and women in general, and non-gender-conforming individuals and women of color specifically remain underrepresented in elected politics (see Center for American Women and Politics 2014; Lawless and Fox 2012).

From a race, gender, and governance perspective, neoliberal politics and ide-ologies help reinforce a culture of exclusive masculinity, in which competition, autonomy, risk, individualism, and economic priorities structured what and who are valued in cities. This local governance culture was a historical main-stay in Milwaukee, although research suggests it was disrupted slightly during the Socialist period of governance and again during the 1970s and 1980s. In recent years, through a neoliberal emphasis on privatization and public-private partnerships and a development-centric agenda, male-dominated sectors (the business and development community) acquired greater influence and greater flexibility in pursuing their agendas in the name of urban growth. Others were excluded. Among other issues, the framing of architectural design and devel-opment as a solution to urban decay, close networks among male elites, and the position of Milwaukee as a second-tier city situated local developers and investors as redemptive. In this climate, not only did certain developers profit intensively, but they had informal access to officials and city staff and were of-ten able to set the rules and frame the discourse, making them in some cases among the most powerful men in Milwaukee. These practices were reinforced through development politics that centered around a triad of interconnected new urbanist, neoliberal, and creative-class agendas (or group think), each of which reproduced exclusionary subjectivities, relationships, and policies with regard to gender and race.

Not only were women and gender-nonconforming individuals often ex-cluded in Milwaukee's urban politics, but so too were feminist ethics of care and collectivity, attention to social reproduction and often social equity, and a range of diverse view points and policies. This was a problem of representative democracy (where the population is not represented in elected leadership), but it was also more than that. The tight circuits of often like-minded urban players helped reinforce certain internal logics and rationalities and subjectivities, mak-ing others nearly invisible. Several studies have shown that, in part because of their socialized roles, women often govern differently and prioritize different issues than men. For example, they tend to be more liberal on social welfare and incarceration, prioritize issues like women's health and education, and tend to solicit more opinions and engage more with constituents. Furthermore, the more women elected officials are visible, the more young girls and other women are inspired to run for office (see chapter 3).

And elite, white masculinist power is both more silent and salient. It produces a limited field and agenda of politics that helps subvert alternatives, potential challenges, and marginalized voices. It contributes to what Isoke (2013) labels "heteropatriarchy" in urban governance, and adduces normative behaviors and rationalities. Dominant discourses, informal networks instantiated in part through neoliberalism, the subtle nature of gendered power, and a backlash or boredom with feminism and antiracism made these exclusions elusive, invisible, and difficult to challenge (e.g., Brodie 2007; Brush 2003; Douglas 2010; Greed 2006; Isoke 2013). Indeed, many of my interviewees saw little concern with women's absences, and the persistence of patriarchy was rarely countered. This attitude erased many issues, not only about presence and absence, but about what rules women or nonwhite individuals have to follow, who will take them seriously, their access without the capacity to transform the apparatus, and the reproduction of masculinity and femininity and power differentials within these institutions. And critically, low-income racialized women in cities often bore the brunt of urban policy decisions and power configurations.

Even among activist groups and institutions, gendered and intersectional inequalities in Milwaukee were often the most marginalized and least visible. In some cases, this involved a conscious choice by activists to prioritize concerns of race or class or jobs (narrowly construed) over gender. In other cases, it was the result of a number of subtle, "subconscious" individual, organizational, and institutional processes or historical exclusions in which women's needs and voices—however complex—were subsumed by other political agendas and the invoked subject was male.

In summary, under patriarchal, raced, and neoliberal policies in Milwaukee, certain women (especially poor racialized women) and feminist and alternative values have suffered multiplier exclusion effects. Many women endured amplified burdens and labors, from insecure paid jobs to caring for multiple children and enduring intimate violence. At the same time, prevailing discourses of gender neutrality, market equality, and the invisibility of social reproduction "erased" and abdicated support for these labors, framing them as individual choices and/or deficiencies. In a similar way, urban development policies, such as new urbanism and creative-class agendas, normalized male, racialized subjectivities and legitimate expenditures on urban elites and downtown, while racialized women, families, and neighborhoods remain ignored.

Furthermore, women, especially nonwhite women, and feminist agendas may be triply excluded in neoliberal political realms. There has been a deepening and reification of economic realms and norms of competition and autonomy through neoliberal policies and discourses. As black feminists remind us, such norms have always been problematically based on conceptions of a white, liberal male subject. Their reification has contributed to unbalanced and often unjust cities and political environments and helped insulate dominant policies from challenges. Simultaneously and dialectically, in part because women were theoretically and politically excluded in neoclassical and economic-focused politics, there was a deepening of masculinist realms. At the same time, feminist strategies of collectively politicizing the economic, the masculine, and other power relations and subjectivities have often been devalued through discourses of individualization.

While this book is largely a tale of deep inequality in Milwaukee, it is not one without fissures, negations, and paradoxes. Urban processes and politics in Milwaukee reveal important findings about multiple scales and types of resistance. First, in contradiction to some literature, I found a denial of neoliberal subjectivities and values by some actors and activists in Milwaukee. While it is clear that the state engaged in ongoing subject interpellation and rearranged its demands on racialized bodies in particular ways, the African American women that I interviewed rejected popular discourses about work, choice, independence, and "good" motherhood. They pointed consistently to racism and its effects in local and national arenas; they articulated their own ideas about motherhood, love, and responsibility. And they made it clear that caring for children and family was work. In navigating many violences and inequalities, they made choices they thought best served their children and their households. Their perspectives are perhaps better understood through black feminism, which pays attention to the historical contradictions and dilemmas of black women and black motherhood, and emphasizes human life, relationality, and intersectionality.

Similarly, while mainstream and elite organizations like the Young Professionals of Milwaukee generally propagated synthetic or simplistic ideas about diversity, they did not go uncontested. In several interviews, members of the organization demonstrated more complex understandings of inequality in Milwaukee and a desire to push back against individualist and neoliberal ideas about race and diversity.

Progressive community activists, organizations, and coalitions also rejected and resisted power relations, policies, and dominant values in Milwaukee. A community-based mobilization against a planned neoliberal downtown development explicitly challenged racial inequality and poverty in the city's development agenda. This mobilization was connected to and learned from progressive movements and activities in other cities across the United States. The coalition argued that this project would be subsidized by the government but serve the needs of elites, as racism and poverty exploded in the city. They brought a message of morality against the markets. In protests and negotiations, the Good Jobs and Livable Neighborhoods Coalition lobbied for affordable housing, decent jobs, and opportunities for minorities to be attached to the development project. Arguing that public subsidies should benefit the public, they held signs reading "This land is our land."

However, the development project came with a history. It represented a deep material investment and historically engrained coalescence of vision among

masculine, elite actors within Milwaukee, accompanied by persuasive but contradictory neoliberal rationalities and the absence of alternative visions for the
city. This meant that the resistance of community members to the plan was met
in some cases with genuine surprise, and with concerted defense. City leaders
and media proclaimed that the market must rule. They argued that Milwaukee must compete with other cities, praised local developers as risk-taking city
saviors, and fought heartily against regulations on development. They questioned the allegiances of activists, labeling them as socialists who would turn
Milwaukee into a "wasteland." Even as developers revealed that they would still
develop if they faced regulations and restrictions, city officials insisted on a
"free market."

The paradoxes, practices, and projects in Milwaukee further affirm that
neoliberalism was and is *not* a monolithic monster that chomps up all in its
path. Rather, a *tenacious, historical, and perhaps underestimated blend* of patriarchal, racist, state, and neoliberal practices has made for a rocky terrain for
progressive, antiracist, and feminist activists in Milwaukee. As described above,
feminist backlashes and ongoing antipathy toward feminism, combined with
neoliberal and racist policies, discourses, and funding practices to help demobilize and delegitimize community mobilizations and resistance throughout
the 1980s; a punitive mayor enhanced the effects. Organizations that provided
direct social services were both rewarded with funds and distracted from political agendas by the sheer human need and their commitment and capacity
to provide gender and race or culturally sensitive services. Additional raced,
gendered, and neoliberal discourses and practices made resistance more difficult and divided communities. Furthermore, for Milwaukee's poorest, African
American women, much energy was consumed in everyday struggles to care for
themselves and households. The demands of their unpaid and paid labors; the
drain of ongoing health problems brought on by trauma, poverty, and racialized
violence; and the needs of their communities nearly but not completely crushed
by incarceration were substantive. The punitive position of the state with regard to welfare and incarceration also precluded feminist and other forms of
community organizing. While activism and spatialized practices of resistance
persisted among low-income African American women, they were pulled in
multiple directions and challenged multiple violences.

In fact, patriarchal and racist legacies and practices persisted in progressive
or antineoliberal efforts, including unions and black churches. As feminists collaborated with organizations to try to forward progressive agendas and meet the
needs of low-income women, they often found themselves sidelined or silencing themselves. Several studies have critiqued masculinism, racism, and misogyny in progressive efforts, including in the labor movement, in political and
humanitarian relief work, and in mobilizations like the Occupy movement and
the World Social Forum. At an academic level, similar violences occur via si-

lence or absence, as narratives of neoliberalism erase gendered and raced power relations. Those who point out sexism, racism, or heterosexism (especially in progressive politics) are construed as killjoys that detract from happiness and solidarity (see Ahmed 2010; Parker 2016b). In Milwaukee, feminists in a progressive coalition sometimes silenced themselves for this reason. The framing of killjoy subjectivities fit neatly with the unpopularity of feminism and disinterest in gender in urban theory, politics, and planning.[2]

This raises issues about affinities among power relations and resistance. Some have argued that there has been a perverse affinity between feminism and neoliberalism (e.g., Fraser 2009). While not fully exploring this issue, my research found little evidence in favor of that argument. Rather, in Milwaukee, I observed rather strong affinities among certain kinds of masculinities and patriarchy, racism, and capitalism. These collective powers were often able to frame or subdue feminist and antiracist efforts (of which there were many) in ways that suited their needs. In the United States, masculinity and male power are deeply bound up with capitalist practices like individualism and competition, and white male power has been concentrated in markets, while African American communities have experienced significant economic dispossession.

An adjusted reading of the emergence and growth of neoliberal policies and power relations might suggest that when white patriarchy was threatened, it tightened its alliances and the extension of markets. Especially as feminism made inroads into the government and public sphere, the state increasingly shifted to serve markets. As feminists have articulated, the expansion and concentration of capitalist markets tend to shift power toward men, while redistribution benefits women, especially low-income women. Thus, a historical perspective might consider whether neoliberalism and its economic arguments emerged so forcefully in response to feminist and civil rights organizing that threatened to destabilize concentrated masculine and racialized power. Similar backlashes had occurred before.

Regardless, collectively (but not without contradictions) racism, patriarchy, and neoliberal capitalism simultaneously devalue cooperation, care, and collectivity, marshalling material resources and political power to instantiate this devaluation. As I explore throughout this book, all male-identifying people don't win and all female-identifying people don't lose under such a configuration. There are dominant and subordinate masculinities and racial and classed hierarchies, and ideologies don't perfectly attach to actual bodies. Some middle-class and white women often "did fine" in Milwaukee, sometimes succeeding under capitalism and neoliberal policy environments and benefitting from their racial and class privilege. However, dominant and imbalanced values and discourses (around competition, for example) help adduce conformity to them and are often attached to historical and material privilege and related bodies. For example, it is easiest for white, elite, heteronormative men, who have benefitted from slavery, capitalism, white flight, women's unpaid labors, and the dispossession of communities of color, to perform neoliberal subjectivities related to autonomy and competition and to secure related material resources. In part because of history, these same bodies often shape the institutions, like governments, that reproduce such discourses, norms, and practices. Hence, power brokers in Milwaukee before and under neoliberal policies were usually male-dominated institutions like development firms, corporations, elite organizations, foundations, think tanks, and local government.

Meanwhile, women—who conduct the majority of caring labors—generally benefit from ideologies and practices that value social reproduction and devote state resources toward them. This is especially true for women of color, who have encountered years of sustained violence and dispossession that have affected their bodies, families, and communities, even as they engage in relational acts of resistance and connection. However, social reproduction has been increasingly deprioritized and devalued under neoliberalism, and the state has often been a source of oppression rather than liberation.

And as I argued in the introduction, for *all* people and cities, we need a more balanced and integrative approach to urban politics that values and performs social reproduction, human life, care, collectivity, and justice. It will take canny attention to complex power relations by scholars and activists and tenacious and creative versions of antiracist feminism and other resistance politics to shift this balance.

Beyond Hegemonies and Hopelessness? Feminist Politics and Imaginaries

In 1902, urban reformer Jane Addams wrote that "social advance depends as much upon the process in which it is secured as the result itself." Not long after, George Orwell wrote a biting satire of the Russian Revolution, in which animals stage a rebellion against an oppressive human farmer. In the end, an elite regime of whiskey-drinking pigs with an army of rabid dogs rules the farm, terrorizing all animals that disagree. Only one of seven principles of the rebellion remain: *all animals are equal, but some are more equal than others*. Addams and Orwell offer important warnings about singular understandings of power, resistance, and alternative futures.

Nearly a hundred years earlier, when the world was seemingly growing cold from commerce, Henry David Thoreau spent years in solitude, reflecting on not only nature, but also community and society. Thoreau observed that so many processes seemed invisible or mechanical through the dominating forces of capitalism. And rather than simply critiquing these processes, he shifted his perspective entirely, and in doing so he unveiled a different but related landscape with its own logics and knowledge. Perhaps such a shift is needed now.

In this book, I have offered one that is ever so slight, rounding out and reorienting our theories and critiques of urban neoliberalism and resistance, which at times are too singular. Using a feminist partial political economy of place approach, I have used stories, analyses, and reflection to look at different processes and multiple power relations from different angles. I have examined the city and the people and practices that constitute it with care and attention. In doing so, I committed to labels and inscriptions, and to a certain description of constraining truths of which I am wary. By paying attention to even the particularities of difference, I have perhaps created categories of exclusion and silences (like women and race) at my own peril. It is possible they are incomplete or inaccurate, or already changed. However, informed and inspired by feminist sensibilities and Thoreau's careful observations, and using a feminist partial political economy approach, I committed to observing and understanding the raced, gendered, and neoliberal processes long enough and with sufficient detail for something useful to be revealed. These were my small efforts at pushing against imbalance. Gillian Rose once argued about feminism, "Different strategies are needed for different circumstances. We do not have to take sides when we have had so little say in the rules of the game" (Rose 1993, 83). Thoreau also argued that in the end, nature can support many orders of understanding. So too can our critical approaches to the urban, and our hopes for a better future.

In the early 1900s, feminist anarchists critiqued multiple oppressions perpetrated by the state, institutions, and individuals. Lucy Parsons (1905/2003, 79), a nonwhite feminist anarchist who wrote fearlessly against slavery and violence, also wrote, "We [women] are slaves of the slaves. We are exploited more ruthlessly than men. Whenever wages are to be reduced, the capitalist class uses women to reduce them." In 2016, as scholars and activists, we might try to simultaneously see the individual and intertwining trajectories of racism, patriarchy, heteronormativity, state power, neoliberal capitalism, and more, drawing from feminist political economists, antiracist black feminists, queer theorists, anarchists, and other intellectual and political traditions. By way of a humble example, I have shown how some of these relations have linked, unlinked, and relinked across different spaces and times in Milwaukee. In doing so, I have suggested that we have perhaps noticed too much change and not enough continuity and connection in our narratives of neoliberalism and urban power relations. I have also suggested that we focus on both the particularities of place and time as well as the relations and lessons across them.

It seems also imperative to try to see beyond neoliberalism and other power relations and to imagine alternative futures. This involves both politics and poetry. We need perhaps legions of feminist killjoys, willing to study, call out, and challenge inequalities in mainstream and progressive urban politics (see Ahmed 2010; Parker 2016b). We need sharp observations and inclusive and reflective political organizing that transforms individuals, deconstructs power in place, and inspires collective action. In this book, I have suggested that urban power is both more distributed and connected than often interpreted. I may have exposed some vulnerabilities, contingencies, and contradictions in the current power relations, and I have given voice to varied actors and the possibilities and constraints in progressive politics, including feminism. Along with others, I've argued that feminist ethics of care, connection, and collectivity are needed as important correctives in urban politics (e.g., Gibson-Graham 2006; Lawson 2007; McDowell 2004). But perhaps we need poetry as much as politics.

> Free love? . . . Man has subdued bodies, but all the power on earth has been unable to subdue love. Man has conquered whole nations, but all his armies could not conquer love. Man has chained and fettered the spirit, but he has been utterly helpless before love.
>
>   Goldman (1910, 211)

> It has rained for five days
> running
> the world is
> a round puddle
> of sunless water
> where small islands
> are only beginning
> to cope
> a young boy
> in my garden
> is bailing out water
> from his flower patch
> when I ask him why
> he tells me
> young seeds that have not seen sun
> forget
> and drown easily.
>   Audre Lorde

Perhaps it is time to speak in different languages about feminist politics, justice, and hope. It seems that we need not just analytics, but also poetry, stories, and experiences that stir the soul. I have argued that current power configurations have erased, devalued, and (re)appropriated many values and visions of feminists, including care, cooperation, human life, community, sustainability, connection, and even love. Increasing the visibility of these values and practices offers one way to shift balances, to challenge compounding inequities, and to reclaim possibilities of feminist politics of hope. Communication in multiple languages and forms is needed too.

With their emphasis on everyday life, renewal, and human experience, *social reproduction activities* and *nature* can be both politics and poetry. We might organize around tangible injustices around everyday life and labor in cities, where one woman sends her child to college and another sends hers to prison. As an analytical construct, social reproduction has limits. And politically, we need to be wary of romanticizing reproduction as an enabler of global capitalism and state power (see Fraser 2014; Molyneux 2006). However, social reproduction and nature provide languages and activities by which we can connect to the common tasks and the emotions that make us human and vulnerable: the feeding of newborn babies, the gathering of neighbors for a common purpose, the grieving over a loved one who has been lost, the hope for spring or a gentle rain. Of course, this awareness of shared vulnerability and experience is not sufficient grounds for ethical action, as Judith Butler (2006) argues. However with attention to equity and justice, social reproduction is a space for political investment and care amid the anomie of competition, autonomy, and capitalism in cities. And so too is the hope of a seed, of a perpetual morning.

NOTES

Chapter One. Masculinities and Markets

1. Research laying out these neoliberal discourses and subjectivities and the restructuring of neoliberal citizenship is extensive. See, for example, Brodie 2004; Brown 2015; Collins and Mayer 2010; Cowen 2006; Dardot and Laval 2013; Kingfisher 2007b; Larner 2000, 2005; McCluskey 2003; Miraftab 2004; Mirowski 2013; Mitchell 2004; Peck, Theodore, and Brenner 2012; Peck and Tickell 2002; Rankin 2001. This project augments such research with a feminist lens, considering how discourses and practices related to neoliberalism and neoliberal citizenship are also gendered and raced.

2. There is abundant literature on neoliberalization trends in U.S. cities and their transformations and tenacity over time and in the wake of varied crises. See, for example, Brown 2015; Derickson 2014; Gotham 2013; Gotham and Greenberg 2014; Hackworth 2007; Isoke 2007, 2011; Katz 2008; Kingfisher 2002; Larner 2000, 2003, 2011; Larner and Butler 2007; Leitner, Peck, and Sheppard 2007; Lipman 2002, 2011, 2013; Macleod and Johnstone 2012; Peck 2006a, 2006b, 2015; Peck and Theodore 2002; Peck, Theodore, and Brenner 2013; Sites 2003, 2012; Springer 2010, 2012; Ward 2006, 2007b, 2010; Ward and England 2007; Warner and Hefitz 2007; Weber 2002). This project takes this and other research as background to examine the particular workings of neoliberalism in Milwaukee and to extend the literature where relevant.

3. Many scholars have argued for the importance of exploring and acknowledging variation, historicity, contingencies, contradictions, exceptions, and relationalities in cities (for a few examples, see England and Ward 2011; Kingfisher and Maskovsky 2008; Larner 2003; Larner and Butler 2007; Larner et al. 2013; Leitner, Peck, and Sheppard 2007; Ong 2006; Peake and Rieker 2013; Robinson 2011; Roy 2015; Springer 2010). While acknowledging such variation, others have argued also for a focus on commonality and consistent features of neoliberalism and are more wary of urban particularism (see, for example, Brenner and Theodore 2002; Peck 2006a, 2015; Peck and Theodore 2002). Later in this chapter I explore the tensions between situated and more totalizing theories reflected in these arguments. In this book, I focus on the geography of the United States, identifying some common elements across U.S. cities and the broader policy framework, but I highlight specific discourses, policies, and practice in Milwaukee and the relations between local, national, and international contexts.

4. On the former, see Barnett 2005; Castree 2005. On the latter, see Gibson-Graham 2000, 2006, 2007, among others.

5. However, even as patriarchy and other power relations persist in urban politics and planning (Jupp 2014; Peake 2015; Sánchez de Madariaga and Roberts 2013; Wright 2013), academic attention has waned. To give just a few examples, the literature on creative-class politics includes only handfuls of articles that address gender and race (e.g., Leslie and Catungal 2012; McLean 2014a, 2014b; Parker 2008). Literature on "the new urban politics" in North American and European contexts has few references to gender. Although a provocative interdisciplinary literature on gender, feminism, and neoliberalism exists (e.g., Brown 2006; Campbell 2014; Eisenstein 2009; Fraser 2013; Kantola and Squires 2012; Kingfisher 2007a; Lind 2005; Newman 2013; Prügl 2014; Simon-Kumar 2013; Walby 2011), (1) it infrequently focuses on cities, urban planning, and politics and (2) it is far outnumbered by mainstream political economic literature on urban neoliberalism in which feminist insights are not often integrated, especially among studies that focus on U.S. cities. Similarly in U.S.-based urban planning journals and conferences, feminism and gender make rare appearances. Finally, a growing "urban explorer" culture and literature not only ignores gender, but also perhaps perpetuates hypermasculine practices and stereotypes (Mott and Roberts 2014).

6. See, for example, Bondi 1999, 2005; Bondi and Christie 2000; Buckley 2014; Derickson 2014, 2015; Domosh 1991, 2003; Fincher 1990; Fincher and Jacobs 1998; Hayden 2002; Isoke 2007, 2011; Kern 2010b; Little, Peake, and Richardson 1988; Peake 1993, 1997, 2015; Peake and Rieker 2013; Spain 2002, 2004; Wekerle 2005a; Wilson 2009; Wright 2013.

7. This critique has been made in different forms by various feminist scholars. See, for example, Bondi and Peake 1988; Clarke, Staeheli, and Brunell 1995; Derickson 2009, 2015; Fincher 1990; Gilbert 1999; Hayden 1981; Isoke 2011; Kern 2010b; Kern and Mullings 2013; Kern and Wekerle 2008; Little, Peake, and Richardson 1988; Massey 1991; McDowell 1991; Parker 2008, 2011; Peake and Rieker 2013; Sandercock and Forsyth 2005; Spain 2002; Whitzman 2007; Wright 2013.

8. For elaborations on arguments and specific critiques that show how urban theory has marginalized feminist contributions and intersecting power relations, see, for example, Bondi and Peake 1988; Clarke, Staeheli, and Brunell 1995; Derickson 2009, 2015; Domosh 1990; Fincher 1990; Gilbert 1999; Hubbard 2004; Isoke 2007, 2011; Jupp 2014; Kern 2010b; Kern and Mullings 2013; Kern and Wekerle 2008; Little, Peake, and Richardson 1988; Massey 1991; McDowell 1991; Parker 2011; Peake 2015; Peake and Rieker 2013; Roy 2015; Sánchez de Madariaga and Roberts 2013; Spain 2002; Wright 2013. This study follows in the tradition of these studies without rehearsing arguments contained within them as to the omissions of much of extant research.

9. For example, see England 1991; Fincher 1990; Gittell and Shtob 1980; Hayden 1980; Markusen 1980; McDowell 1983; Spain 1992, 2002, 2004, 2014.

10. McDowell 2001, 233–34; also see Burke and Major 2014; Rutherford 2011, 2014.

11. See Lawless and Fox (2012) for an overview of some of these issues, which I explore in more detail in chapter 4. Also see Atkeson 2003; Atkeson and Carrillo 2007; Bashevkin 2011; Bratton 2005; Broockman, 2014; Brush 2003; Campbell and Wolbrecht 2006; Gerrity, Osborn, and Mendez 2007; Isoke 2011; Lister 1990; Orloff 1996; Weikart et al. 2007). A recent study found that females and African Americans and Latinos

mitigate the most restrictive and punitive aspects of welfare reform and incarceration. Women of color will also have the strongest countervailing effect on state welfare reform (Reingold and Smith 2012). Isoke (2011) found that even though African American men dominate the city council in the New Jersey city that she studied, this did not disrupt the heteropatriarchal nature of urban government or incline the city to attend to the needs of low-income African American residents.

12. Bondi and Peake 1988; Cope 1997; Derickson 2009; Fincher 1990; Gibson-Graham 2000, 2006; Haraway 1988; Harding 1993; Isoke 2007; Little, Peake, and Richardson 1988; Massey 1991; McDowell 1991; Peake and Rieker 2013; Rose 1997; Spain 2002, 2004; Wright 2013.

13. See, for example, Cahill 2007; Derickson 2009; Domosh 2003; Haraway 1988; Harding 1991; Hesse-Biber 2012; Jarvis 2009; McKittrick 2006; Miraftab 2006; Mohanty 2003; Naples 2003; Rose 1997; Smith 2005; Swarr and Nagar 2010; Wright 2013.

14. Holland 2012; hooks 2000; Isoke 2007, 2011; McKittrick 2011; Mohanty 1988; Puar 2007, 2012; Richie 2000.

15. Campbell 2014; Fraser 2009; Gill 2011; Valentine, Jackson, and Mayblin 2014; Walby 2011.

16. See, for example, Bondi 1999; Cordova 1993; Crenshaw 1989, 1991; Fincher and Jacobs 1998; Gilmore 2007; McDowell 2008; McKittrick 2011; Puar 2007; Richie 2000, 2012.

17. Holland 2012; Puar 2012. For various discussions of intersectionality, see Cho, Crenshaw, and McCall 2013; Holland 2012; Isoke 2013; McCall 2005; McDowell 2008; Puar 2012; Russell 2007; Valentine 2007.

18. On critiques of intersectionality and/or the problematic nature of categories, see, for example, Cho, Crenshaw, and McCall 2013; Derickson 2009; Holland 2012; McCall 2005; Puar 2012; Sharp et al. 2000; and Valentine 2007.

19. Hill Collins 2002, 2004; hooks 2000; Isoke 2007, 2011; McKittrick 2006, 2011; Richie 2012.

20. Jones 2009; Richie 2012; U.S. Census Bureau 2010; Williams and Hegewisch 2011.

21. See Cho, Crenshaw, and McCall 2013; McDowell 2008; Valentine 2007. In particular, there has been considerable discussion and debate about affinities and alliances between feminism and neoliberalism. Kantola and Squires (2012) have argued that feminists have adapted to the neoliberal environment and shifted state feminism and surrounding strategies to market feminism and related tactics. Scholars like Nancy Fraser and Hester Eisenstein have argued that feminism inadvertently fueled and/or was co-opted by neoliberalism. Scholars like Janet Newman (2012) and Sylvia Walby (2011) have rejected this view, and in some cases argued for nuanced interpretations of diverse feminisms and associated politics and practices. The literature is abundant and growing, but see, for example, Campbell 2014; Eisenstein 2009; Fraser 2009, 2013; Newman 2012; Prügl 2014; Simon-Kumar 2013; Walby 2011.

22. See, for example, Fincher 2006; Gill 2011; McDowell 2008; Walby 2011.

23. See, for example, Goode and Maskovsky 2001; Kern and Mullings 2013; Lipman 2011; Wilson 2006; Wilson 2009.

24. Katz 1994, 2004; McDowell 2001; McKittrick 2011; Miraftab 2006; Mountz and Hyndman 2006; Naples 2003; Nast 1994; Smith 1990, 1999; Staeheli and Lawson 1994; Swarr and Nagar 2010; Walby 2000, 2011; Wright 2009, 2010.

25. See, for example, Hoffman 2014; Massey 1999; Peake and Rieker 2013; Robinson 2011; Rodgers, Barnett, and Cochrane 2014; Roy 2015.

26. Also see Katz 1994, 2004; McDowell 2001, 2008; Mountz 2011; Mountz and Hyndman 2006; Naples 2003; Nast 1994; Pratt and Rosner 2006; Rose 1997; Smith 2005; Wright 2006, 2009.

27. On this critique, see Domosh 2003; Fincher 1990; Isoke 2013; Jarvis 2009; Kern 2010b; McDowell 1991; Peake and Rieker 2013; Spain 2002; Wilson 1991; Wright 2013.

28. See, for example, Burgess 2008; Douglas 2010; Gill 2011; McRobbie 2009; Rahder and Altilia 2004; Sánchez de Madariaga and Roberts 2013; Valentine, Jackson, and Mayblin 2014; Walby 2011; Wankiewicz 2013.

29. Many scholars have explored the merits of this openness to learning while in the field and from other forms of scholarship and theories. See, for example, Burawoy 2009; di Leonardo 1993; Harding 1998; Naples 2003; Rose 1997; Sanjek 2000; Smith 1999; Strega 2005; Wright 2006.

Chapter Two. Reconsidering History

1. See, for example, Brown 1999; Fraser 2013; Maskovsky 2001; Neubeck and Cazenave 2001; Orloff 1996; Quadagno 2000; Roberts 1996; Venkatesh 2000; Wilson 2009.

2. As Greenberg (2008, 125), points out, "this development involved the purposeful deindustrialization of New York's still thriving port district, the elimination of some 30,000 blue-collar jobs, and the overall transformation of a historically mixed-used district into a global financial center."

3. Brenner and Theodore 2002; Brown 2006; Hackworth 2007; Harvey 2005; Peck and Theodore 2002; Sites 2003.

4. Feminists have explored these intersections more fully with regard to national policies and ideologies in the United States with relevant findings for this book (see, for example, Bashevkin 1998; Boyer 2003; Brown 2006, 2015; Collins, di Leonardo, and Williams 2008; Duggan 2012; Fraser 2013; Fraser and Gordon 1994; Kingfisher 2002, 2011; Mink 1990; Simon-Kumar 2011; Williams 1995). However, the emphasis of these studies has less commonly been on *urban* politics. A recent and growing body of literature attends closely to racialized neoliberal urban practices and formations in the United States and Canada (e.g., Boyd 2008; Buckley 2014; Derickson 2014; Parker 2008; Roberts and Mahtani 2010).

5. See, for example, Bashevkin 1998; Morgan and Maskovsky 2003; University of Wisconsin–Milwaukee 2001; Wolch and Dear 1993.

6. Tax incremental financing (TIF) and business improvement districts (BIDs) are excellent examples of these new kinds of formations, which allow tax dollars to be used toward private business and urban and neighborhood development that is organized by and provides profits for the private sector (see Ward 2007a, 2007b on BIDs and Weber 2010 on TIF). In the late 1990s and early 2000s, Milwaukee had the highest number of BIDs for a city of its size.

7. On the gendered and raced nature of welfare reform and austerity, see Bashevkin 1998; Fraser and Gordon 1994; Gilens 1995; Kingfisher 1996, 2002; Mink 1990; Neubeck and Cazenave 2001; Noble 1997; Quadagno 1994; Roberts 2002; Williams 1995. Many of these authors detail the ways that stereotypical media images of poor women of color

shape welfare policies and public support for them. Gilens (1995) found that racism was the most important factor in shaping white opposition to welfare, and that "negative attitudes toward blacks lead many whites who support spending for education, health care, and the elderly to oppose means-tested programs aimed exclusively at the poor."

8. See, for example, chapter 7; Douglas 2010; Gill 2007, 2011; McRobbie 2011; Walby 2011.

9. See Burgess 2008; Greed 2005; Hayden 2002; Kern 2010b; Parker 2011; Rahder and Altilia 2004; Sánchez de Madariaga and Roberts 2013.

10. See Fraser 2013; Kingfisher 1996; McDowell 2004; Mink 1990; Okin 1989; Orloff 1996; Walby 2011; Williams 1995.

11. See, among others, Campbell 2014; Cho, Crenshaw, and McCall 2013; Fraser 2013; McDowell 2008; Walby 2011.

12. There are extensive and varied literatures that illustrate the important role of values, discourses, and "frames" in shaping national and urban policies, subjectivities, and inequalities related to gender, race, sexuality, neoliberalism, and other relations. Here I am less interested in sifting through the precise differences in these arguments and more interested in articulating key values and surrounding discourses associated with U.S. urban politics and urban neoliberalism and how they work (not uncontested) in concert with specific practices, materialities, and relations of ruling to marginalize particular individuals, groups, alternatives, etc. See, for example, Bacchi 1999; Brown 2006, 2015; Dardot and Laval 2013; Fraser and Gordon 1994; Gill 1995; Kingfisher 2007a, 2007b; Laclau and Mouffe 2001; Larner 2003; Larner et al. 2013; Mirowski 2013; Naples 2003; Peck 2008; Rose 1999; Smith 2005; Springer 2012.

13. See, for example, Brodie 2007; Brown 2015; Dardot and Laval 2013; Hackworth 2008; Larner 2003; Lawson 2007; Mirowski 2013; Rodriguez 2014.

14. See, for example, Boyer 2003; Fraser 2013; Fraser and Gordon 1994; Kingfisher 2002; Orloff 1996; Williams 1995.

15. See, for example, Campbell 2014; Fraser 2013; Lawson 2007; Lister 1990; McDowell 1999, 2004; McEwan and Goodman 2010; Orloff 1996; Roberts 2013; Walby 2011.

16. See, for example, Boyer 2003; Brodie 2007; Collins and Mayer 2010; Fraser 2013; Katz 2004, 2008; McDowell 2004; Meehan and Strauss 2015; Mitchell, Marston, and Katz 2004; Orloff 1996; Simon-Kumar 2013. See also chapter 6.

17. See, for example, Davila 2004; Davis 2007; Parker 2008; Peck 2006a; Wilson 2009.

18. Social reproduction is discussed in more detail in chapter 6. On feminist theories of social reproduction, also see Bakker and Gill 2003; Bakker and Silvey 2012; Katz 2001, 2008; Laslett and Brenner 1989; Luxton and Bezanson 2006; Meehan and Strauss 2015; Mitchell, Marston, and Katz 2004.

19. E.g., Boyer 2003; Collins and Mayer 2010; Ferree, Lorber, and Hess 1999; McDowell 2004.

20. See, for example, Bashevkin 1998; Boyer 2003; Fraser and Gordon 1994; Gilens 1995; Kingfisher 2002; Mink 1990; Williams 1995.

21. The literature on urban entrepreneurialism and interurban competition is deep. For some examples, see Hall and Hubbard 1998; Harvey 1989; Peck 2001, 2006a; Rennie-Short 2003; Weber 2002, 2010; Wilson 2009. These issues are also discussed in chapters 4 and 7.

22. See, for example, Bashevkin 1998; Brodie 2007; Campbell 2014; Himmelweit and Land 2011; Kingfisher 2002; Orloff 1996; Walby 2011. Different bodies experience this "suffering" differently, dependent on social reproductive duties, race or ethnicity, sexuality, age, class, and other factors.

23. See Brownlow 2009; Campbell 2014; Douglas 2010; Gill 2007, 2011; Isoke 2011; Kern 2010b; Valentine, Jackson, and Mayblin 2014.

24. See Fincher 1990; McKittrick 2011; Spain 2004; Wright 2013.

25. See Brownill 2000; Fainstein 2001; Fincher 2006; Kern 2010a; Kern and Wekerle 2008; Sánchez de Madariaga and Roberts 2013.

26. These arguments differ from those presented by some feminist theorists who suggest the state is no longer marked by masculinities and associated politics of exclusion, individualization, and domination (e.g., Simon-Kumar 2011). In at least some U.S. cities, these associations still ring rather true, progressive politics of inclusion are not particularly salient, and the "man" still lurks in the state (see Brown 1992).

27. See, for example, Correll, Benard, and Paik 2007; Dovidio and Gaertner 2000; Handelsman et al., 2005; Hegewisch and Hartmann 2014; Leitner, Peck, and Sheppard 2007; Lips 2013; Pager 2007; Peck and Theodore 2001; Tomaskovic-Devey, Thomas, and Johnson 2005; Valian 1999; Wenneras and Wold 1997.

28. See Crittenden 2001; Douglas 2010; Douglas and Michaels 2005; Hays 1996.

29. Brodie 2007, 2008; Burnham and Theodore 2012; McDowell 2007, 2013; Orloff 1996; Pratt 2004; Walby 2011.

30. See Gilmore 2007; Hill Collins 2002; Isoke 2011; Luxton and Bezanson 2006; Nagar et al. 2002; Naples 1992; Stall and Stoecker 1998.

31. See, for example, Alvarez 1999; Bashevkin 1998; Eisenstein 2009; Eschle and Maiguashca 2014; Fraser 2009, 2013; McRobbie 2009; Newman 2013; Runyan and Peterson 2013; Walby 2011; Whitzman 2007. See also chapter 7.

32. See Elwood 2006; Klodawsky, Siltanen, and Andrew 2013; Leitner and Sheppard 2008; Purcell 2008; Sites 2007.

33. See, for example, Eisenstein 2009; Fraser 2009; Marchand and Runyan 2010; Martin 2004; Melamed 2006; Newman and Lake 2006; Stoecker 2004.

Chapter Three. From Sewer Socialism to "Sewers for Sale"

1. While this decline for Milwaukee was dramatic, it was not as marked as in other cities such as Detroit, where the entire manufacturing base was nearly decimated. In fact, in 1990, Milwaukee still had nearly a hundred thousand manufacturing jobs. In 1992, it was fourth among fourteen Frost Belt cities in manufacturing employment (Levine and Callaghan 1998).

2. Importantly, the unique design of Milwaukee's county and city governments—which had split governance responsibilities in the 1930s—helped facilitate this limited success for the city during the Depression. Milwaukee County, rather than Milwaukee City, had the onerous task of ensuring that social services were provided to all citizens and for providing care of the indigent.

3. As chapter 7 shows, this same tactic is used in contemporary urban politics. Milwaukee activists who sought to include community benefits like affordable housing into

development projects were labeled socialists who were trying to impede progress and development in Milwaukee.

4. In fact, women seemed to hold consistently about 25 percent of Common Council seats throughout the 1980s. This number peaked in 1992, and gradually declined afterward to reach zero percent in 2004 (data furnished by the Office of the City Clerk, Milwaukee 1980–2004).

5. As Collins and Mayer (2010, 22) explain, most studies (within and outside of Milwaukee) do not show significantly improved circumstances for participants who have left welfare. Furthermore, studies cannot account for many women who have left welfare—"who show up neither in unemployment insurance data nor on social service rosters."

6. See Courtney and Dworsky 2006; Mulligan-Hansel and Fendt 2003; State of Wisconsin, Department of Workforce Development 2005.

7. "Within Wisconsin, it's difficult to find a nonprofit voucher group that hasn't received significant Bradley money. For example, the Institute for the Transformation of Learning, led by Howard Fuller, has been granted more than $1 million by Bradley since 1995. The Black Research Organization, started by Mike Holt of the pro-voucher Community Journal, received a total of $319,000 in 1995 and 1996. Partners Advancing Values in Education, a pro-voucher scholarship group based in Milwaukee, has received roughly $10 million from Bradley over the years" (cited in Miner 2001).

8. Also, while there are limited data and analysis on gendered and raced practices within urban think tanks (particularly neoconservative and neoliberal foundations) and their associated networks, and although this is outside of the scope of this book, some suggestive evidence does exist. First, the majority of these think tanks are dominated by men and whites, in terms of both boards and staff composition. Second, as I have alluded to in this chapter, these think tanks have been involved in funding organizations and projects with sexist and racialized agendas and overtones, producing and disseminating related discourses and publications. For example, Bill Bennett, in a Heritage Foundation–sponsored debate on family values, made the following comments: "Just as no amount of feminist demagogy will ever make it possible for women to be anything other than what they ineluctably are, with the result that the recent effort to help them 're-define' themselves has left them little more than a bellyful of bitterness" (Heritage Foundation 1992).

9. Urban geographer Jamie Peck argues that foundations and think tanks have played an increasing and critical role in framing and marketing neoliberal policies, most recently in reorienting discussions of racism and redistribution in New Orleans following Katrina toward revanchism, renewal, and restricted government.

10. See, among others, Brenner and Theodore 2002; Harvey 2006; Larner 2003; McLean 2014a, 2014b; Parker 2008; Weber 2002.

11. See Barrett and Greene 1994; Daykin 2006a, 2006b; Gould 2003; Norquist 2003; Parker 2008; Zimmerman 2008; see also chapters 4 and 5.

Chapter Four. Rationalities of Rule

1. Excluding the most expensive projects, the average condo sold in 2005 was 1,441 square feet and $312,000. See Daykin 2006a, 2007.

2. On parasitic suburbanism, see Beauregard 2006.

3. For example, Norquist wrote an article titled "The Self-Reliant City" in 1994 in *City Journal* and an article in *Civic Bulletin* in 1998, both published by the Manhattan Institute. Furthermore, his book was reviewed favorably by these same publication outlets. Norquist also contributed to a book titled *The Entrepreneurial City*, which was authored by Stephen Goldsmith, a senior fellow and chairman for civic innovation at the Manhattan Institute. Finally, he was a keynote speaker at events sponsored by the Manhattan Institute and an advisory board member. For a fuller discussion on the role of think tanks (especially the Manhattan Institute) in the dissemination and production of neoliberal ideologies and the neoliberal framing of urban crises and responses, see Peck 2006b.

4. See, for example, Al-Hindi 2001; Cabrera and Najarian 2013; Goetz 2003; Johnson and Talen 2008; Markovich and Hendler 2006.

5. Recent quasi-public developments have emerged in response to Milwaukee's housing crisis, which was exacerbated by a significant decline in federal support for housing. For example, a housing trust fund was launched in 2006 after significant lobbying by Milwaukee's activist organizations.

6. See Atkeson 2003; Atkeson and Carrillo 2007; Bratton 2005; Broockman, 2014; Campbell and Wolbrecht 2006; Gerrity, Osborn, and Mendez 2007; Weikart et al. 2007.

Chapter Five. Could the Violent Femmes Save Milwaukee?

1. For some exceptions, see Leslie and Catungal 2012; McLean 2014a, 2014b; Negrey and Rausch 2009; Parker 2008.

2. The concept of embodiment acknowledges that "our awareness is profoundly influenced by the fact that we have a body, which is shaped by connections and larger networks of meanings at multiple scales" (Cresswell 1999, 175–76).

3. There is an extensive literature that discusses bias and unearned privilege related to race, gender, class, and physical appearance, including studies where reviewers looked at identical resumes or applications, and those with male-sounding and white-sounding names were ranked higher than those female-sounding or black-sounding names (see Bertrand and Mullainathan 2003; Biernat 2003; Dovidio and Gaertner 2000; Pager and Quillian 2005; Steinpreis, Anders, and Ritzke 1999; Valian 1999; Wenneras and Wold 1997).

4. Also see Correll, Benard, and Paik 2007; Dovidio and Gaertner 2000; Handelsman et al. 2005; Hegewisch and Hartmann 2014; Lips 2013; Pager 2007; Parker 2008; Steinpreis, Anders, and Ritzke 1999; Tomaskovic-Devey, Thomas, and Johnson 2005; Valian 1999; Wenneras and Wold 1997.

Chapter Six. Getting By in Milwaukee

1. Marx framed social reproduction as the backdrop processes that produce laborers and enable capitalist production, a perspective that still reverberates through much scholarship. Engagement with social reproduction has helped feminists displace hierarchical assumptions and the primacy of production in much academic work and raise critical questions of value (Brodie 2007; Dalla Costa and James 1972; Meehan and Strauss 2015; Mitchell, Marston, and Katz 2004). Feminists have highlighted the multiple forms of power, structures, and processes—within, "outside," and connected to capitalism—that shape the social reproduction of life and communities (e.g., Acker

2006; Gibson-Graham 1996; Katz 2008). In particular, antiracist and black feminists help make visible ways that the capitalist system, the state, and all forms of reproductive and provisioning activity are dialectically constructed in and through the multiply situated social actions of race, gender, sexuality, and class (e.g., Acker 2006; Hill Collins 2000a, 2000b; hooks 2000; Kobayashi 2004). Recent feminist work calls for an integrative, empirical, comprehensive, and contemporary analysis of social reproduction, also labeled "life's work" (Bakker 2007; Luxton and Bezanson 2006; Meehan and Strauss 2015; Mitchell, Marston, and Katz 2004). Meehan and Strauss (2015) ask how social reproduction studies might come into conversation with literatures related to embodiment, multiple forms of materiality (including human/nonhuman), and the complex forms of economic life and provisioning that occur in households and communities. Furthermore, they remind us that social reproduction theories have sometimes "been blind to the nitty gritty of material life." It is with these critiques and analytical spirit that I explore social reproduction and neoliberalism in Milwaukee in this chapter.

2. See Alexander 2010; Brown 1999; Jones 2009; McCluskey 2003; Quadagno 1994; Richie 2012; Roberts 1993, 2008. Also see chapters 2 and 3.

3. All names of interviewees, children, and family members have been changed.

4. There is a rich literature that discusses discrimination in labor markets as well as the paradoxes and problems for women in the gendered, raced, and uneven neoliberal economy. Feminists have argued that support for caregiving and economic autonomy is necessary for women's equality, but these have not manifested under neoliberalism. To various degrees, socialist, black, radical, and other feminists have long pointed out that liberalism and capitalism (and the subjectivities and assumptions in which they are rooted) cannot produce justice and equity. On the latter arguments, see, for example, Brown 1995; Ferree and Mueller 2003; Lorde 1984; MacKenzie 1984; McKittrick 2011; Young 1987. On gendered and raced inequalities in neoliberal labor markets and economies, see Brown 2015; Collins and Mayer 2010; Larner et al. 2013; McDowell 2013; Meehan and Strauss 2015; Pager and Quillian 2005; Pager and Western 2012; Roberts 2013, 2015; Runyan and Peterson 2013; Simon-Kumar 2011. See also chapter 2.

5. See Richie (2012) for more on racialized and gendered differentiation, fear, and African American women's experience with the criminal justice system.

6. See, among others, Alexander 2010; Bonds 2007; Cowen and Siciliano 2011; Gilmore 2007; Isoke 2013; McKittrick 2011; Richie 2012; Roberts 2008.

Chapter Seven. "This Land Is Our Land"

1. This represented a sixteen-million-dollar increase from projected expenditures in a resolution passed in March 2002.

2. Author's notes, December 15, 2003; presentation of Park East Development Plan to RACM, December 15, 2003.

3. Interview, community activist, White, female, December 2003.

4. See *Economist* 2004, where he was described as a fiscally conservative socialist.

5. Bonds does not fully detail why he thinks that black community organizations were more subject to the punitive actions of the mayor, although he does argue that the presence of African American leaders in the City Council did nothing to mitigate this trend.

6. As described by Pedroni (2005), desegregation efforts (resisted at first) in Milwau-

kee Public Schools entailed long bus rides for black students to primarily white suburban schools. White students primarily remained in their nearby local schools. Black students were exhausted, lost time for homework due to bus rides, and felt culturally alienated, as did their families.

7. Several studies have explored the way that community-based organizations have been co-opted, shifting toward service provision and training initiatives and away from activism in a neoliberal climate. See, for example, Alvarez 1999; Eick 2007; Kantola and Squires 2012; Lake and Martin 2003; Martin 2004; Mayer 2007; Melamed 2006; Stoecker 2004.

8. Both the historic dominance of patriarchy and racism and the fact that liberalism has always been premised on a white male subject and distributed its benefits accordingly have helped enable this reinvigoration.

9. Some scholars lay the supposed demise of feminism at neoliberalism's feet or suggest that neoliberalism provided the roots for more neoconservative and antiwomen agendas to flourish. See, for example, Brown 2006; Eisenstein 2009; Fraser 2009. My argument is closer to that of Sylvia Walby (2011), who argues that neoliberalism is relevant for gender relations and has made feminist and social justice organizing more difficult in specific ways, but is not all-determining. See also, among others, Gibson-Graham 2007; Larner and Butler 2007; Leitner, Peck, and Sheppard 2007; Newman 2013; Marchand and Runyan 2010; and Smith, Stenning, and Willis 2009 for arguments about feminist and social justice organizing influences on the state and the two-way relationships between neoliberalism and "resistance."

10. Brown 2006; Davis 2007; Derickson 2014; Duggan 2012; Wajcman 2013.

11. Bashevkin 1998; Davis 2007; Gilens 1995; Kingfisher 1996; Larner 2003; Mink 1990; Moody 1997; Rose 1999; Walby 2011; and Williams 1995.

12. See, for example, Bakker 2007; Bashevkin 1998; Brodie 2005, 2007; Davis 2007; Faludi 1991; Fraser 2013; Hewitt 2005; Runyan and Peterson 2013; Walby 2011; and Wilson 2009.

13. On antipathy and the structural fading of feminism, backlashes, claims of a postfeminist moment, reluctance of women to declare themselves feminist, withdrawal of the state from equity and gender claims, and other issues, see Braithwaite 2004; Brodie 2008; Bumiller 2009; Douglas 2010; Faludi 2006; Fraser 2009, 2013; Gill 2011; Kingfisher 2002; McRobbie 2009; Roth 2004; Tinsley et al. 2009; and Walby 2011. There is a smaller literature that looks more specifically at hostility and indifference toward feminist or gender-focused agendas in urban planning and politics. See Burgess 2008; Parker 2011; Rahder and Altilia 2004; Sánchez de Madariaga and Roberts 2013; and Whitzman 2007. Also see chapter 2.

14. This is not to say that racism ever dissipated in the United States, but to suggest that there was a backlash and deepening and reformulation of specific kinds of racist practices in the 1980s and 1990s, along with discourses and policies that claimed equality existed, especially via the market. See Alexander 2010; Duggan 2012; Gilmore 2007; Hewitt 2005; McKittrick 2006, 2011; and Richie 2012.

15. See chapter 2.

16. For example, see Brodie 2007; Hyatt 2001, 2011; Jennings 2002; Lyon-Callo 2008;

Morgan and Maskovsky 2003; Mulligan-Hansel and Fendt 2003; Nagar et al. 2002; Runyan and Peterson 2013; Walby 2011.

17. See note 7.

18. See Elwood and Leitner 1998; Leitner, Peck, and Sheppard 2007; and Smith, Stenning, and Willis 2009.

19. I don't wish to assert that everyone in city leadership held the exact same opinion, as there was dissent among different actors. Rather, I present the dominant themes that came through in interviews, public documents, and testimonies of city officials and employees, which often coincided with the views of developers.

20. Hackworth 2007; Sager 2011; Weber 2002; Wyly and Hammel 2004; and Zimmerman 2008. See also chapters 3, 4, and 5.

21. Collins and Mayer 2010; Hackworth 2007; Jessop 1996; Peck and Tickell 2002.

22. Testimony, Steering and Rules Committee of Common Council, June 10, 2004.

23. Testimony, Steering and Rules Committee of Common Council, June 10, 2004.

24. Developer's testimony, Steering and Rules Committee of Common Council, June 10, 2004.

25. Letter addressed to Common Council members from the Office of the Comptroller, January 20, 2004.

26. Developer's testimony, Steering and Rules Committee of the Common Council, June 10, 2004, emphasis added.

27. Not all members of the Good Jobs and Livable Neighborhoods Coalition shared the exact same views, and in some cases the imaginaries of individuals and the coalition coincided with those of the city leaders.

28. See Good Jobs and Livable Neighborhoods Coalition (2003).

29. See Good Jobs and Livable Neighborhoods Coalition (2004b), presented to City Council members on November 12, 2004.

30. Following the two-year period, the debates moved on to the county level and a series of events ensued, which were not part of this research process.

31. Verbal comments, elected official C, Common Council meeting, June 10, 2004.

32. Verbal testimony, commercial representative, Common Council meeting, June 10, 2004. During this meeting (one of many where the Park East Development was debated), community members, developers, and other interested parties were invited to give verbal testimony. Elected officials asked questions of those giving testimony, and also had some discussion among themselves. I attended the meeting, requested an audiotape from the City Clerk's office, and then transcribed the comments, exchanges, and testimonies made during the meeting.

33. Verbal comments, elected official A, Common Council meeting, June 10, 2004.

34. Verbal testimony, business owner, Common Council meeting, June 10, 2004.

35. Handelsman et al. 2005; Kay and Shipman 2014; Okimoto and Brescoll 2010; and Wenneras and Wold 1997.

36. See, for example, Brenner and Theodore 2002; Hackworth 2007; Hubbard 2004; Kern 2010b; Kern and Wekerle 2008; and Tickell and Peck 1996. See also chapter 5.

37. Author's field notes, June 10, 2004. Similar patterns were apparent in previous meetings I attended.

38. Comments, elected official C, City Council meeting, June 10, 2004.

39. Testimony, City Council meeting, June 10, 2004.

40. Testimony, labor activist, City Council meeting, June 10, 2004.

41. Author's field notes, March 18, 2004.

42. A substitute ordinance related to the promotion and creation of benefits to the community as a result of development occurring in the city (Number 031050, Substitute 5).

43. Also see, for example, Burgess 2008; Greed 2006; Isoke 2007; Rahder and Altilia 2004; Sánchez de Madariaga and Roberts 2013; Wankiewicz 2013; Whitzman 2007; and Wright 2013.

44. Testimony, contractor, City Council meeting, June 10, 2004.

45. Testimony, contractor, City Council meeting, June 10, 2004.

46. Testimony, union representative, City Council meeting, June 10, 2004.

47. See, for example, Bhattacharjya et al. 2013; Isoke 2007; Luft 2008; *MS* 2011; and Stall and Stoecker 1998.

48. Author's field notes, January 20, 2004; June 10, 2004; and December 16, 2004.

49. Pastor's name is a pseudonym. Author's field notes, January 20, 2004.

50. See Barnes 2006; Collins et al. 2004; Ngunjiri, Gramby-Sobukwe, and William-Gegner, 2012.

51. Dominance of white and Western women has been a long-standing issue for women of color and women from the non-Western world with regard to feminism (see, among others, Cordova 1993; Crenshaw 1989, 1991; Hill Collins 2002; Isoke 2013; McKittrick 2006, 2011; Mohanty 1988; Mohanty and Russo 1991; and Moraga and Anzaldúa 2015).

Conclusion. Feminist Urban Narratives, Politics, and Imaginaries

1. In some Milwaukee zip codes, over 60 percent of African American men had experienced incarceration by age thirty-four.

2. As discussed in chapter 1. Also see, among others, Burgess 2008; Parker 2016; Rahder and Altilia 2004; Sánchez de Madariaga and Roberts 2013; and Wright 2013.

BIBLIOGRAPHY

Abu-Lughod, J. L. (1999). *New York, Chicago, Los Angeles: America's global cities.* Minneapolis: University of Minnesota Press.

Acker, J. (2006). Inequality regimes gender, class, and race in organizations. *Gender & Society,* 20(4), 441–64.

Addams, J. (2002/1902). *Democracy and social ethics.* Urbana: University of Illinois Press.

Ahlers, J. (2007, September 7). When I was 30; Tim Sheehy; Bringing Milwaukee to the world. *Milwaukee Journal Sentinel,* Z35.

Ahmed, S. (2010). *The promise of happiness.* Durham, N.C.: Duke University Press.

Alexander, M. (2012). *The new Jim Crow: Mass incarceration in the age of colorblindness.* New York: New Press.

Al-Hindi, K. F. (2001). The new urbanism: Where and for whom? Investigation of an emergent paradigm. *Urban Geography,* 22(3), 202–19.

Alvarez, S. E. (1999). Advocating feminism: The Latin American feminist NGO "boom." *International Feminist Journal of Politics,* 1(2), 181–209.

American Civil Liberties Union. (2013, June). The war on marijuana in black and white. https://www.aclu.org/sites/default/files/field_document/1114413-mj-report-rfs-rel1.pdf.

Ashton, P. (2009). An appetite for yield: The anatomy of the subprime mortgage crisis. *Environment and Planning A,* 41(6), 1420–41.

Ashton, P., Doussard, M., and Weber, R. (2012). The financial engineering of infrastructure privatization: What are public assets worth to private investors? *Journal of the American Planning Association,* 78(3), 300–312.

Atkeson, L. R. (2003). Not all cues are created equal: The conditional impact of female candidates on political engagement. *Journal of Politics,* 65(4), 1040–61.

Atkeson, L. R., and Carrillo, N. (2007). More is better: The impact of female representation on citizen attitudes toward government responsiveness. *Gender and Politics,* 3(1), 79–101.

Bacchi, C. L. (1999). *Women, policy and politics: The construction of policy problems.* Thousand Oaks, Calif.: Sage.

Baker, A. C. (2014). Eroding the wealth of women: Gender and the subprime foreclosure crisis. *Social Service Review*, 88(1), 59–91.

Bakker, I. (2007). Social reproduction and the constitution of a gendered political economy. *New Political Economy*, 12(4), 541–56.

Bakker, I., and Gill, S. (Eds.). (2003). *Power, production, and social reproduction: Human in/security in the global political economy*. London: Palgrave Macmillan.

Bakker, I., and Silvey, R. (Eds.). (2012). *Beyond states and markets: The challenges of social reproduction*. New York: Routledge.

Ball, M. (2014, April 23). The privatization backlash. *Atlantic Monthly*. http://www .theatlantic.com/politics/archive/2014/04/city-state-governments-privatization -contracting-backlash/361016/.

Barnes, S. L. (2006). Whosoever will let her come: Social activism and gender inclusivity in the Black Church. *Journal for the Scientific Study of Religion*, 45(3), 371–87.

Barnett, C. (2005). The consolations of "neoliberalism." *Geoforum*, 36(1), 7–12.

Barrett, K., and Greene, R. (1994). The state of the cities: Managing for results. *Financial World Magazine*, 163, 40–42.

Bashevkin, S. B. (1998). *Women on the defensive: Living through conservative times*. Chicago: University of Chicago Press.

———. (2011). *Tales of two cities: Women and municipal restructuring in London and Toronto*. Vancouver: University of British Columbia Press.

Beauregard, R. A. (2006). *When America became suburban*. Minneapolis: University of Minnesota Press.

Beck, E. A., and Zeidler, F. (1982). *The sewer socialists: A history of the Socialist Party of Wisconsin, 1897–1940* (Vol. 1). Fennimore, Wis.: Westburg Associates.

Beckis, U. (2001). Interview with Ulrich Beck. *Journal of Consumer Culture*, 1(2), 261–77.

Berardi, F. (2009). *The soul at work: From alienation to autonomy*. Los Angeles: Semiotext(e).

Berger, M. S. (2001). *A Milwaukee woman's life on the left: The autobiography of Meta Berger*. Madison: Wisconsin Historical Society.

Bertrand, M., and Mullainathan, S. (2003). Are Emily and Greg more employable than Lakisha and Jamal? A field experiment on labor market discrimination (w9873). Cambridge, Mass.: National Bureau of Economic Research.

Berube, A. (1990). Marching to a different drummer: Lesbian and gay GIs in World War II. In M. Duberman, M. Vicinus, and G. Chauncey, Jr. (Eds.), *Hidden from history: Reclaiming the gay and lesbian past*, 383–92. New York: Meridian.

Bhattacharjya, M., Birchall, J., Caro, P., Kelleher, D., and Sahasranaman, V. (2013). Why gender matters in activism: Feminism and social justice movements. *Gender & Development*, 21(2), 277–93.

Bianchi, S. M., Sayer, L. C., Milkie, M. A., and Robinson, J. P. (2012). Housework: Who did, does or will do it, and how much does it matter? *Social Forces*, 91(1), 55–63.

Biernat, M. (2003). Toward a broader view of social stereotyping. *American Psychologist*, 58(12), 1019.

Blackstone, E., and Hakim, S. (1997, February 1). Private ayes: A tale of four cities. *American City and County.* http://americancityandcounty.com/mag/government _private_ayes_tale.

Boles, J. K. (1991). Form follows function: The evolution of feminist strategies. *Annals of the American Academy of Political and Social Science,* 515, 38–49.

———. (1992). Local feminist coalitional strategies: Three models. Paper prepared for delivery at the annual meeting of the American Political Science Association, September 3–6.

———. (2001). Local elected women and policymaking: Movement delegates or feminist trustees? In S. J. Carroll (Ed.), *The impact of women in public office,* 68–88. Bloomington: Indiana University Press.

Bondi, L. (1999). Gender, class, and gentrification: Enriching the debate. *Environment and Planning D: Society and Space,* 17(3), 261–82.

———. (2005). Gender and the reality of cities: Embodied identities, social relations and performativities. Institute of Geography Online Paper Series GEO-005. https://www.era.lib.ed.ac.uk/handle/1842/822.

Bondi, L., and Christie, H. (2000). Working out the urban: Gender relations and the city. In G. Bridge and S. Watson (Eds.), *A companion to the city,* 292–306. Oxford: Blackwell.

Bondi, L., and Peake, L. (1988). Gender and the city: Urban politics revisited. In J. Little, L. Peake, and P. Richardson (Eds.), *Women in cities: Gender and the urban environment,* 21–40. London: Macmillan.

Bondi, L., and Rose, D. (2003). Constructing gender, constructing the urban: A review of Anglo-American feminist urban geography. *Gender, Place & Culture,* 10(3), 229–45.

Bonds, A., and Inwood, J. (2015). Beyond white privilege: Geographies of white supremacy and settler colonialism. *Progress in Human Geography.* Early online version.

Bonds, M. (2004). *Race, politics and community development funding: The discolor of money.* New York: Haworth Social Work Practice Press.

———. (2007). Black political power reassessed: Race, politics, and federal funds. *Journal of African American Studies,* 11, 189–203.

Borowski, G. (2001, May 9). Nationwide efficiency survey ranks Milwaukee in top 20; While city comes in 13th out of 44, council wrestles with $7 million budget shortfall. *Milwaukee Journal Sentinel.*

Bourdieu, P. (1989). Social space and symbolic power. *Sociological Theory,* 7(1), 14–25.

———. (1998). *Acts of resistance: Against the tyranny of the market.* New York: New Press.

Boyd, M. R. (2008). *Jim Crow nostalgia: Reconstructing race in Bronzeville.* Minneapolis: University of Minnesota Press.

Boyer, K. (2003). At work, at home? New geographies of work and care-giving under welfare reform in the US. *Space and Polity,* 7(1), 75–86.

Bradley Foundation. (1997). Annual report. http://www.bradleyfdn.org.

———. (2004). Annual report. http://www.bradleyfdn.org.

———. (2005). Annual report. http://www.bradleyfdn.org.

———. (2006). Grantee showcase: President Bush visits Holy Redeemer in Milwaukee, touts "faith-based" social services work there. http://www.bradleyfdn.org.

Braithwaite, A. (2004). Politics of/and backlash. *International Journal of Women's Studies*, 5(5), 18–33.

Bratton, K. A. (2005). Critical mass theory revisited: The behavior and success of token women in state legislatures. *Politics & Gender*, 1(1), 97–125.

Bratton, K. A., Haynie, K. L., and Reingold, B. (2007). Agenda setting and African American women in state legislatures. *Journal of Women, Politics & Policy*, 28(3–4), 71–96.

Brenner, N. (2001). The limits to scale? Methodological reflections on scalar structuration. *Progress in Human Geography*, 25(4), 591–614.

Brenner, N., and Theodore, N. (Eds.). (2002). *Spaces of neoliberalism: Urban restructuring in North America and Western Europe*. London: Blackwell.

Brodie, J. (2003). Globalization, in/security, and the paradoxes of the social. In I. Bakker and S. Gill (Eds.), *Power, production, and social reproduction: Human in/security in the global political economy*, 47–65. London: Palgrave Macmillan.

———. (2004). Introduction: Globalization and citizenship beyond the national state. *Citizenship Studies*, 8(4), 323–32.

———. (2005). Globalization, governance, and gender: Rethinking the agenda for the twenty-first century. In L. Amoore (Ed.), *The global resistance reader*, 244–56. New York: Routledge.

———. (2007). Reforming social justice in neoliberal times. *Studies in Social Justice*, 1(2), 93–107.

———. (2008). We are all equal now: Contemporary gender politics in Canada. *Feminist Theory*, 9(2), 145–64.

Broockman, D. E. (2014). Do female politicians empower women to vote or run for office? A regression discontinuity approach. *Electoral Studies*, 34, 190–204.

Brown, M. (1999). *Race, money, and the American welfare state*. Ithaca, N.Y.: Cornell University Press.

Brown, W. (1992). Finding the man in the state. *Feminist Studies*, 18(1), 7–34.

———. (1995). *States of injury: Power and freedom in late modernity*. (Vol. 6). Princeton, N.J.: Princeton University Press.

———. (2006). American nightmare: Neoliberalism, neoconservatism, and de-democratization. *Political Theory*, 34(6), 690–714.

———. (2015). *Undoing the demos: Neoliberalism's stealth revolution*. Cambridge, Mass.: MIT Press.

Brownill, S. (1994). Selling the inner city: Regeneration and place marketing in London's Docklands. In J. R. Gold and S. V. Ward (Eds.), *Place promotion: The use of publicity and marketing to sell towns and regions*, 133–52. New York: John Wiley.

———. (2000). Regen(d)eration: Women and urban policy in Britain. In J. Darke, S. Ledwith, and R. Woods (Eds.), *Women and the city*, 11–40. Houndmills: Palgrave.

Brownlow, A. (2009). Keeping up appearances: Profiting from patriarchy in the nation's "safest city." *Urban Studies*, 46(8), 1680–1701.

Brush, L. (2003). *Gender and governance*. Walnut Creek, Calif.: AltaMira.

Buckley, M. (2014). On the work of urbanization: Migration, construction labor, and the commodity moment. *Annals of the Association of American Geographers*, 104(2), 338–47.

Buenker, J. (1981). The politics of mutual frustration: Socialists and suffragists in New York and Wisconsin. In S. Miller (Ed.), *Flawed liberation: Socialism and feminism*, 113–44. Westport, Conn.: Greenwood.

Buhle, M. (1983). *Women and American socialism, 1870–1920*. Champaign: University of Illinois Press.

Bumiller, K. (2009). *In an abusive state: How neoliberalism appropriated the feminist movement against sexual violence*. Durham, N.C.: Duke University Press.

Burawoy, M. (2000). *Uncertain transition: Ethnographies of change in the postsocialist world*. Lanham, Md.: Rowman & Littlefield.

———. (2009). *The extended case method: Four countries, four decades, four great transformations, and one theoretical tradition*. Berkeley: University of California Press.

Bureau of Labor Statistics. (2010). Geographic profile of employment and unemployment. http://www.bls.gov/gps/.

Burgess, G. (2008). Planning and the gender equality duty—Why does gender matter? *People, Place & Policy*, 2(3), 112–21.

Burke, R. J., and Major, D. A. (Eds.). (2014). *Gender in organizations: Are men allies or adversaries to women's career advancement?* Cheltenham: Edward Elgar.

Burnham, L., and Theodore, N. (2012). *Home economics: The invisible and unregulated world of domestic work*. Chicago: National Domestic Workers Alliance.

Butler, J. (2006). *Precarious life: The powers of mourning and violence*. New York: Verso.

Cabrera, J. F., and Najarian, J. C. (2013). Can new urbanism create diverse communities? *Journal of Planning Education and Research*, 33, 427–41.

Cahill, C. (2007). The personal is political: Developing new subjectivities through participatory action research. *Gender, Place & Culture*, 14(3), 267–92.

Campbell, B. (2014). After neoliberalism: The need for a gender revolution. *Soundings*, 56(1), 10–26.

Campbell, D. E., and Wolbrecht, C. (2006). See Jane run: Women politicians as role models for adolescents. *Journal of Politics*, 68(2), 233–47.

Castree, N. (2005). The epistemology of particulars: Human geography, case studies, and "context." *Geoforum*, 36, 541–44.

Center for American Women and Politics. (2010). Current numbers. http://www.cawp.rutgers.edu/

———. (2014). Women in public office. http://www.cawp.rutgers.edu/.

Centers for Disease Control and Prevention. (2012). National health statistics report: Fertility of men and women aged 15–44 years in the United States: National Survey of Family Growth, 2006–2010. http://www.cdc.gov/nchs/data/nhsr/nhsr051.pdf.

Charlton, S. E. M., Everett, J. M., and Staudt, K. A. (Eds.). (1989). *Women, the state, and development*. Albany: State University of New York Press.

Chaskin, R. J., and Joseph, M. L. (2009). Building "community" in mixed-income developments: Assumptions, approaches, and early experiences. *Urban Affairs Review*, 45, 299–335.

Cho, S., Crenshaw, K. W., and McCall, L. (2013). Toward a field of intersectionality studies: Theory, applications, and praxis. *Signs*, 38(4), 785–810.

Chun, J. J., Lipsitz, G., and Shin, Y. (2013). Intersectionality as a social movement strategy: Asian immigrant women advocates. *Signs*, 38(4), 917–40.

Clarke, S., Staeheli, L., and Brunell, S. (1995). Women redefining urban politics. In D. Judge, G. Stoker, and H. Wolman (Eds.), *Theories of urban politics*, 205–27. London: Sage.

Clawson, R. A., and Trice, R. (2000). Poverty as we know it: Media portrayals of the poor. *Public Opinion Quarterly*, 64(1), 53–64.

Collins, J., David, R., Handler, A., Wall, S., and Andes, S. (2004). Very low birthweight in African American infants: The role of maternal exposure to interpersonal racial discrimination. *American Journal of Public Health*, 9(12), 2132–38.

Collins, J. L., di Leonardo, M., and Williams, B. (Eds.). (2008). *New landscapes of inequality: Neoliberalism and the erosion of democracy in America*. Santa Fe, N. Mex.: School for Advanced Research Press.

Collins, J., and Mayer, V. (2010). *Both hands tied: Welfare reform and the race to the bottom in the low-wage labor market*. Chicago: University of Chicago Press.

Congress for New Urbanism. (1999, January/February). Pumping life into a city with better design. *Better Cities and Towns*.

———. (2001). Charter of new urbanism. http://www.cnu.org/charter.

Connell, C. (2010). Doing, undoing, or redoing gender? Learning from the workplace experiences of transpeople. *Gender & Society*, 24(1), 31–55.

Connell, R. W. (2013). *Gender and power: Society, the person and sexual politics*. New York: John Wiley.

Conroy, K., Sandel, M., and Zuckerman, B. (2010). Poverty grown up: How childhood socioeconomic status impacts adult health. *Journal of Developmental & Behavioral Pediatrics*, 31(2), 154–60.

Cooper, M. (2000). Being the "go-to-guy": Fatherhood, masculinity, and the organization of work in Silicon Valley. *Qualitative Sociology*, 23(4), 379–405.

Cope, M. (1997). *Feminist epistemology*. Lanham, Md.: Rowman & Littlefield.

Cordova, T. (1993). *Chicana voices: Intersections of class, race, and gender*. Albuquerque: University of New Mexico Press.

Correll, S., Benard, S., and Paik, I. (2007). Getting a job: Is there a motherhood penalty? *American Journal of Sociology*, 112, 1297–1338.

Courtney, M., and Dworsky, A. (2006). Findings from the Milwaukee TANF Applicant Study. Chicago: Chapin Hall Center for Children, University of Chicago.

Cowen, D. E. (2006). Fighting for "freedom": The end of conscription in the United States and the neoliberal project of citizenship. *Citizenship Studies*, 10(2), 167–83.

Cowen, D., and Siciliano, A. (2011). Surplus masculinities and security. *Antipode*, 43(5), 1516–41.

Crenshaw, K. (1989). Demarginalizing the intersection of race and sex: A black feminist critique of antidiscrimination doctrine, feminist theory and antiracist politics. *University of Chicago Legal Forum*, 1989(1), 139–67.

———. (1991). Mapping the margins: Intersectionality, identity politics, and violence against women of color. *Stanford Law Review*, 43, 1241–99.

Cresswell, T. (1999). Embodiment, power and the politics of mobility: The case of female tramps and hobos. *Transactions of the Institute of British Geographers*, 24(2), 175–92.

Crittenden, A. (2001). *The price of motherhood: Why the most important job in the world is still the least valued.* New York: Metropolitan Books.

Cronon, W. (2009). *Nature's metropolis: Chicago and the Great West.* New York: Norton.

Cummings, J. D. (2008). The stained glass ceiling in the black Baptist church: The continuing paradox of liberation. Doctoral dissertation, Asbury Theological Seminary.

Cuordileone, K. A. (2000). "Politics in an age of anxiety": Cold War political culture and the crisis in American masculinity, 1949–1960. *Journal of American History*, 87, 515–45.

Dalla Costa, M., and James, S. (1972). *The power of women and the subversion of the community.* London: Falling Wall Press.

Dardot, P., and Laval, C. (2013). *The new way of the world: On neoliberal society.* New York: Verso.

Davila, A. (2004). *Barrio dreams: Puerto Ricans, Latinos, and the neoliberal city.* Berkeley: University of California Press.

Davis, D. (2007). Narrating the mute: Racializing and racism in a neoliberal moment. *Souls*, 9(4), 346–60.

Day, K. (2003). New urbanism and the challenges of designing for diversity. *Journal of Planning Education and Research*, 23(1), 83–95.

Daykin, T. (2002, April 12). New life on the river. *Milwaukee Journal Sentinel*.

———. (2006a, January 13). Real estate execs predict strong year for downtown condo market: Demand also will grow for retail business. *Milwaukee Journal Sentinel*, D1.

———. (2006b, April 10). Illinois buyers feel at home in Milwaukee condos, on weekends. *Milwaukee Journal Sentinel*.

———. (2007, April 24). 1 more hotel is proposed: Park East plan calls for long-term lodging, condos. *Milwaukee Journal Sentinel*, D1.

Derickson, K. D. (2009). Gendered, material, and partial knowledges: A feminist critique of neighborhood-level indicator systems. *Environment and Planning A*, 41(4), 896–910.

———. (2014). The racial politics of neoliberal regulation in post-Katrina Mississippi. *Annals of the Association of American Geographers*, 104(4), 889–902.

———. (2015). On the politics of recognition in critical urban scholarship. *Urban Geography*. http://www.tandfonline.com/doi/abs/10.1080/02723638.2015.1105483 ?journalCode=rurb20#.V3G482NCaDA.

Desmond, M. (2016). *Evicted: Poverty and profit in the American city.* New York: Crown.

Dierenfield, B. (2008). *The civil rights movement.* Harlow: Pearson.

di Leonardo, M. (1993). What a difference political economy makes: Feminist anthropology in the postmodern era. *Anthropological Quarterly*, 66, 76–80.

Dixon, B. (2005, July 14). Ten worst places to be black. *Black Commentator*, 146. www .blackcommentator.com/146/146_cover_dixon_worst.html.

Dodson, L., and Bravo, E. (2005). When there is no time or money: Work, family, and community lives of low-income families. In J. Heymann and C. Beem (Eds.),

Unfinished work: Building equality and democracy in an era of working families, 122–55. New York: New Press.

Dombeck, J. M. (1987). The women's coalition of Milwaukee, 1972–1987: Feminist activism at the local level. Master's thesis, University of Wisconsin–Milwaukee.

Domosh, M. (1990). Shaping the commercial city: Retail districts in nineteenth-century New York and Boston. *Annals of the Association of American Geographers,* 80(2), 268–84.

———. (1991). Toward a feminist historiography of geography. *Transactions of the Institute of British Geographers,* 16, 95–104.

———. (2003). Toward a more fully reciprocal feminist inquiry. ACME, 2(1), 107–11.

Domosh, M., and Seager, J. (2001). *Putting women in place: Feminist geographers make sense of the world.* New York: Guilford.

Donegan, M., and Lowe, N. (2008). Inequality in the creative city: Is there still a place for "old-fashioned" institutions? *Economic Development Quarterly,* 22(1), 46–62.

Douglas, S. (2010). *Enlightened sexism: The seductive message that feminism's work is done.* New York: Henry Holt.

Douglas, S., and Michaels, M. (2005). *The mommy myth: The idealization of motherhood and how it has undermined all women.* New York: Free Press.

Dovidio, J., and Gaertner, S. (2000). Aversive racism and selection decisions: 1989 and 1999. *Psychological Science,* 11, 315–19.

Duggan, L. (2012). *The twilight of equality? Neoliberalism, cultural politics, and the attack on democracy.* Boston: Beacon.

Economist. (2004, January 8). Hard act to follow.

Edsall, T., and Edsall, M. (1991). *Chain reaction: The impact of race, rights, and taxes on American politics.* New York: Norton.

Eick, V. (2007). Space patrols—The new peace-keeping functions of nonprofits: Contesting neoliberalism or the urban poor? In H. Leitner, J. Peck, and E. S. Sheppard (Eds.), *Contesting neoliberalism: Urban frontiers,* 266–90. New York: Guilford.

Eisenstein, H. (2009). *Feminism seduced: How global elites use women's labor and ideas to exploit the world.* Boulder, Colo.: Paradigm.

Elwood, S. (2006). Beyond cooptation or resistance: Urban spatial politics, community organizations, and GIS-based spatial narratives. *Annals of the Association of American Geographers,* 96(2), 323–41.

Elwood, S., and Leitner, H. (1998). GIS and community-based planning: Exploring the diversity of neighborhood perspectives and needs. *Cartography and Geographic Information Systems,* 25(2), 77–88.

England, K. V. (1991). Gender relations and the spatial structure of the city. *Geoforum,* 22(2), 135–47.

England, P., and Folbre, N. (1999). The cost of caring. *Annals of the American Academy of Political and Social Science,* 561(1), 39–51.

England, K., and Ward, K. (Eds.). (2011). *Neoliberalization: States, networks, peoples* (Vol. 30). New York: John Wiley.

Eschle, C., and Maiguashca, B. (2014). Reclaiming feminist futures: Co-opted and progressive politics in a neo-liberal age. *Political Studies,* 62(3), 634–51.

Evans, K. (2006, October 17). City disillusions young minority professionals. *Milwaukee Journal Sentinel.*

Fainstein, S. S. (2001). *The city builders: Property development in New York and London, 1980–2000.* Lawrence: University Press of Kansas.

Fairclough, N. (2002). *Discourse and social change.* London: Polity.

Faludi, S. (1991). *Backlash: The undeclared war against American women.* New York: Crown.

———. (2006). *Backlash: The undeclared war against American women* (15th anniversary ed.). New York: Random House.

Fendt, P. S., Mulligan-Hansel, K. M., and White, M. A. (2001). Passing the buck: w-2 and emergency services in Milwaukee County. Milwaukee: Institute for Wisconsin's Future.

Fenster, T. (2005). The right to the gendered city: Different formations of belonging in everyday life. *Journal of Gender Studies,* 14(3), 217–31.

Fenton, A. (1930). The Mexicans of the City of Milwaukee. Report published by the Young Women's Christian Association. Available through the Wisconsin Historical Museum.

Ferree, M. M., Lorber, J., and Hess, B. B. (Eds.). (1999). *Revisioning gender* (Vol. 5). Walnut Creek, Calif.: AltaMira.

Ferree, M. M., and Mueller, C. (2003). Feminism and the women's movement: A global perspective. In D. Snow, S. Soule, and H. Kriesi (Eds.), *The Blackwell companion to social movements,* 576–607. London: Blackwell.

Fincher, R. (1990). Women in the city: Feminist analyses of urban geography. *Australian Geographical Studies,* 28(1), 29–37.

———. (2006). Space, gender and institutions in processes creating difference. *Gender, Place & Culture,* 14(1), 5–27.

Fincher, R., and Jacobs, J. M. (Eds.). (1998). *Cities of difference.* New York: Guilford.

Florida, R. (2002a). *The rise of the creative class.* New York: Basic Books.

———. (2002b, May). The rise of the creative class: Why cities without gays and rock bands are losing the economic development race. *Washington Monthly.*

———. (2004). Revenge of the squelchers. *Next American City,* 5, i–viii.

———. (2005). *Cities and the creative class.* New York: Routledge.

Foucault, M. (1977). *Discipline and punish: The birth of the prison.* New York: Random House.

Fraser, N. (1989). *Unruly practices: Power, discourse and gender in contemporary social theory.* Minneapolis: University of Minnesota Press.

———. (2009). Feminism, capitalism and the cunning of history. *New Left Review,* 56, 97–117.

———. (2013). *Fortunes of feminism: From state-managed capitalism to neoliberal crisis.* New York: Verso.

———. (2014). Behind Marx's hidden abode: For an expanded conception of capitalism. *New Left Review,* 86, 55–72.

Fraser, N., and Gordon, L. (1994). A genealogy of dependency: Tracing a keyword of the US welfare state. *Signs,* 19(2), 309–36.

FUEL Milwaukee. (2007). Fuel events. http://www.fuelmilwaukee.org.

Fure-Slocum, E. (2000). Cities with class? Growth politics, the working-class city, and debt in Milwaukee during the 1940s. *Social Science History*, 24(1), 257–305.

García, A. M. (1997). *Chicana feminist thought: The basic historical writings*. New York: Psychology Press.

Gerrity, J. C., Osborn, T., and Mendez, J. M. (2007). Women and representation: A different view of the district? *Politics & Gender*, 3(2), 179–200.

Gibson-Graham, J. K. (1996). Querying globalization. *Rethinking Marxism*, 9(1), 1–27.

———. (2000). Poststructural interventions. In E. Sheppard and T. J. Barnes (Eds.), *A companion to economic geography*, 95–110. New York: John Wiley.

———. (2006). *"The" end of capitalism (as we knew it): A feminist critique of political economy*. Minneapolis: University of Minnesota Press.

———. (2007). Cultivating subjects for a community economy. In A. Tickell, E. Sheppard, J. Peck, and T. Barnes (Eds.), *Politics and practice in economic geography*, 106–18. Thousand Oaks, Calif.: Sage.

Gilbert, M. (1998). Race, space, and power: The survival strategies of working poor women. *Annals of the Association of American Geographers*, 88(4), 595–602.

———. (1999). Place, politics, and the production of urban space: A feminist critique of the growth machine thesis. In A. E. G. Jonas and D. Wilson (Eds.), *The urban growth machine: Critical perspectives, two decades later*, 95–108. Albany: State University of New York Press.

Gilens, M. (1995). Racial attitudes and opposition to welfare. *Journal of Politics*, 57(4), 994–1014.

Gill, R. (2002). Cool, creative and egalitarian? Exploring gender in project-based new media work in Europe. *Information, Communication, and Society*, 5, 70–89.

———. (2007). Postfeminist media culture: Elements of a sensibility. *European Journal of Cultural Studies*, 10(2), 147–66.

———. (2011). Sexism reloaded; or, It's time to get angry again! *Feminist Media Studies*, 11(1), 61–71.

Gill, S. (1995). Globalisation, market civilization, and disciplinary neoliberalism. *Journal of International Studies*, 24(3), 399–423.

Gilmore, R. W. (2007). *Golden gulag: Prisons, surplus, crisis, and opposition in globalizing California*. Berkeley: University of California Press.

Gilroy, P. (2000). *Against race: Imagining political culture beyond the color line*. Cambridge, Mass.: Harvard University Press.

———. (2013). *There ain't no black in the Union Jack*. New York: Routledge.

Gittell, M., and Shtob, T. (1980). Changing women's roles in political volunteerism and reform of the city. *Signs*, 5(3), S67–78.

Glaze, L., and Maruschak, L. (2008). *Parents in prison and their minor children*. Washington, D.C.: Bureau of Justice Statistics.

Goetz, E. G. (2003). *Clearing the way: Deconcentrating the poor in urban America*. Boston: Urban Institute.

Goldin, C. (2002). The rising (and then declining) significance of gender (w8915). Cambridge, Mass.: National Bureau of Economic Research.

Goldin, C., and Rouse, C. (1997). Orchestrating impartiality: The impact of "blind" auditions on female musicians (W5903). Cambridge, Mass.: National Bureau of Economic Research.

Goldman, E. (1910). Marriage and love. In A. Shulman (Ed.), *Red Emma speaks: An Emma Goldman reader* (3rd ed.), 204–13. Amherst, N.Y.: Humanity Books.

Goode, J., and Maskovsky, J. (Eds.). (2001). *New poverty studies: The ethnography of power, politics, and impoverished people in the United States.* New York: New York University Press.

Good Jobs and Livable Neighborhoods Coalition. (2003, April 13). Community benefits in the Park East Corridor. Two-page brochure developed by the Good Jobs and Livable Neighborhoods Coalition.

———. (2004a). Community benefits in the Park East Corridor. Updated document developed by the Good Jobs and Livable Neighborhoods Coalition.

———. (2004b, November 12). The need for an affordable housing component in the Park East Redevelopment Project.

Gotham, K. F. (2013). Dilemmas of disaster zones: Tax incentives and business reinvestment in the Gulf Coast after Hurricanes Katrina and Rita. *City & Community,* 12(4), 291–308.

Gotham, K. F., and Greenberg, M. (2014). *Crisis cities: Disaster and redevelopment in New York and New Orleans.* New York: Oxford University Press.

Gottesdiener, L. (2013). *A dream foreclosed: Black America and the fight for a place to call home.* New York: Zuccotti Park Press.

Gould, W. (1999a, May 4). Grunau keeps a hand in downtown's reshaping from Schlitz Park to Midwest Express Center. *Milwaukee Journal Sentinel.*

———. (1999b, June 1). Advocates of new urbanism aim to recapture the coziness of city life. *Milwaukee Journal Sentinel.*

———. (2003, June 30). Norquist's legacy is a livelier city. *Milwaukee Journal Sentinel.*

Gourley, S. (2008). *Ms. and the material girl: Perceptions of women from the 1970s to the 1990s.* Minneapolis, Minn.: Twenty-First Century Books.

Greed, C. (2005). Overcoming the factors inhibiting the mainstreaming of gender into spatial planning policy in the United Kingdom. *Urban Studies,* 42(4), 719–49.

———. (2006). Institutional and conceptual barriers to the adoption of gender mainstreaming within spatial planning departments in England. *Planning Theory and Practice,* 7(2), 179–97.

Greenberg, M. (2008). *Branding New York: How a city in crisis was sold to the world.* New York: Routledge.

Gurda, J. (1999). *The making of Milwaukee.* Brookfield, Wis.: Burton & Mayer.

Hackworth, J. (2007). *The neoliberal city: Governance, ideology, and development in American urbanism.* Ithaca, N.Y.: Cornell University Press.

———. (2008). The neoliberal city: Governance, ideology, and development in American urbanism. *Economic Geography,* 84(1), 121–22.

Hackworth, J., and Moriah, A. (2006). Neoliberalism, contingency and urban policy: The case of social housing in Ontario. *International Journal of Urban and Regional Research,* 30(3), 510–27.

Hall, S. (2013). Business education and the (re)production of gendered cultures of work in the city of London. *Social Politics,* 20(2), 222–41.

Hall, T., and Hubbard, P. (1998). *The entrepreneurial city: Geographies of politics, regime, and representation.* New York: John Wiley.

Handelsman, J., Cantor, N., Carnes, M., Denton, D., Fine, E., Grosz, B., . . . Sheridan, J. (2005). More women in science. *Science*, 309(5378), 1190–91.

Hanlon, J. (2010). Success by design: HOPE VI, new urbanism, and the neoliberal transformation of public housing in the United States. *Environment and Planning A*, 42(1), 80.

Haraway, D. (1988). Situated knowledges: The science question in feminism and the privilege of partial perspective. *Feminist Studies*, 14(3), 575–99.

Harding, S. G. (1991). *Whose science? Whose knowledge? Thinking from women's lives.* Ithaca, N.Y.: Cornell University Press.

———. (Ed.). (1993). *The "racial" economy of science: Toward a democratic future.* Bloomington: Indiana University Press.

———. (1998). *Is science multicultural? Postcolonialisms, feminisms, and epistemologies.* Bloomington: Indiana University Press.

Harvey, D. (1985). *The urban experience.* Baltimore: Johns Hopkins University Press.

———. (1989). From managerialism to entepreneurialism: The transformation in urban governance in late capitalism. *Geografiska Annaler*, 71B, 3–18.

———. (2005). *A brief history of neoliberalism.* Oxford: Oxford University Press.

Hay, J. (2003). Unaided virtues: The (neo)liberalization of the domestic sphere and the new architecture of community. In Z. Bratich, J. Packer, and C. McCarthy (Eds.), *Foucault, cultural studies, and governmentality*, 166–205. Albany: State University of New York Press.

Hayden, D. (1980). What would a non-sexist city be like? Speculations on housing, urban design, and human work. *Signs*, 5(3), s170–87.

———. (1981). *The grand domestic revolution: A history of feminist design for homes, neighborhoods, and cities.* Cambridge, Mass.: MIT Press.

———. (1984/2002). *Redesigning the American dream: Gender, housing, and family life* (2nd ed., rev.). New York: Norton.

Hays, S. (1996). *The cultural contradictions of motherhood.* New Haven, Conn.: Yale University Press.

Hegewisch, A., and Hartmann, H. (2014). Occupational segregation and the gender wage gap: A job half done. Briefing Paper IWPR C, 419. Washington, D.C.: Institute for Women's Policy Research.

Held, T. (2002, February 23). Milwaukee County: New directions. Ament's legacy: Broken promises, predictable paths. *Milwaukee Journal Sentinel.*

Hennessy, R., and Ingraham, C. (Eds.). (1997). *Materialist feminism: A reader in class, difference, and women's lives.* New York: Psychology Press.

Heritage Foundation. (1992, September 15). Shaping American Values Debate. http://www.heritage.org/Research/Religion/HL428.cfm.

Hesse-Biber, S. N. (Ed.). (2012). *Handbook of feminist research: Theory and praxis.* Thousand Oaks, Calif.: Sage.

Hewitt, R. (2005). *White backlash and the politics of multiculturalism.* Cambridge: Cambridge University Press.

Hill Collins, P. (2000a). *Black feminist thought: Knowledge, power and the politics of empowerment*. New York: Routledge.

———. (2000b). Gender, black feminism, and black political economy. *Annals of the American Academy of Political and Social Science*, 568(1), 41–53.

———. (2001). Like one of the family: Race, ethnicity, and the paradox of US national identity. *Ethnic and Racial Studies*, 24(1), 3–28.

———. (2002). *Black feminist thought: Knowledge, power and the politics of empowerment* (2nd ed.). New York: Routledge.

———. (2004). *Black sexual politics: African Americans, gender, and the new racism*. New York: Routledge.

Himmelweit, S., and Land, H. (2011). Reducing gender inequalities to create a sustainable care system. *Kurswechsel*, 4, 49–63.

Hindman, N. C. (2010, September 2). The 11 cities where women out-earn men by the biggest margin. *Huffington Post*.

HNTB Corporation and Planning & Design Institute. (2003, October 16). Park East Redevelopment Plan. Documents one and three: Renewal plan. Final draft, 5.

Hoffman, L. (2014). The urban, politics and subject formation. *International Journal of Urban and Regional Research*, 38(5), 1576–88.

Holland, S. P. (2012). *The erotic life of racism*. Durham, N.C.: Duke University Press.

hooks, b. (1981). *Ain't I a woman: Black women and feminism* (Vol. 3). Boston: South End Press.

———. (1994). Postmodern blackness. In P. Williams and L. Chrisman (Eds.), *Colonial discourse and post-colonial theory: A reader*, 421–27. London: Longman.

———. (2000). *Feminist theory: From margin to center*. London: Pluto Press.

Hooper, C. (2001). *Manly states: Masculinities, international relations, and gender politics*. New York: Columbia University Press.

Hubbard, P. (2004). Revenge and injustice in the neoliberal city: Uncovering masculinist agendas. *Antipode*, 36(4), 665–86.

Hyatt, S. B. (2001). From citizen to volunteer: Neoliberal governance and the erasure of poverty. In J. Goode and J. Maskovsky (Eds.), *New poverty studies: The ethnography of power, politics, and impoverished people in the United States*, 435–69. New York: New York University Press.

———. (2011). What was neoliberalism and what comes next? The transformation of citizenship in the law-and-order state. In C. Shore, S. Wright, and D. Però (Eds.), *Policy worlds: Anthropology and the analysis of contemporary power*, 105–24. New York: Berghahn Books.

Ilcan, S., Oliver, M., and O'Connor, D. (2007). Spaces of governance: Gender and public sector restructuring in Canada. *Gender Place and Culture*, 14(1), 75–92.

In the Public Interest. (2014). Shift: How taxpayers began reclaiming control of their public services. http://www.inthepublicinterest.org/shift-how-taxpayers-began -reclaiming-control-of-their-public-services/.

Interfaith Conference of Milwaukee. (2006). Milwaukee housing trust fund video. http://www.interfaithconference.org/housing_trust_fund.htm.

Isoke, Z. (2007). The political spaces of black women in the city: Identity, agency, and the flow of social capital in Newark, N.J. Doctoral dissertation, Rutgers University.

———. (2011). The politics of homemaking: Black feminist transformations of a cityscape. *Transforming Anthropology*, 19(2), 117–30.

———. (2013). *Urban black women and the politics of resistance*. New York: Palgrave Macmillan.

Janega, J. (2009, December 11). Meter freeze-ups have residents fuming. *Chicago Tribune*, 8.

Jarvis, H. (2002). Lunch is for wimps: What drives parents to work long hours in "successful" British and U.S. Cities? *AREA* 34(3), 340–52.

Jarvis, H., with Cloke, J., and Kantor, P. (2009). *Cities and gender*. New York: Routledge.

Jennings, J. (2002). Welfare reform and neighborhoods: Race and civic participation. In R. Alberda and R. Withorn (Eds.), *Lost ground: Welfare reform, poverty, and beyond*, 129–44. Cambridge, Mass.: South End Press.

Jessop, B. (1996). A Neo-Gramscian approach to regulation of urban regimes: Accumulation strategies, hegemonic projects and governance. In M. Lauria (Ed.), *Reconstructing urban regime theory: Regulation urban politics in a global economy*, 51–74. London: Sage.

Johnson, J., and Talen, E. (2008). Affordable housing in new urbanist communities: A survey of developers. *Housing Policy Debates*, 19(4), 583–615.

Jones, J. (2009). *Labor of love, labor of sorrow: Black women, work, and the family from slavery to the present* (2nd ed., rev.). New York: Basic Books.

Jupp, E. (2014). Women, communities, neighbourhoods: Approaching gender and feminism within UK urban policy. *Antipode*, 46(5), 1304–22.

Kantola, J., and Squires, J. (2012). From state feminism to market feminism? *International Political Science Review*, 33(4), 382–400.

Karamessini, M., and Rubery, J. (2013). *Women and austerity: The economic crisis and the future for gender equality*. New York: Routledge.

Kasparek, J., Malone, B., and Schock, E. (2004). *Wisconsin history highlights: Delving into the past*. Madison: Wisconsin Historical Society Press.

Katz, C. (1994). Playing the field: Questions of fieldwork in geography. *Professional Geographer*, 46(1), 67–72.

———. (2001). Vagabond capitalism and the necessity of social reproduction. *Antipode*, 33(4), 709–28.

———. (2004). *Growing up global: Economic restructuring and children's everyday lives*. Minneapolis: University of Minnesota Press.

———. (2008). Bad elements: Katrina and the scoured landscape of social reproduction. *Gender, Place & Culture*, 15(1), 15–29.

Katz, P., Scully, V. J., and Bressi, T. W. (1994). *The new urbanism: Toward an architecture of community* (Vol. 10). New York: McGraw-Hill.

Kay, K., and Shipman, C. (2014, May). The confidence gap. *Atlantic*. http://www.theatlantic.com/magazine/archive/2014/05/the-confidence-gap/359815/.

Kenny, J., and Zimmerman, J. (2004). Constructing the "genuine American city": Neotraditionalism, new urbanism and neo-liberalism in the remaking of downtown Milwaukee. *Cultural Geographies*, 11(1), 73–98.

Kern, L. (2007). Reshaping the boundaries of public and private life: Gender, condominium development, and the neoliberalization of urban living. *Urban Geography*, 28(7), 657–81.

———. (2010a). Selling the "scary city": Gendering freedom, fear and condominium development in the neoliberal city. *Social & Cultural Geography*, 11(3), 209–30.

———. (2010b). *Sex and the revitalized city: Gender, condominium development, and urban citizenship*. Vancouver: University of British Columbia Press.

Kern, L., and Mullings, B. (2013). Urban neoliberalism, urban insecurity and urban violence: Exploring the gender dimensions. In L. Peake and M. Rieker (Eds.), *Rethinking feminist interventions into the urban*, 23–40. New York: Routledge.

Kern, L., and Wekerle, G. (2008). Gendered spaces of redevelopment: Gender politics of city building. In J. DeSena and R. Hutchinson (Eds.), *Gender in an urban world*, 233–62. Bingley: Emerald.

Kingfisher, C. P. (1996). Women on welfare: Conversational sites of acquiescence and dissent. *Discourse & Society*, 7(4), 531–57.

———. (Ed.). (2002). *Western welfare in decline: Globalization and women's poverty*. Philadelphia: University of Pennsylvania Press.

———. (2007a). Spatializing neoliberalism: Articulations, recapitulations, and (a very few) alternatives. In K. England and K. Ward (Eds.), *Neoliberalization: States, networks, peoples*, 195–222. New York: John Wiley.

———. (2007b). What D/discourse analysis can tell us about neoliberal constructions of (gendered) personhood: Some notes on commonsense and temporality. *Gender and Language*, 1(1), 93–105.

———. (2011). *Women in the American welfare trap*. Philadelphia: University of Pennsylvania Press.

Kingfisher, C., and Maskovsky, J. (2008). Introduction: The limits of neoliberalism. *Critique of Anthropology*, 28(2), 115–26.

Klodawsky, F. (2009). Home spaces and rights to the city: Thinking social justice for chronically homeless women. *Urban Geography*, 30(6), 591–610.

Klodawsky, F., Aubry, T., and Farrell, S. (2006). Care and the lives of homeless youth in neoliberal times in Canada. *Gender, Place & Culture*, 13(4), 419–436.

Klodawsky, F., Siltanen, J., and Andrew, C. (2013). Urban contestation in a feminist register. *Urban Geography*, 34(4), 541–59.

Knowles, E. D., and Lowery, B. S. (2012). Meritocracy, self-concerns, and whites' denial of racial inequity. *Self and Identity*, 11(2), 202–22.

Kobayashi, A. (2004). Anti-racist feminism in geography: An agenda for social action. In L. Nelson and J. Seager (Eds.), *The companion to feminist geography*, 32–40. London: Routledge.

Kruse, K. M. (2013). *White flight: Atlanta and the making of modern conservatism*. Princeton, N.J.: Princeton University Press.

L'Aberge, A. (1995). Seeking a place to stand: Political power and activism among Wisconsin women. Doctoral dissertation, University of Wisconsin–Madison.

Laclau, E., and Mouffe, C. (2001). *Hegemony and socialist strategy: Towards a radical democratic politics*. New York: Verso.

Lakoff, G. (2002). *Moral politics*. Chicago: University of Chicago Press.

Langdon, P. (2007, January). More developers, better results: A lesson in orchestration. *New Urban News.*

Larner, W. (2000). Theorising neoliberalism: Policy, ideology and governmentality. *Studies in Political Economy,* 63, 5–26.

———. (2003). Neoliberalism: Guest editorial. *Environment and Planning D: Society and Space,* 21, 509–12.

———. (2005). Neoliberalism in (regional) theory and practice: The stronger communities action fund in New Zealand. *Geographical Research,* 43(1), 9–18.

———. (2011). C-change? Geographies of crisis. *Dialogues in Human Geography,* 1(3), 319–35.

Larner, W., and Butler, M. (2007). The places, people and politics of partnership: After neoliberalism in Aotearoa New Zealand. In H. Leitner, J. Peck, and E. S. Sheppard (Eds.), *Contesting neoliberalism: Urban frontiers,* 71–89. New York: Guilford.

Larner, W., Fannin, M., MacLeavy, J., and Wang, W. (2013). New times, new spaces: Gendered transformations of governance, economy, and citizenship. *Social Politics,* 20(2), 157–64.

Laslett, B., and Brenner, J. (1989). Gender and social reproduction: Historical perspectives. *Annual Review of Sociology,* 15, 381–404.

Lawless, J. L., and Fox, R. L. (2012). *Men rule: The continued under-representation of women in US politics.* Washington, D.C.: Women and Politics Institute.

Lawson, V. (2007). Geographies of care and responsibility. *Annals of the Association of American Geographers,* 97(1), 1–11.

Leitner, H., Peck, J., and Sheppard, E. S. (Eds.). (2007). *Contesting neoliberalism: Urban frontiers.* New York: Guilford.

Leitner, H., Sheppard, E., and Sziarto, K. M. (2008). The spatialities of contentious politics. *Transactions of the Institute of British Geographers,* 33(2), 157–72.

Leslie, D., and Catungal, J. P. (2012). Social justice and the creative city: Class, gender and racial inequalities. *Geography Compass,* 6(3), 111–22.

Levine, M. (2003a). "Stealth depression": Joblessness in the city of Milwaukee since 1990. A report prepared by the University of Wisconsin–Milwaukee Center for Economic Development.

———. (2003b). Two Milwaukees. A report prepared by the University of Wisconsin– Milwaukee Center for Economic Development.

———. (2006). The economic state of Milwaukee's inner city: 2006. A report prepared by the University of Wisconsin–Milwaukee Center for Economic Development.

———. (2013a). Perspectives on the state of the Milwaukee economy. A report prepared for Wisconsin Voices, Milwaukee Center for Economic Development.

———. (2013b, December 14). Race and inequality at the crossroads. Presentation to YWCA Racial Justice Summit, Milwaukee.

Levine, M., and Callaghan, S. (1998). The economic state of Milwaukee: The city and the region. A report prepared by the University of Wisconsin–Milwaukee Center for Economic Development.

Levine, M., and Zipp, J. (1994). Downtown redevelopment in Milwaukee: Has it delivered for the city? A report prepared by the University of Wisconsin– Milwaukee Center for Economic Development.

Levrant de Bretteville, S. (1981). The woman's building: Physical forms and social implications. In S. Keller (Ed.), *Building for women*, 37–49. Lexington, Mass.: Heath.

Lind, A. (2005). *Gendered paradoxes: Women's movements, state restructuring, and global neoliberalism*. University Park: Pennsylvania State University Press.

Lipman, P. (2002). Making the global city, making inequality: The political economy and cultural politics of Chicago school policy. *American Educational Research Journal*, 39(2), 379–419.

———. (2011). *The new political economy of urban education: Neoliberalism, race, and the right to the city*. New York: Taylor & Francis.

———. (2013). Economic crisis, accountability, and the state's coercive assault on public education in the USA. *Journal of Education Policy*, 28(5), 557–73.

Lips, H. M. (2013). The gender pay gap: Challenging the rationalizations. Perceived equity, discrimination, and the limits of human capital models. *Sex Roles*, 68(3–4), 169–85.

Lister, R. (1990). Women, economic dependency and citizenship. *Journal of Social Policy*, 19(04), 445–67.

Little, J., Peake, L., and Richardson, P. (1988). *Women in cities: Gender and the urban environment*. New York: New York University Press.

Lorde, A. (1984). Age, race, class, and sex: Women redefining difference. In *Sister outsider*, 114–24. New York: Crown Press.

Loyd, J. M., Mitchelson, M., and Burridge, A. (Eds.). (2013). *Beyond walls and cages: Prisons, borders, and global crisis* (Vol. 14). Athens: University of Georgia Press.

Luft, R. E. (2008). Looking for common ground: Relief work in post-Katrina New Orleans as an American parable of race and gender violence. *NWSA Journal*, 20(3), 5–31.

Luxton, M., and Bezanson, K. (Eds.). (2006). *Social reproduction: Feminist political economy challenges neo-liberalism*. Montreal: McGill-Queen's University Press.

Lyon-Callo, V. (2008). *Inequality, poverty, and neoliberal governance: Activist ethnography in the homeless sheltering industry*. Toronto: University of Toronto Press.

MacKenzie, S. (1984). A socialist feminist perspective on gender and the environment. *Antipode*, 16(3), 3–10.

Macleod, G., and Johnstone, C. (2012). Stretching urban renaissance: Privatizing space, civilizing place, summoning "community." *International Journal of Urban and Regional Research*, 36(1), 1–28.

Maranville, D. A. (1990). Welfare and federalism. *Loyola Law Review*, 36, 1–53.

Marchand, M. H., and Runyan, A. S. (Eds.). (2010). *Gender and global restructuring: Sightings, sites and resistances*. New York: Routledge.

Markovich, J., and Hendler, S. (2006). Beyond "soccer moms": Feminist and new urbanist critical approaches to suburbs. *Journal of Planning Education and Research*, 22, 410–27.

Markusen, A. (1980). City spatial structure, women's household work, and national urban policy. *Signs*, 5(3), S22–44.

Martin, D. (2004). Nonprofit foundations and grassroots organizing: Reshaping urban governance. *Professional Geographer*, 56, 394–405.

Maruschak, L. (2008). *Medical problems of prisoners*. Washington, D.C.: Bureau of Justice Statistics.

Maskovsky, J. (2001). The other war at home: The geopolitics of U.S. poverty. *Urban Anthropology*, 30(2–3), 215–38.

Massey, D. (1991). *A global sense of place*. Minneapolis: University of Minnesota Press.

———. (1993). *Power-geometry and a progressive sense of place*. London: Routledge.

———. (1995). Masculinism, dualisms, and high technology. *Transactions of the Institute of British Geographers*, 20, 487–99.

———. (1999). Cities in the world. In D. Massey, J. Allen, and S. Pile (Eds.), *City worlds*, 94–150. London: Routledge.

———. (2008). When theory meets politics. *Antipode*, 40(3), 492–97.

Massey, D., and McDowell, L. (1994/1984). *A woman's place*. Minneapolis: University of Minnesota Press.

Mayer, M. (2007). Contesting the neoliberalization of urban governance. In H. Leitner, J. Peck, and E. S. Sheppard (Eds.), *Contesting neoliberalism: Urban frontiers*, 90–115. New York: Guilford.

Mbembé, J. A., and Nuttall, S. (2004). Writing the world from an African metropolis. *Public Culture*, 16(3), 347–72.

McCall, L. (2005). The complexity of intersectionality. *Signs*, 30(3), 1771–1800.

McCluskey, M. (2003). Efficiency and social citizenship: Challenging the neoliberal attack on the welfare state. *Indiana Law Review*, 78, 783–876.

McDowell, L. (1983). Towards an understanding of the gender division of urban space. *Environment and Planning D: Society and Space*, 1(1), 59–72.

———. (1991). Life without father and Ford: The new gender order of post-Fordism. *Transactions of the Institute of British Geographers*, 1, 400–19.

———. (1997). *Capital culture: Gender at work in the city*. Oxford: Blackwell.

———. (1999). *Gender, identity, and place: Understanding feminist geographies*. Minneapolis: University of Minnesota Press.

———. (2001). Linking scales; or, How research about gender and organizations raises new issues for economic geographers. *Journal of Economic Geography*, 1, 229–50.

———. (2004). Workfare, work/life balance, and an ethic of care. *Progress in Human Geography*, 28, 145–63.

———. (2007). Spaces of the home: Absence, presence, new connections and new anxieties. *Home Cultures*, 4(2), 129–46.

———. (2008). Thinking through work: Complex inequalities, constructions of difference and trans-national migrants. *Progress in Human Geography*, 32(4), 491–507.

———. (2011). *Capital culture: Gender at work in the city* (Vol. 65). New York: John Wiley.

———. (2013). *Working lives: Gender, migration and employment in Britain, 1945–2007*. New York: John Wiley.

McEwan, C., and Goodman, M. K. (2010). Place geography and the ethics of care: Introductory remarks on the geographies of ethics, responsibility and care. *Ethics, Place and Environment*, 13(2), 103–12.

McGuirk, P. (2012). Geographies of urban politics: Pathways, intersections, interventions. *Geographical Research*, 50(3), 256–68.

McKittrick, K. (2006). *Demonic grounds: Black women and the cartographies of struggle*. Minneapolis: University of Minnesota Press.

———. (2011). On plantations, prisons, and a black sense of place. *Social & Cultural Geography*, 12(8), 947–63.

McLean, H. (2014a). Cracks in the creative city: The contradictions of community arts practice. *International Journal of Urban and Regional Research*, 38(6), 2156–73.

———. (2014b). Digging into the creative city: A feminist critique. *Antipode*, 46(3), 669–90.

McRobbie, A. (2009). *The aftermath of feminism: Gender, culture and social change*. London: Sage.

———. (2011). Reflections on feminism, immaterial labour and the post-Fordist regime. *New Formations*, 70(1), 60–76.

Mead, L. (2004). *Government matters: Welfare reform in Wisconsin*. Princeton, N.J.: Princeton University Press.

Meehan, K., and Strauss, K. (Eds.). (2015). *Precarious worlds: Contested geographies of social reproduction*. Athens: University of Georgia Press.

Melamed, J. (2006). The spirit of neoliberalism: From racial liberalism to neoliberal multiculturalism. *Social Text*, 24, 1–24.

Memorandum from Alyssa Talanker (UWM) to John Goldstein Regarding Community Benefits in the Park East Redevelopment Plan. (2003, February 23).

Memorandum from the Office of City Attorney to Julie Penman, Commissioner of the Department of City Development. (2003, January 24).

Metzger, J. (2010). *What would Jane say? City-building and a tale of two Chicagos*. Chicago: Lake Claremont Press.

Miller, S. (Ed.). (1981). *Flawed liberation: Socialism and feminism*. Westport, Conn.: Greenwood.

———. (1983). Other socialists: Native-born and immigrant women in the Socialist Party of America, 1901–1917. *Labor History*, 24, 84–102.

———. (2002). For white men only: The Socialist Party of America and issues of gender, ethnicity, and race. *Journal of the Gilded Age and Progressive Era*, 2(3), 283–302.

Milwaukee Center for Urban Health. (2010). Milwaukee health report 2010: Health disparities in Milwaukee by socioeconomic status. http://www.cuph.org/mhr/2010-milwaukee-health-report.pdf.

Milwaukee City Council Records. (2000). City Council member records, provided by City of Milwaukee by personal request.

Milwaukee Department of City Development. (n.d.). Invest in downtown Milwaukee. www.mkedcd.org/downtown/.

———. (1999). Milwaukee downtown plan. www.mkedcd.org/planning/plans/downtown/index.html.

———. (2007). Business improvement districts. wwww.mkedcd.org/business/busbid.html.

Milwaukee Downtown (Business Improvement District 21). (2006). 2006 annual report. www.milwaukeedowntown.com/pdf/2006-annual-report.pdf.

Milwaukee Journal Sentinel. (2006, February 27). Editorial: Man behind a movement.

Milwaukee Magazine. (2008, January 1). No holds barred: A quarter-century of brutally honest assessments of politicians and their campaigns.

——. (2012, March 9). He built this city.

Miner, B. (2001). Voucher's money man. *Rethinking Schools*, 16(1). http://www.rethinkingschools.org/archive/16_01/Joyc161.shtml.

——. (2002a, Spring). Payment surcharge gives extra 28 million dollars to voucher schools. *Rethinking Schools.* http://www.rethinkingschools.org/special_reports/voucher_report/v_paym163.shtml.

——. (2002b, October). Politics trumps religion: Bush's faith-based initiative. Race wire. *Color Lines.*

——. (2004, February). Old guard, new guard. *Milwaukee Magazine.*

Mink, G. (1990). The lady and the tramp: Gender, race, and the origins of the American welfare state. In L. Gordon (Ed.), *Women, the state, and welfare*, 92–122. Madison: University of Wisconsin Press.

Miraftab, F. (2004). Invited and invented spaces of participation: Neoliberal citizenship and feminists' expanded notion of politics. *Wagadu*, 1, 1–7.

——. (2006). Feminist praxis, citizenship and informal politics: Reflections on South Africa's anti-eviction campaign. *International Feminist Journal of Politics*, 8(2), 194–218.

Mirowski, P. (2013). *Never let a serious crisis go to waste: How neoliberalism survived the financial meltdown.* New York: Verso.

Mitchell, K. (2004). *Crossing the neoliberal line: Pacific Rim migration and the metropolis.* Philadelphia: Temple University Press.

Mitchell, K., Marston, S. A., and Katz, C. (Eds.). (2004). *Life's work: Geographies of social reproduction* (Vol. 52). New York: Wiley-Blackwell.

MMAC FUEL Milwaukee. (2008). About us. http://www.fuelmilwaukee.org/CWT/External/About/Index.aspx.

Mohanty, C. T. (1988). Under Western eyes: Feminist scholarship and colonial discourses. *Feminist Review*, 30, 61–88.

——. (2003). *Feminism without borders: Decolonizing theory, practicing solidarity.* New Delhi: Zubaan.

Mohanty, C., Russo, A., and Torres, L. (1991). *Third-World women and the politics of feminism.* Bloomington: Indiana University Press.

Molina, S. (2001). Attracting and retaining women in high technology. Survey report commissioned by Deloitte and Touch. Polling conducted by Roper Starch Worldwide.

Molyneux, M. (2006). Mothers at the service of the new poverty agenda: Progresa/Oportunidades, Mexico's conditional transfer programme. *Social Policy & Administration*, 40(4), 425–49.

Moody, K. (1997). *Workers in a lean world.* New York: Verso.

Moraga, C., and Anzaldúa, G. (Eds.). (2015). *This bridge called my back: Writings by radical women of color.* Albany: State University of New York Press.

Morgan, S., and Maskovsky, J. (2003). The anthropology of welfare "reform": New perspectives on U.S. urban poverty. *Annual Review of Anthropology*, 32, 315–38.

Morris, M. (1998). *Too soon too late: History in popular culture* (Vol. 22). Bloomington: Indiana University Press.

Mott, C., and Roberts, S. M. (2014). Not everyone has (the) balls: Urban exploration and the persistence of masculinist geography. *Antipode*, 46(1), 229–45.

Mountz, A. (2011). Where asylum-seekers wait: Feminist counter-topographies of sites between states. *Gender, Place & Culture*, 18(3), 381–99.

Mountz, A., and Hyndman, J. (2006). Feminist approaches to the global intimate. *Women's Studies Quarterly*, 34, 446–63.

Mulligan-Hansel, K., and Fendt, P. (2003). Unfair sanctions: Does w-2 punish people of color? A report by the Institute for Wisconsin's Future and the University of Wisconsin–Milwaukee Center for Economic Development.

Muzik, Edward J. (1960). Victor L. Berger: A biography. Doctoral dissertation, Northwestern University.

Nagar, R., Lawson, V., McDowell, L., and Hanson, S. (2002). Locating Globalization: Feminist (re)readings of the subjects and spaces of globalization. *Economic Geography*, 78(3), 257–84.

Naples, N. A. (1992). Activist mothering: Cross-generational continuity in the community work of women from low-income urban neighborhoods. *Gender & Society*, 6(3), 441–63.

———. (1997). The "new consensus" on the gendered "social contract": The 1987–1988 US congressional hearings on welfare reform. *Signs*, 22(4), 907–45.

———. (2002). Materialist feminist discourse analysis and social movement research: Mapping the changing context for "community control." In D. S. Meyer, N. Whittier, and B. Robnett (Eds.), *Social movements: Identity, culture, and the state*, 226–46. Oxford: Oxford University Press.

———. (2003). *Feminism and method: Ethnography, discourse analysis, and activist research*. New York: Routledge.

Nast, H. J. (1994). Women in the field: Critical feminist methodologies and theoretical perspectives. *Professional Geographer*, 46(1), 54–66.

Negrey, C., and Rausch, S. (2009). Creativity gaps and gender gaps: Women and place in the U.S. *Gender, Place & Culture*, 16(5), 517–33.

Neubeck, K. J., and Cazenave, N. A. (2001). *Welfare racism: Playing the race card against America's poor*. New York: Psychology Press.

Newman, J. (2012). *Working the spaces of power: Activism, neoliberalism and gendered labour*. New York: Bloomsbury.

———. (2013). Spaces of power: Feminism, neoliberalism and gendered labor. *Social Politics*, 20(2), 200–221.

Newman, K., and Lake, R. W. (2006). Democracy, bureaucracy and difference in US community development politics since 1968. *Progress in Human Geography*, 30(1), 44–61.

Ngunjiri, F. W., Gramby-Sobukwe, S., and William-Gegner, K. (2012). Tempered radicals: Black women's leadership in the church and community. *Journal of Pan African Studies*, 5(2), 84–109.

Nixon, S., and Crewe, B. (2004). Pleasure at work? Gender, consumption and work-based identities in the creative industries. *Consumption, Markets, and Culture*, 7(2), 129–47.

Noble, C. (1997). *Welfare as we know it: A political history of the welfare states*. Oxford: Oxford University Press.

Norman, J. (1989). Congenial Milwaukee: A segregated city. In G. Squires (Ed.), *Unequal partnerships: The political economy of urban redevelopment in postwar America*, 178–201. New Brunswick, N.J.: Rutgers University Press.

Norman, J., and Borowski, G. J. (1999, March 21). Where have all the houses gone? *Milwaukee Journal Sentinel*, A1–5.

Norquist, J. (1994, Summer). The self-reliant city—Milwaukee. *City Journal*. www.city-journal.org/article02.php?aid=1438.

———. (1998a, March 1). The wealth of cities. *New Democrat*.

———. (1998b, December 15). The wealth of cities. *Manhattan Institute Civic Bulletin*.

———. (1999a). *The wealth of cities: Revitalizing the centers of urban life*. Cambridge, Mass.: Perseus.

———. (1999b, January 26). Restoring the wealth of our cities. Speech for the Landmark Series Public Affairs Forum, Saint Paul, Minn.

———. (2003, December 14). The Norquist years: His legacy: Rebuilding the marketplace. *Milwaukee Journal Sentinel*.

———. (2014, November 14). Roadblock on main street. *American Conservative*. http://www.theamericanconservative.com/articles/roadblock-on-main-street/.

Office of the City Clerk, Milwaukee. (1980–2004). Legislative Reference Bureau.

Okimoto, T. G., and Brescoll, V. L. (2010). The price of power: Power seeking and backlash against female politicians. *Personality and Social Psychology Bulletin*, 36(7), 923–36.

Okin, S. M. (1989). *Justice, gender, and the family*. New York: Basic Books.

Omi, M., and Winant, H. (2014). *Racial formation in the United States*. New York: Routledge.

Ong, A. (2006). *Neoliberalism as exception: Mutations in citizenship and sovereignty*. Durham, N.C.: Duke University Press.

Orloff, A. (1996). Gender in the welfare state. *Annual Review of Sociology*, 1, 51–78.

Orum, A. M. (1995). *City-building in America*. Boulder, Colo.: Westview Press.

Orwell, G. (1945). *Animal farm*. London: Secker and Warburg.

Pager, D. (2007). *Marked: Race, crime, and finding work in an era of mass incarceration*. Chicago: University of Chicago Press.

Pager, D., and Quillian, L. (2005). Walking the talk? What employers say versus what they do. *American Sociological Review*, 70(3), 355–80.

Pager, D., and Western, B. (2012). Identifying discrimination at work: The use of field experiments. *Journal of Social Issues*, 68(2), 221–37.

Parker, B. (2008). Beyond the class act: Gender and race in the creative class discourse. In J. DeSena and R. Hutchinson (Eds.), *Gender in an urban world*, 201–32. Bingley: Emerald.

———. (2011). Material matters: Gender and the city. *Geography Compass*, 5(6), 433–47.

———. (2016a). Feminist forays in the city: Imbalance and intervention in urban research methods. *Antipode* 48(5): 1337–58.

———. (2016b). The feminist geography researcher as killjoy: Excavating gendered urban power relations. *Professional Geographer*. Published online.

Parreñas, R. S. (2001). *Servants of globalization: Women, migration and domestic work.* Stanford, Calif.: Stanford University Press.

Parsons, L. (1905/2003). Speeches at the founding convention of the Industrial Workers of the World. In G. Ahrens (Ed.), *Lucy Parsons: Freedom, equality, and solidarity—Writings and speeches, 1878–1937,* 77–85. Chicago: Charles H. Kerr.

Pateman, C. (1989). *The disorder of women: Democracy, feminism, and political theory.* Stanford, Calif.: Stanford University Press.

Peake, L. (1993). "Race" and sexuality: challenging the patriarchal structuring of urban social space. *Environment and Planning D*, 11(4), 415–32.

———. (1997). Toward a social geography of the city: Race and dimensions of urban poverty in women's lives. *Journal of Urban Affairs*, 19(3), 335–61.

———. (2015). On feminism and feminist allies in knowledge production in urban geography. *Urban Geography.* http://www.tandfonline.com/doi/abs/10.1080 /02723638.2015.1105484?journalCode=rurb20.

Peake, L., and Rieker, M. (Eds.). (2013). *Rethinking feminist interventions into the urban.* New York: Routledge.

Peck, J. (2001). *Workfare states.* New York: Guilford.

———. (2005). Struggling with the creative class. *International Journal of Urban and Regional Research*, 29(4), 740–70.

———. (2006a). Countering neoliberalism. *Urban Geography*, 27(8), 729–33.

———. (2006b). Liberating the city: Between New York and New Orleans. *Urban Geography*, 27(8), 681–713.

———. (2007, June 28). The creativity fix. *Eurozine.* http://www.eurozine.com/articles /2007-06-28-peck-en.html.

———. (2008). Remaking laissez-faire. *Progress in Human Geography*, 32(1), 3–43.

———. (2014). Pushing austerity: State failure, municipal bankruptcy and the crises of fiscal federalism in the USA. *Cambridge Journal of Regions, Economy and Society*, 7(1), 17–44.

———. (2015). Cities beyond compare? *Regional Studies*, 49(1), 160–82.

Peck, J., and Theodore, N. (2001). Contingent Chicago: Restructuring the spaces of temporary labor. *International Journal of Urban and Regional Research*, 25(3), 471–96.

———. (2002). The temporary staffing industry: Growth imperatives and limits to contingency. *Economic Geography*, 78(4), 463–93.

Peck, J., Theodore, N., and Brenner, N. (2012). Neoliberalism resurgent? Market rule after the Great Recession. *South Atlantic Quarterly*, 111(2), 265–88.

———. (2013). Neoliberal urbanism redux? *International Journal of Urban and Regional Research*, 37(3), 1091–99.

Peck, J., and Tickell, A. (2002). Neoliberalizing space. *Antipode*, 34(3), 380–404.

Pedroni, T. (2005). Market movements and the dispossessed: Race, identity and subaltern agency among black women voucher advocates. *Urban Review*, 37(2), 83–105.

Pifer, R. L. (2003). *A city at war: Milwaukee labor during World War II*. Madison: Wisconsin Historical Society.

Pratt, G. (2004). *Working feminism*. Philadelphia: Temple University Press.

Pratt, G., and Johnston, C. (2013). Staging testimony in Nanay. *Geographical Review*, 103(2), 288–303.

Pratt, G., and Rosner, V. (2006). Introduction: The global & the intimate. *Women's Studies Quarterly*, 34(1/2), 13.

Prügl, E. (2014). Neoliberalising feminism. *New Political Economy*, 20, 614–31.

Puar, J. (2007). *Terrorist assemblages: Homonationalism in queer times*. Durham, N.C.: Duke University Press.

———. (2012). "I would rather be a cyborg than a goddess": Becoming-intersectional in assemblage theory. *philoSOPHIA*, 2(1), 49–66.

Pulido, L. (2000). Rethinking environmental racism: White privilege and urban development in Southern California. *Annals of the Association of American Geographers*, 90, 12–40.

Purcell, M. (2008). *Recapturing democracy: Neoliberalization and the struggle for alternative urban futures*. New York: Routledge.

Quadagno, J. (1994). *The color of welfare: How racism undermined the war on poverty*. Oxford: Oxford University Press.

———. (2000). Another face of inequality: Racial and ethnic exclusion in the welfare state. *Social Politics*, 7(2), 229–37.

Rahder, B., and Altilia, C. (2004). Where is feminism in planning going? Appropriation or transformation. *Planning Theory*, 3, 107–16.

Rankin, K. N. (2001). Governing development: Neoliberalism, microcredit, and rational economic woman. *Economy and Society*, 30(1), 18–37.

———. (2009). Critical development studies and the praxis of planning. *City*, 13(2–3), 219–29.

Rast, Joel. (2006). Governing the regimeless city: The Frank Zeidler administration in Milwaukee, 1948–1960. *Urban Affairs Review*, 42(1), 81–112.

Reading, R. (2006). The enduring effects of abuse and related adverse experiences in childhood: A convergence of evidence from neurobiology and epidemiology. *Child: Care, Health and Development*, 32(2), 253–56.

Reason Foundation. (2007). Annual privatization report.

Rector, R. (1997, March 4). Wisconsin's welfare miracle. Backgrounder. A report of the Heritage Foundation.

Reese, W. J. (1981). "Partisans of the proletariat": The socialist working class and the Milwaukee schools, 1890–1920. *History of Education Quarterly*, 24, 3–51.

Reingold, B., and Smith, A. R. (2012). Welfare policymaking and intersections of race, ethnicity, and gender in US state legislatures. *American Journal of Political Science*, 56(1), 131–47.

Rennie-Short, J. (2013). *Global metropolitan: Globalizing cities in a capitalist world*. New York: Routledge.

Reynolds, D. (2002). *Taking the high road: Communities organize for economic change.* London: M.E. Sharpe.

Rich, M. (1993). *Federal policymaking and the poor: National goals, local choices, and distributional outcomes.* Princeton, N.J.: Princeton University Press.

Richie, B. E. (2000). A Black feminist reflection on the antiviolence movement. *Signs,* 25(4), 1133–37.

———. (2012). *Arrested justice: Black women, violence, and America's prison nation.* New York: New York University Press.

Rigakos, G., and Greener, D. (2000). Bubbles of governance: Private policing and the law in Canada. *Canadian Journal of Law and Society,* 15(1), 145–85.

Roberts, A. (2013). Financing social reproduction: The gendered relations of debt and mortgage finance in twenty-first-century America. *New Political Economy,* 18(1), 21–42.

———. (2015). Gender, financial deepening and the production of embodied finance: Towards a critical feminist analysis. *Global Society,* 29(1), 107–27.

Roberts, D. E. (1993). Racism and patriarchy in the meaning of motherhood. *American University Journal of Gender, Social Policy & the Law,* 1(1), 1–38.

———. (1996). Welfare and the problem of black citizenship. *Yale Law Journal,* 105(6), 1563–1602.

———. (2000). Criminal justice and black families: The collateral damage of over-enforcement. University of California Davis Law Review, 34, 1005–28.

———. (2002). Shattered bonds: The color of child welfare. *Children and Youth Services Review,* 24(11), 877–80.

———. (2008). The racial geography of child welfare: Toward a new research paradigm. *Child Welfare,* 87(2), 125–50.

Roberts, D. J., and Mahtani, M. (2010). Neoliberalizing race, racing neoliberalism: Placing "race" in neoliberal discourses. *Antipode,* 42(2), 248–57.

Robinson, J. (2011). 2010 Urban Geography Plenary Lecture—The travels of urban neoliberalism: Taking stock of the internationalization of urban theory. *Urban Geography,* 32(8), 1087–1109.

Rodgers, S., Barnett, C., and Cochrane, A. (2014). Where is urban politics? *International Journal of Urban and Regional Research,* 38(5), 1551–60.

Rodriguez, J. A. (2014). *Bootstrap new urbanism: Design, race, and redevelopment in Milwaukee.* Lexington, Mass.: Lexington Books.

Rose, G. (1993). *Feminism and geography.* London: Polity.

———. (1997). Situating knowledges: Positionality, reflexivities and other tactics. *Progress in Human Geography,* 21(3), 305–20.

Rose, N. (1999). *Powers of freedom: Reframing political thought.* Cambridge: Cambridge University Press.

Rosser, S. (2004). *The science glass ceiling: Academic women scientists and the struggle to succeed.* New York: Routledge.

Roth, B. (2004). Thinking about challenges/limits to feminist activism in extra-feminist settings. *Social Movement Studies,* 3(2), 147–66.

Roy, A. (2003). *City requiem: Calcutta.* Minneapolis: University of Minnesota Press.

————. (2015). The universal and its others: Reflections on twenty-first-century planning. In J. Hillier and J. Metzger (Eds.), *Connections: Exploring contemporary planning theory and practice with Patsy Healey*, 295–304. Burlington, Vt.: Ashgate.

————. (2015). What is urban about critical theory? AAG 2015 Urban Geography Plenary Lecture. *Urban Geography*. Published online.

Runyan, A. S., and Peterson, V. S. (2013). *Global gender issues in the new millennium* (4th ed.). Boulder, Colo.: Westview Press.

Russell, K. (2007). Feminist dialectics and Marxist theory. *Radical Philosophy Review*, 10(1), 33–54.

Rutherford, S. (2011). *Women's work, men's cultures: Overcoming resistance and changing organizational cultures*. New York: Palgrave Macmillan.

————. (2014). Gendered organizational cultures, structures and processes: The cultural exclusion of women in organizations. In R. J. Burke and D. A. Major (Eds.), *Gender in organizations: Are men allies or adversaries to women's career advancement?*, 193–216. Cheltenham: Edward Elgar.

Sager, T. (2011). Neo-liberal urban planning policies: A literature survey 1990–2010. *Progress in Planning*, 76(4), 147–99.

Sánchez de Madariaga, I. (2013). Opening the gates: A case study of decision-making and recognition in architecture. In I. Sánchez de Madariaga and M. Roberts (Eds.), *Fair shared cities: The impact of gender planning in Europe*, 129–47. Burlington, Vt.: Ashgate.

Sánchez de Madariaga, I., and Roberts, M. (Eds.). (2013). *Fair shared cities: The impact of gender planning in Europe*. Burlington, Vt.: Ashgate.

Sandercock, L., and Forsyth, A. (2005). A gender agenda: New directions for planning theory. In S. S. Fainstein and L. J. Servon (Eds.), *Gender and planning: A reader*, 67–85. New Brunswick, N.J.: Rutgers University Press.

Sanjek, R. (2000). Keeping ethnography alive in an urbanizing world. *Human Organization*, 59(3), 280–88.

Satter, B. (2009). *Family properties: Race, real estate, and the exploitation of black urban America*. New York: Macmillan.

Schmid, J. (2006, November 12). Study slams city job efforts: Policy vacuum, real-estate emphasis harm economic growth. *Milwaukee Journal Sentinel*.

————. (2007a, June 20). Region to ask: "What do you think of us?" *Milwaukee Journal Sentinel*.

————. (2007b, September 6). Building a base abroad: Kahler Slater spreads a hometown success. *Milwaukee Journal Sentinel*.

Schultze, S. (2005, June 28). Sewer user fees could climb 25% or more: Energy prices cut into contractor revenue. *Milwaukee Journal Sentinel*.

Seidel, E. (1916–44). Autobiography part I, part II and part III, unpublished manuscript. Emil Seidel Papers, 1916–1944. Milwaukee Manuscript Collection G. University of Wisconsin–Milwaukee Archives.

————. (n.d.). Defense of the socialist regime in Milwaukee. Emil Seidel Papers, 1916–1944. Milwaukee Manuscript Collection G. University of Wisconsin–Milwaukee Archives.

Sharp, J. P., Routledge, P., Philo, C., and Paddison, R. (Eds.) (2000). *Entanglements of power: Geographies of domination/resistance*. New York: Routledge.

Sherman, J. (2002, August 13). Florida praises Milwaukee. http://mobile.onmilwaukee.com/buzz/articles/florida.

Shriver, M., and Center for American Progress. (2014). *The Shriver report: A woman's nation pushes back from the brink*. Washington, D.C.: Center for American Progress.

Simon-Kumar, R. (2011). The analytics of "gendering" the post-neoliberal state. *Social Politics*, 18(3), 441–68.

Sites, W. (2003). *Remaking New York: Primitive globalization and the politics of urban community*. New York: Routledge.

———. (2007). Beyond trenches and grassroots? Reflections on urban mobilization, fragmentation, and the anti-Wal-Mart campaign in Chicago. *Environment and Planning A*, 39(11), 2632–51.

———. (2012). God from the machine? Urban movements meet machine politics in neoliberal Chicago. *Environment and Planning A*, 44(11), 2574–90.

Smith, A., Stenning, A., and Willis, K. (2009). *Social justice and neoliberalism: Global perspectives*. London: Zed Books.

Smith, D. E. (1990). *The conceptual practices of power: A feminist sociology of knowledge*. Toronto: University of Toronto Press.

———. (1999). *Writing the social: Critique, theory, and investigations*. Toronto: University of Toronto Press.

———. (2005). *Institutional ethnography: A sociology for people*. Walnut Creek, Calif.: AltaMira.

Smith, K. (2003). From Socialism to racism: The politics of class and identity in postwar Milwaukee. *Michigan Historical Review*, 29(1), 71–95.

Spain, D. (1992). *Gendered spaces*. Chapel Hill: University of North Carolina Press.

———. (2002). What happened to gender relations on the way from Chicago to Los Angeles? *City and Community*, 1(2), 155–69.

———. (2004). *How women saved the city*. Minneapolis: University of Minnesota Press.

———. (2014). Gender and urban space. *Annual Review of Sociology*, 40, 581–98.

Sparke, M. (2013). *Introducing globalization: Ties, tensions, and uneven integration*. New York: Wiley-Blackwell.

Springer, S. (2010). Neoliberalism and geography: Expansions, variegations, formations. *Geography Compass*, 4(8), 1025–38.

———. (2012). Neoliberalism as discourse: Between Foucauldian political economy and Marxian poststructuralism. *Critical Discourse Studies*, 9(2), 133–47.

Staeheli, L. A., and Lawson, V. A. (1994). A discussion of "women in the field": The politics of feminist fieldwork. *Professional Geographer*, 46(1), 96–102.

Stall, S., and Stoecker, R. (1998). Community organizing or organizing community? Gender and the crafts of empowerment. *Gender & Society*, 12(6), 729–56.

State of Wisconsin, Department of Workforce Development. (2005). An evaluation of the Wisconsin Works (w-2) program.

Steinem, G. (2008, January 8). Women are never front-runners. *New York Times*.

Steinpreis, R., Anders, K., and Ritzke, D. (1999). The impact of gender on the review of the curricula vitae of job applicants and tenure candidates: A national empirical study. *Sex Roles*, 41, 509–28.

Stevens, A. B. (2011, October 11). We are the 99% too: Creating a Feminist Space within Occupy Wall Street. *MS*. http://msmagazine.com/blog/2011/10/11/we-are-the-99 -too-creating-a-feminist-space-within-occupy-wall-street/.

Stewart, A., Stubbs, J., and Malley, J. (2002). *Assessing the academic work environment for women scientists and engineers*. Ann Arbor: University of Michigan, Institute for Research on Women and Gender.

Stoecker, R. (2004). The mystery of the missing social capital and the ghost of social structure: Why community development can't win. In R. Silverman (Ed.), *Community-based organizations: The intersection of social capital and local context in contemporary urban society*, 53–66. Detroit: Wayne State University Press.

Stone, C. (1989). *Governing Atlanta, 1946–1988*. Lawrence: University Press of Kansas.

Strega, S. (2005). The view from the poststructural margins. In L. Brown and S. Strega (Eds.), *Research as resistance: Critical, indigenous, and anti-oppressive approaches*, 199–236. Toronto: Canadian Scholars' Press.

Sue, D. W. (2010). *Microaggressions in everyday life: Race, gender, and sexual orientation*. Hoboken, N.J.: John Wiley.

Sundstrom, W. A. (1992). Last hired, first fired? Unemployment and urban Black workers during the Great Depression. *Journal of Economic History*, 52(2), 415–29.

Swarr, A. L., and Nagar, R. (2010). *Critical transnational feminist praxis*. Albany: State University of New York Press.

Talen, E. (1999). Sense of community and neighborhood form: An assessment of the social doctrine of new urbanism. *Urban Studies*, 36(8), 1361–79.

Thomas, R. (1992). *Citizenship, gender and work: Social organization of industrial agriculture*. Berkeley: University of California Press.

Thoreau, H. D. (1854/1971). *Walden* (J. Lyndon Shanley, Ed.). Princeton, N.J.: Princeton University Press.

Thornton, E. (2007, May 7). Roads to riches: Why investors are clamoring to take over America's highways, bridges, and airports—and why the public should be nervous. *Business Week*.

Tickell, A., and Peck, J. (1996). The return of the Manchester men: Men's words and men's deeds in the remaking of the local state. *Transactions of the Institute of British Geographers*, 21, 595–616.

Time. (1936, April 6). Marxist mayor, 18–19.

———. (1991, August 19). Social programs: Learn, work and wed. http://www.time .com/time/magazine/article/0,9171,973642–1,00.html#ixzzozKJIbK5b.

Tinsley, C. H., Cheldelin, S. I., Schneider, A. K., and Amanatullah, E. T. (2009). Women at the bargaining table: Pitfalls and prospects. *Negotiation Journal*, 25(2), 233–48.

Tomaskovic-Devey, D., Thomas, M., and Johnson, K. (2005). Race and the accumulation of human capital across the career: A theoretical model and fixed-effects application. *American Journal of Sociology*, 111(1), 58–89.

Tomlinson, B. (2013). To tell the truth and not get trapped: Desire, distance, and intersectionality at the scene of argument. *Signs*, 38(4), 993–1017.

Tone, A. (1997). *The business of benevolence: Industrial paternalism in progressive America*. Ithaca, N.Y.: Cornell University Press.

Trotter, J. (1985). *Black Milwaukee: The making of an industrial proletariat, 1915–1945*. Chicago: University of Illinois Press.

University of Wisconsin–Milwaukee Center for Economic Development. (2001, December). Emergency services utilization in Milwaukee County: 1995 to 2000. Prepared for the Emergency Services Utilization Research Project and Policy Education Initiative.

University of Wisconsin–Milwaukee Center for Employment and Training. Drilldown. (2011). Drilldown. Emergency services utilization in Milwaukee County: 1995 to 2000: A report prepared for the Emergency Services Utilization Research Project and Policy Education Initiative.

U.S. Census Bureau. (2010). Quick facts: Wisconsin. www.census.gov/quickfacts/map.

Valentine, G. (2007). Theorizing and researching intersectionality: A challenge for feminist geography. *Professional Geographer*, 59(1), 10–21.

Valentine, G., Jackson, L., and Mayblin, L. (2014). Ways of seeing: Sexism the forgotten prejudice? *Gender, Place & Culture*, 21(4), 401–14.

Valian, V. (1999). *Why so slow? The advancement of women in science*. Princeton, N.J.: Princeton University Press.

Van de Kamp Nohl, M. (2001, April). Marilyn's story. *Milwaukee Magazine*.

———. (2002, April). Women and power: The shocking truth about being a female professional in Milwaukee and the ominous implications for the future of Wisconsin. *Milwaukee Magazine*.

Venkatesh, S. A. (2000). *American project: The rise and fall of a modern ghetto*. Cambridge, Mass.: Harvard University Press.

Voigt, K. (2006, May). Applying new urbanism street principles in Downtown Milwaukee, Wis., USA. *Institute of Transportation Engineers Newsletter*.

Wajcman, J. (2013). *Managing like a man: Women and men in corporate management*. New York: John Wiley.

Walby, S. (2000). Beyond the politics of location: The power of argument. *Feminist Theory*, 1(2), 109–207.

———. (2011). *The future of feminism*. Cambridge: Polity.

———. (2013). *Patriarchy at work: Patriarchal and capitalist relations in employment, 1800–1984*. New York: John Wiley.

Walton, J. (1993). The contributions and limits of political economy. *Annual Reviews in Sociology*, 19, 301–20.

Wankiewicz, H. (2013). European regional development programmes for cities and regions: Driving forces for gender planning? In I. Sánchez de Madriaga and M. Roberts (Eds.), *Fair shared cities: The impact of gender planning in Europe*, 131–54. Burlington, Vt.: Ashgate.

Ward, K. (2006). "Policies in motion," urban management and state restructuring: The trans-local expansion of business improvement districts. *International Journal of Urban and Regional Research*, 30(1), 54–75.

———. (2007a). Business improvement districts: Policy origins, mobile policies and urban liveability. *Geography Compass*, 1(3), 657–72.

———. (2007b). "Creating a personality for downtown": Business improvement districts in Milwaukee. *Urban Geography*, 28(8), 781–808.

———. (2008). Editorial—toward a comparative (re)turn in urban studies? Some reflections. *Urban Geography*, 29(5), 405–10.

———. (2010). Entrepreneurial urbanism and business improvement districts in the state of Wisconsin: A cosmopolitan critique. *Annals of the Association of American Geographers*, 100(5), 1177–96.

Ward, K., and England, K. (2007). Introduction: Reading neoliberalization. In K. England and K. Ward (Eds.), *Neoliberalization: States, networks, peoples*, 1–22. New York: John Wiley.

Warner, M., and Hefitz, A. (2007). Trends in contracted and public government services, 2002–2007. Report prepared by the Reason Foundation.

Weber, R. (2002). Extracting value from the city. *Antipode*, 34(3), 519–40.

———. (2010). Selling city futures: The financialization of urban redevelopment policy. *Economic Geography*, 86(3), 251–74.

Weikart, L. A., Chen, G., Williams, D. W., and Hromic, H. (2007). The democratic sex: Gender differences and the exercise of power. *Journal of Women, Politics & Policy*, 28(1), 119–40.

Weir, M. (1999). Politics, money, and power in community development. In R. F. Ferguson and W. T. Dickens (Eds.), *Urban problems and community development*, 139–92. Washington, D.C.: Brookings Institution Press.

Weiss, M. (2005). Who sets social policy in metropolis? Economic positioning and social reform in Singapore. *New Political Science*, 27(3), 267–89.

Wekerle, G. (2005a). Domesticating the neoliberal city: invisible genders, food and the politics of place. In A. Escobar and W. Harcourt (Eds.), *Women and the politics of place*, 86–99. Sterling, Va.: Kumarian Press.

———. (2005b). Gender and the city: Urban restructuring, social exclusion, and gender claims. In H. H. Hiller (Ed.), *Urban Canada*, 211–33. Oxford: Oxford University Press.

Wenneras, C., and Wold, A. (1997). Nepotism and sexism in peer-review. *Nature*, 387, 341–43.

White, S. (1995, February). Black public opinion in Milwaukee. Wisconsin Policy Research Institute Report (Vol. 8, no. 2).

Whitzman, C. (2007). The loneliness of the long-distance runner: Long-term feminist planning initiatives in London, Toronto, Montreal, and Melbourne. *Planning Theory and Practice*, 8(2), 205–27.

Williams, C., and Hegewisch, A. (2011). Women, poverty, and economic insecurity in Wisconsin and the Milwaukee-Waukesha-West Allis MSA. Washington, D.C.: Institute for Women's Policy Research.

Williams, D., Neighbors, H., and Jackson, J. (2008). Racial/ethnic discrimination and health: Findings from community studies. *American Journal of Public Health*, 98, S29–37.

Williams, J. (2000). *Unbending gender: Why family and work conflict and what to do about it*. New York: Oxford University Press.

———. (2002). *Unbending gender: Why family and work conflict and what to do about it*. Oxford: Oxford University Press.

Williams, J. C., Blair-Loy, M., and Berdahl, J. L. (2013). Cultural schemas, social class, and the flexibility stigma. *Journal of Social Issues*, 69(2), 209–34.

Williams, J., and Boushey, H. (2010). The three faces of work-family conflict: The poor, the professionals, and the missing middle. A report by the Work Life Law Center and the Center for American Progress.

Williams, L. A. (1995). Race, rat bites and unfit mothers: How media disclosure informs welfare legislation debate. *Fordham Urban Law Journal*, 22(4), 1159–96.

Wilson, A. (2013). Feminism in the space of the World Social Forum. *Journal of International Women's Studies*, 8(3), 10–27.

Wilson, D. (2009). Introduction: Racialized poverty in U.S. cities: Toward a refined racial economy perspective. *Professional Geographer*, 61, 139–49.

Wilson, D., and Keil, R. (2008). The real creative class. *Social & Cultural Geography*, 9(8), 841–47.

Wilson, E. (1991). *The sphinx in the city: Urban life, the control of disorder, and women*. Berkeley: University of California Press.

———. (2006). The work of antidepressants: Preliminary notes on how to build an alliance between feminism and psychopharmacology. *Biosocieties*, 1(1), 125–31.

Wirka, S. M. (1996). The city social movement: Progressive women reformers and early social planning. In M. C. Sies and C. Silver (Eds.), *Planning the twentieth-century American city*, 55–75. Baltimore: Johns Hopkins University Press.

———. (1998). City planning for girls: Exploring the ambiguous nature of women's planning history. In L. Sandercock (Ed.), *Making the invisible visible: A multicultural planning history*, 150–62. Berkeley: University of California Press.

Wisconsin DWD. (2005). Wisconsin Department of Workforce Development. https://dwd.wisconsin.gov.

Wisconsin Legislative Audit Bureau. (2005, April). An evaluation of Wisconsin Works (W-2) Program.

Wisconsin Women's Council and Women's Fund of Greater Milwaukee. (2006). The status of women in Milwaukee county. A report produced by the Wisconsin Women's Council and Women's Fund of Greater Milwaukee.

Wolch, J., and Dear, M. (1993). *Malign neglect: Homelessness in an American city*. New York: Jossey-Bass.

Wolf-Powers, L. (2010). Community benefits agreements and local government: A review of recent evidence. *Journal of the American Planning Association*, 76(2), 141–59.

Women and Poverty Public Education Initiative. (2003, October). The plight of families in Milwaukee living only on food stamps. Report produced by the Women and Poverty Public Education Initiative.

Women's Prison Association, Institute on Women & Criminal Justice. (2011). *Shackling brief*. New York: Women's Prison Association.

Wood, D. (2003). Effect of family and child poverty on health outcomes in the United States. *Pediatrics*, 112, 707–11.

Woods, C. (2002). Life after death. *Professional Geographer*, 54(1), 62–66.

Wright, M. W. (2006). *Disposable women and other myths of global capitalism*. New York: Taylor & Francis.

———. (2009). Gender and geography: Knowledge and activism across the intimately global. *Progress in Human Geography*, 33(3), 379–86.

———. (2010). Geography and gender: Feminism and a feeling of justice. *Progress in Human Geography*, 34(6), 818–27.

———. (2013). Feminism, urban knowledge, and the killing of politics. In L. Peake and M. Rieker (Eds.), *Rethinking feminist interventions into the urban*, 41–52. New York: Routledge.

Wyly, E. K., and Hammel, D. J. (2004). Mapping neo-liberal American urbanism. In R. Atkinson and G. Bridge (Eds.), *Gentrification in a global context: The new urban colonialism*, 18–39. London: Routledge.

Young, I. M. (1987). Difference and policy: Some reflections in the context of new social movements. *University of Cincinnati Law Review*, 56, 535–59.

———. (1995). Mothers, citizenship, and independence: A critique of pure family values. *Ethics*, 105(3), 535–56.

Young Professionals of Milwaukee. (2004a). A brain gain best practice: Young Professionals of Milwaukee success story from 0–2,600 in 26 months. Provided by the Young Professionals of Milwaukee.

———. (2004b, August 26). Membership survey—Who we are. Provided by the Young Professionals of Milwaukee.

Zimmerman, J. (2008). From brew town to cool town: Neoliberalism and the creative city development strategy in Milwaukee. *Cities*, 25, 230–42.

INDEX

activism: barriers to, 136–38, 142–43; black, 23, 127, 131, 136–137, feminist, 23, 65–66, 138–39; gay and lesbian, 65; neighborhood, 65
Addams, Jane, 175
Ahmed, Sara, 140, 161
Allis-Chalmers, 48, 57
amplification, 118–24
antifeminism. *See* backlash: against women/feminism
Atlanta, 63, 68
autonomy, 28–31, 41, 70, 82, 83, 98; black women, 119–120, 121

backlash: against civil rights movement, 24, 41, 140, 188n14; against gays and lesbians, 59; against labor movement, 24; against welfare, 27; against women/feminism, 17, 24, 27, 41, 54, 57, 58–59, 66, 83, 139–40
Baltimore, 63, 68
Barrett, Tom, 101–2
Bashevkin, Sylvia, 139
Beerline B, 80
Benson, John, 72–73
Berardi, Franco, 103
Berger, Meta, 52, 53
Berger, Victor, 53, 54, 55
black feminist theory, 8–9, 12, 14, 16, 117–19
black migration, 48, 58, 60
Black Research Organization, 185n7
Boles, Janet, 65
Bondi, Liz, 18
Bonds, Michael, 136, 187n5
Bradley Foundation, 71–73, 137–39, 185n7
Braithwaite, Ann, 140
Bronzeville, 84
Brown, Wendy, 127

Brownlow, Alec, 91
Brush, Lisa, 169
Burawoy, Michael, 15, 16
Bush, George W., 137
Butler, Judith, 132, 178

Campaign for Sustainable Milwaukee, 135
Campbell, Beatrix, 36
caregiving, 29, 30, 34, 38, 104, 112–13, 125; low-income black women, 118–19; for sick family, 130–31. *See also* social reproduction; unpaid labor
Castree, Noel, 8
Charlton, Sue Ellen, 94
Chicago, 2, 25, 39–40
Child Protective Services, 121
Chun, Jennifer Jihye, 11
churches, 127–28, 135, 137–38; gender inequality, 159; opposition to neoliberal urban development, 158–59. *See also* religion and spirituality
citizenship, 2, 29, 31, 70, 101, 153
civil rights movement. *See* activism: black
Collins, Patricia Hill, 18–119, 159
colonialism, 4, 32, 35, 47, 83, 89, 167
community benefits agreement, 151; final agreement, 154–55; lack of feminist gains, 156–57; Park East demands, 147–49; Park East Development opposition, 145–46; rejection of, for Park East Development, 144–45. *See also* Good Jobs and Livable Neighborhoods Coalition
community work, 38–39
competition, 32–34, 68, 98; between cities, 24; masculinity, 33, 40
Congress for New Urbanism, 80, 82

consumption, 46, 54, 58, 81, 95, 98, 100–102, 116, 166
contingent work, 48–49, 71, 83
creative class, 33, 73–74, 79, 80, 97; as consumers, 101–2; culture of overwork, 103–4; identity validation, 101; rationality of rule, 100; scripts/discourses, 103, 108, 113, 114
cultural misrecognition, 8–9

Davis, Dana, 110
Day, Kristen, 82
debt, 58–59
deindustrialization, 16, 48, 64–65
Detroit, 22, 55, 184n1
developers: deference to, 149–51; demographic characteristics, 89; market concentration, 88–89; masculinities, 90–91, 150–51; subsidized risks and investments, 150–51
development, 3. See also downtown development
discourses, 17–18, 28n12, 28–34; creative class, 97–105; market, 151–153; new urbanism, 81–85; New York fiscal crisis, 24; rejection of neoliberal discourses, 11, 124; welfare reform, 26, 70–71. See also autonomy; competition; framing; individualism; neoliberal discourses; work, discourses of
Displaced Homemaker Project/Network, 66
diversity, 106–11, 140; as concept that disguises structural racism, 109–10
downtown development, 21, 28, 64–65, 69, 73–75, 88; lack of benefit to community, 85; resistance to, 65
Downtown Plan, 90

Eight Hour League, 47
Eisenhower, Dwight D., 59
Eisenstein, Hester, 181n21
embodiment, 128
entrepreneurialism, 28, 30, 33, 100
Equal Rights Amendment, 57
everyday racism, 8–9
evictions. See housing: evictions

Faludi, Susan, 58, 139, 140
Federal Housing Administration, 60
feminism, 3, 5–8; black, 17, 18, 117, 131, 186–87n1; shift from state to market, 142, 181n21
feminist killjoy, 17, 140, 156–57

feminist partial political economy of place (FPEP), 5, 10, 13, 14, 17; definition, 9–10
feminist planning, 85
feminist praxis, 9
feminist theory, definition, 6–7
feminist urban scholarship, 5–9
Ferree, Myra Marx, 29
Fincher, Ruth, 13
Florida, Richard, 33, 97–99, 103; creativity as leveler, 104–5; diversity, 110; as embodiment of creative class, 99
Foucault, Michel, 103
foundations and think tanks, 25, 71, 82, 120, 137, 185nn8–9. See also specific organizations
Fox, Richard, 92
framing, 24, 34, 61, 81–82, 89–90, 146, 139–40, 158, 185n9. See also discourses
Fraser, Nancy, 181n21
FUEL, Milwaukee. See Young Professionals of Milwaukee

General Federation of Women's Clubs, 53
gentrification, 74, 87, 95, 100, 114
Gilder, George, 72
Gill, Stephen, 146
Goldman, Emma, 177
Good Jobs and Livable Neighborhoods Coalition, 134, 143–46; critique of markets and development, 152–53; feminist values, 147; racism, 158, 160–61; resistance to feminist discourse, 153–54; sexism, 158, 160–61
Gordon, Danae Davis, 91
governance. See urban governance
Grand Avenue Mall, 74
Great Depression, 2, 45, 184n2; Socialist response, 51–52
Greater Milwaukee Committee, 59–60, 63, 65, 67, 74–75, 135
Greenberg, Miriam, 182n2
Gurda, John, 51, 52, 61, 62–63, 65

Harvey, David, 7, 116
Hayden, Dolores, 7, 56, 85
health, 129–31
Heritage Foundation, 72, 185n8
Hesse-Biber, Sharlene, 7
heteronormativity, 28, 58, 140
Hoan, Daniel, 44, 51, 54, 56; racism, 55
Hoan family, 53
homelessness, 86
home ownership, 39–40

hooks, bell, 118
housing, 3; destruction, 85; evictions, 40, 86; gender inequalities in, 39–40; low-income displacement, 86–87; racism 39–40, 60–61, 63–64
housing policy, feminist critique, 85
Houston, 63
Hubbard, Phil, 36
Hudson Institute, 72

incarceration, 8, 27, 190n1; effect on women of color, 123–24; rates for women, 124
income inequality, 37–38
Indianapolis, 2, 25, 68
individualism, 28, 30, 33, 68, 110, 115
Institute for the Transformation of Learning, 185n7
intersectionality, 3, 4, 6, 11
Isoke, Zenzele, 36, 91–92, 129, 131, 171

Joyce, Michael, 71–72, 73

Kantola, Johanna, 142
Katz, Cindi, 15, 117
Kenny, Judith, 83
Kern, Leslie, 84, 90–91
Keynes, John Maynard, 22
Keynesianism, 21, 22–24; feminist critique, 22–27; transition to neoliberalism, 25–27
Knights of Labor, 47
Ku Klux Klan, 54

labor legislation, 47–48
labor movement, 47; gendered exclusion, 158, 160–61; progressive coalitions 135–39, 143–45, 160; purge of radicals, 60; racial exclusion, 158, 160–61; union decline, 48
Larner, Wendy, 4
Lawless, Jennifer, 92
legal activism, 26
Lipsitz, George, 11
"live, work, and play," 80, 87, 88, 95, 100, 155
Lorde, Audre, 177
Los Angeles, 147
low-wage work, 37, 39, 71; black women, 120, 122

Maier, Henry, 63–67; ties to business elite, 65
Manchester, UK, 91
Manhattan Institute, 72, 82, 186n3
Manpower, 48, 71

markets: masculinities, 62; urban policymakers' affinity for, 74, 81–82
Marx, Karl, 31, 186n1
masculinities, 3, 29; autonomy, 28–30; competition, 32–33; creative class, 102–6; postwar Milwaukee, 57–63; urban governance, 90–92, 149–51; work, 31–23. See also competition: masculinity; markets: masculinities
Maskovsky, Jeff, 64
Maywood, California, 25
McCarthy, Joseph, 59
McCluskey, Margaret, 26
McKittrick, Katherine, 8–9
McLean, Heather, 111
Meehan, Katie, 186–87n1
Miller, Sally, 52, 53–54, 56
Milwaukee: child poverty rates, 5; demographics, 46–47; earnings, 50; European immigrants, 47; German immigrants, 47, 49; industrial sector, 47–49; Mexican Americans, 54; Native Americans, 47, 54; occupational structure, 50, 112; racial disparities, 46; suburban annexation, 61–62; suburban job creation, 87; suburbs, 46, 47
Milwaukee Art Museum, 74
Milwaukee Board of Realtors, 61
Milwaukee Brewers, 68
Milwaukee Chamber of Commerce, 100, 108–9
Milwaukee County Public Museum, 68
Milwaukee Property Owners Association, 61
Milwaukee Redevelopment Authority, 69
Milwaukee Redevelopment Corporation, 65
Milwaukee School Board, 52
Milwaukee Women's Coalition, 66
Miner, Barbara, 73
Model Cities Program, 22
municipal employment cuts, 69
Murray, Charles, 72

NAACP, Milwaukee chapter, 54, 55
Naples, Nancy, 15
National Organization for Women, 23, 66
neoliberal discourses, 28n12, 28–34; rejection of, 11. See also autonomy; competition; individualism; work, discourses of
neoliberalism: critique of concept, 2–3, 4; definition, 1–2, 3, 8, 21; U.S. origins, 22, 24
Newark, 22, 91–92
Newman, Janet, 106, 181n21
New Orleans, 185n9

new urbanism, 4, 28, 74; definition, 79–80; gender, 83–86; race, 83–86; romanticizing past, 83

New York City, 63, 68, 73; fiscal crisis, 23–24

9 to 5, 23, 66

Norman, Jack, 60

Norquist, John, 26, 33, 44, 51, 67–72, 78, 84, 100, 186n3; diversity, 107; first election (1988), 135–36; opposition to community benefits agreement, 84; w-2, 120

Orum, Anthony, 52, 65, 67

Orwell, George, 175

Park, Peter, 80

Park East neighborhood, 84

Park East Redevelopment Plan, 90, 134, 157; contestation of, 143–49; discourse of racial inequality, 154, 156–57; market-led development, 144–45, 149; as neoliberal policy, 143–46. See also community benefits agreement

Parsons, Lucy, 176

Partners Advancing Values in Education, 185n7

Peake, Linda, 8

Peck, Jamie, 32, 91, 105, 112, 185n8

Philadelphia, 2, 25, 68

Phillips, Vel, 62–63

policymakers. See political leadership; urban governance

political economy, 5, 6, 9; critique of, 6–7

political exclusion of women, 35–36, 89, 91–92, 185n4

political leadership: gender, 65–66, 91–93, 139, 180–81n11; race, 63–65, 91–93. See also urban governance

Porter, Michael, 84

poverty rates, Wisconsin, 47

Pratt, Geraldine, 15

privatization, 2, 4, 25, 28, 68–73; social services, 137

provisioning, 125–28

public goods, investment in, 23. See also privatization

public-private partnerships, 25, 69

Quinlan, Pierce, 71

rationality of rule, 81–83, 93, 94

Reingold, Beth, 139

relational research, 14–17

religion and spirituality, 127–28

resistance, 3; by African-American low income women, 125–31; barriers to, 135–43; by churches, 127, 158–59; co-optation of, 48; feminist, antiracist, and progressive, 135–43; to neoliberal development, 146–49; to racist state, 125

Richie, Beth, 119, 159

Riverwalk, 74, 87

Roberts, Dorothy, 121

Rose, Gillian, 6, 14, 176

Rosner, Victoria, 15

Roth, Benita, 140

Roy, Ananya, 3, 90

Satter, Beryl, 39–40

school vouchers, 68, 72–73, 137, 142, 185n7

second-wave feminism, 23

segregation, 5, 45; housing, 61, 87

Seidel, Emil, 50–51

service economy, 37, 48

"Sewer Socialism," 2, 25, 49–56

shadow state, 41, 119, 126, 138

Shin, Young, 11

Simon-Kumar, Rachel, 32

slavery, 29, 33, 39, 83, 125

Smith, Adrienne R., 139

Smith, Dorothy, 15

Smith, Kevin, 61

Socialism: decline, 57–62, 63; ideology, 47, 69; reforms, 50–52

Socialist Party: black leadership, 54; black women, 55; female leadership, 52–53, 54, 55; gender equity, 52; race, 54–55; support for women's suffrage, 50, 53–54, 56; women's chapter, 52

social reproduction, 2, 31–32, 34, 38, 53, 55, 83, 112–14, 186–87n1; black women, 119; definition, 117; embodiment, 128–31; informal work, 125; privatization, 113. See also caregiving; unpaid labor

social service cuts, 69–70, 135

Spain, Daphne, 35, 156

Springer, Simon, 17

Squires, Judith, 142

Stokes, Carl, 23

Strauss, Kendra, 186–87n1

subjectivity, 2, 3, 41, 101–2, 105, 131

subprime mortgages, 40

suburbanization, 59–61

Task Force on Battered Women, 66

tax reform, 69

theoretical toolkits, 17–18
think tanks. *See* foundations and think tanks
Thomas, Elizabeth, 52
Thompson, Tommy, 32, 72
Thoreau, Henry David, 175, 176
Tickell, Adam, 90–91
Tomlinson, Barbara, 4
Toronto, 84
Trotter, Joe William, 54

United Water Services, 69
unpaid labor, 29, 31, 33, 36, 38–39, 83, 94, 123–25, 129. *See also* caregiving; social reproduction
urban female reformers, 35, 156
urban governance: gender, 4, 8, 90–94, 139, 149–51; masculinities, 90–92, 149–51
Urban League, 57
urban regime theory, 7
urban renewal, 62, 63–64, 66–67; resistance to, 64

Valentine, Gill, 10
Veterans Administration, 60
Violent Femmes, 33, 98

wage gap, 37, 105, 118
Wajcman, Judy, 110
Walby, Sylvia, 181n21, 188n9
walkability, 87, 88, 95, 167, 187–88n6
Walton, John, 8
Weber, Rachel, 74
Wekerle, Gerda, 91
welfare, 31, 38; cuts, 24–25, 69; disciplining recipients, 120–21; gendered, 71, 119; impediment to markets, 24; racialized, 24, 31–32, 71, 119, 140, 183n7; work requirements, 26

Welfare Policy Center, 72
"welfare queen," 24, 26, 32, 118, 151
welfare reform, 2, 4, 8, 26, 70–73, 137. *See also* Wisconsin Works
welfare-to-work, 48. *See also* Wisconsin Works
white flight, 59–61
whiteness. *See* white privilege
white privilege, 3, 13, 27, 29, 105–6, 110, 115–16, 167
Whitzman, Carolyn, 140
Wilson, David, 26, 145
Wilson, Woodrow, 51
Wisconsin Electric Power, 68
Wisconsin Works (w-2), 70–71, 120–23, 137; work placements, 121–22
Woman's Building, 7
Woman's School Alliance, 53
Women's Crisis Line, 66
women's rights movement. *See* activism: feminism; second-wave feminism
Women's Strike for Equality, 23
work, discourses of, 31–32, 33. *See also* contingent work
World War I, 46, 48, 51
World War II, 48, 56–57, 58
Wright, Melissa, 17

Young Professionals of Milwaukee, 74, 98–99, 100–102; elite access, 112; member characteristics, 106; race and diversity, 106–11

Zeidler, Frank, 59–60, 62
Zimmerman, Jeff, 83

GEOGRAPHIES OF JUSTICE AND SOCIAL TRANSFORMATION

1. *Social Justice and the City*, rev. ed.
   BY DAVID HARVEY

2. *Begging as a Path to Progress: Indigenous Women and Children and the Struggle for Ecuador's Urban Spaces*
   BY KATE SWANSON

3. *Making the San Fernando Valley: Rural Landscapes, Urban Development, and White Privilege*
   BY LAURA R. BARRACLOUGH

4. *Company Towns in the Americas: Landscape, Power, and Working-Class Communities*
   EDITED BY OLIVER J. DINIUS AND ANGELA VERGARA

5. *Tremé: Race and Place in a New Orleans Neighborhood*
   BY MICHAEL E. CRUTCHER JR.

6. *Bloomberg's New York: Class and Governance in the Luxury City*
   BY JULIAN BRASH

7. *Roppongi Crossing: The Demise of a Tokyo Nightclub District and the Reshaping of a Global City*
   BY ROMAN ADRIAN CYBRIWSKY

8. *Fitzgerald: Geography of a Revolution*
   BY WILLIAM BUNGE

9. *Accumulating Insecurity: Violence and Dispossession in the Making of Everyday Life*
   EDITED BY SHELLEY FELDMAN, CHARLES GEISLER, AND GAYATRI A. MENON

10. *They Saved the Crops: Labor, Landscape, and the Struggle over Industrial Farming in Bracero-Era California*
    BY DON MITCHELL

11. *Faith Based: Religious Neoliberalism and the Politics of Welfare in the United States*
    BY JASON HACKWORTH

12. *Fields and Streams: Stream Restoration, Neoliberalism, and the Future of Environmental Science*
    BY REBECCA LAVE

13. *Black, White, and Green: Farmers Markets, Race, and the Green Economy*
    BY ALISON HOPE ALKON

14. *Beyond Walls and Cages: Prisons, Borders, and Global Crisis*
    EDITED BY JENNA M. LOYD, MATT MITCHELSON, AND ANDREW BURRIDGE

15. *Silent Violence: Food, Famine, and Peasantry in Northern Nigeria*
    BY MICHAEL J. WATTS

16. *Development, Security, and Aid: Geopolitics and Geoeconomics at the U.S. Agency for International Development*
    BY JAMEY ESSEX

17. *Properties of Violence: Law and Land-Grant Struggle in Northern New Mexico*
   BY DAVID CORREIA

18. *Geographical Diversions: Tibetan Trade, Global Transactions*
   BY TINA HARRIS

19. *The Politics of the Encounter: Urban Theory and Protest under Planetary Urbanization*
   BY ANDY MERRIFIELD

20. *Rethinking the South African Crisis: Nationalism, Populism, Hegemony*
   BY GILLIAN HART

21. *The Empires' Edge: Militarization, Resistance, and Transcending Hegemony in the Pacific*
   BY SASHA DAVIS

22. *Pain, Pride, and Politics: Social Movement Activism and the Sri Lankan Tamil Diaspora in Canada*
   BY AMARNATH AMARASINGAM

23. *Selling the Serengeti: The Cultural Politics of Safari Tourism*
   BY BENJAMIN GARDNER

24. *Territories of Poverty: Rethinking North and South*
   EDITED BY ANANYA ROY AND EMMA SHAW CRANE

25. *Precarious Worlds: Contested Geographies of Social Reproduction*
   EDITED BY KATIE MEEHAN AND KENDRA STRAUSS

26. *Spaces of Danger: Culture and Power in the Everyday*
   EDITED BY HEATHER MERRILL AND LISA M. HOFFMAN

27. *Shadows of a Sunbelt City: The Environment, Racism, and the Knowledge Economy in Austin*
   BY ELIOT M. TRETTER

28. *Beyond the Kale: Urban Agriculture and Social Justice Activism in New York City*
   BY KRISTIN REYNOLDS AND NEVIN COHEN

29. *Calculating Property Relations: Chicago's Wartime Industrial Mobilization, 1940–1950*
   BY ROBERT LEWIS

30. *In the Public's Interest: Evictions, Citizenship, and Inequality in Contemporary Delhi*
   BY GAUTAM BHAN

31. *The Carpetbaggers of Kabul and Other American-Afghan Entanglements: Intimate Development, Geopolitics, and the Currency of Gender and Grief*
   BY JENNIFER L. FLURI AND RACHEL LEHR

32. *Masculinities and Markets: Raced and Gendered Urban Politics in Milwaukee*
   BY BRENDA PARKER

www.ingramcontent.com/pod-product-compliance
Lightning Source LLC
Chambersburg PA
CBHW010139270326
41926CB00022B/4500